CONTEMPORARY NORTHERN IRISH SOCIETY
An Introduction

Colin Coulter

Pluto  Press

LONDON • STERLING, VIRGINIA

First published 1999 by Pluto Press
345 Archway Road, London N6 5AA
and 22883 Quicksilver Drive, Sterling, VA 20166–2012, USA

British Library Cataloguing in Publication Data
A catalogue record for this book is available from the British Library

ISBN 0 7453 1254 3 hbk

Library of Congress Cataloging in Publication Data
Coulter, Colin, 1966–
    Contemporary Northern Irish society : an introduction / Colin
Coulter.
        p.   cm. — (Contemporary Irish studies)
    Includes bibliographical references.
    ISBN 0–7453–1254–3
    1. Northern Ireland—Social conditions—20th century. 2. Social
conflict—Northern Ireland—History—20th century. I. Title. II.
Series.
    HN400.3.A8 C68 1999
    306'.09416—dc21   99–28413
                                                          CIP

Designed and produced for Pluto Press by
Chase Production Services, Chadlington, OX7 3LN
Typeset from disk by Stanford DTP Services, Northampton
Printed in the EC by TJ International, Padstow

For my parents Sadie & Tommy Coulter

Contents

Acknowledgements

This book is the outcome of living and working in two rather different places: Belfast and Maynooth. I would like to take this opportunity to acknowledge the debts I have accumulated in both places. For the best part of a decade from the mid 1980s on I was a student in the Queen's University of Belfast. I wish to thank those individuals who helped me during that time and indeed who have helped me since: Bob Cormack, Liam O'Dowd, Renee Prendergast, Jim Smyth, Henry McNally, Darin McCrystal, Billy Marcus, Patricia Lundy, Richard Kirkland, Dave Calder, Theresa Callan, Niamh Moore, Fiona O'Neill, Jim McAuley and Mark McGovern. A particular debt is owed to Pete Shirlow and Alan Bairner for providing friendship and assistance when it was needed most. Thanks also to the inimitable Sam Porter who has been a constant, if unlikely, source of both inspiration and fashion advice. Since January of 1995 I have taught in the Department of Sociology in the National University of Ireland, Maynooth. I want to express my gratitude to all the people who have made my time in Maynooth so enjoyable. In particular I wish to thank Tara Coogan, Linda Connolly, Steve Coleman, Mairead Mahon, Gavin McArthur, Noel Kavanagh, Seaghan Pól Mac Fionmhcáin, Claudine Favrat, Cathal MacDonagh, Dave Slattery, Mairead Slattery, Jamie Saris, Lisa McCaffrey, Joe Cleary, Jane Gray, Honor Fagan, Eamonn Slater, Tony Cunningham, Martin Daniel, Ken Duffy and Heather Laird. Last but certainly not least I want to thank the Sociology and CCIS students of NUI Maynooth for their support and indulgence.

Introduction

People living in Northern Ireland are wont to insist that outsiders neither understand nor care about the difficulties that beset the province. This familiar grievance has of course some basis in truth. The contention that the rest of the world remains essentially indifferent to the plight of the six counties has, however, been seriously questioned by modern trends in academic writing. Over the last three decades literally thousands of academic books and articles have sought to address the various issues associated with 'the troubles' (Whyte 1991). Indeed the level of attention devoted to the province has been such that it has become a commonplace assertion that Northern Ireland represents – in proportionate terms at least – the most researched region on the face of the planet. The multiple animosities that frequently contaminate relations between Protestants and Catholics in the six counties have been set out for public perusal. Every turn in the dismal recent history of the province has been documented. The stories of those who have killed or been killed during 'the troubles' have been recorded, often in heartrending detail.

The purpose of this particular book is rather different from most of those that deal with the nature of contemporary Northern Irish society. The chapters that follow do not seek simply to tell yet again the sorry tale of the troubles. At various turns specific incidents and passages from recent Northern Irish history are sketched because they happen to be germane to the discussion at hand. The text that follows does not, however, set out to provide an exhaustive narrative of the horrific events that have overtaken the province since the late 1960s. It is presumed that most readers possess at least a rudimentary knowledge of the occurrences that have ensured that Northern Ireland has come to be synonymous around the world with political violence. It is hoped that the specific moments and sequences mentioned in the text will be documented with sufficient clarity so as to be meaningful even to those who are entirely unfamiliar with the narrative detail of 'the troubles'.

1

The intention of this book then is not to provide yet another political history of the province but rather to offer an overview of the particular social formation that presently exists within the six counties. The focus of the text will hopefully prove somewhat broader than most other existing portraits of contemporary Northern Irish society. Social scientists have frequently fallen prey to a distinctly narrow understanding of social and political identity in the six counties. The people of the province are often depicted simply as the bearers of particular ethnic or national identities that are conventionally designated as 'unionist' or 'nationalist'. The preoccupation of social and political scientists with these particular ontological formations is in part understandable. Ethnonational sentiment has after all made an enormous impact upon the manner in which Northern Irish people think, feel and act. Indeed a large proportion of this book is devoted to examining the nature of the opposition between 'unionism' and 'nationalism'. While eth-nonational feeling evidently represents an essential source of social and political identity in Northern Ireland it is not, however, the only one. The outlook and conduct of people living in the six counties, as elsewhere, are also crucially influenced by class location and gender convention. An adequate understanding of the nature of contemporary Northern Irish society requires, therefore, an appreciation that the distinctive social and political personae prevalent within the six counties emerge out of the complex interplay of a range of seemingly discrete identities. Consequently this book seeks to acknowledge not only the salience of ethnonational persuasion but also the critical importance of class and gender distinctions to the life of the province.

The first three chapters of the book examine the most important sources of community and distinction in Northern Ireland. The final two consider the manner in which the loyalties and hatreds characteristic of the province tend to be perceived. In relative terms at least, the troubles have been a decidedly low level conflict. The violence that has afflicted the six counties in recent generations has of course been horrific and unnecessary. Nonetheless the death toll from the troubles remains minuscule compared to that of other contemporary ethnic conflicts in eastern Europe or central Africa. Indeed it is hard to shake the conviction that it is in part the presumed novelty of white westerners killing other white westerners that has drawn such disproportionate attention to the affairs of Northern Ireland. Were the people of the province the residents of another region beyond the pale of the 'civilised' first world theirs would truly be a forgotten conflict. The comparatively minor scale of the troubles reflects in part an appreciation among the various combatants that they simply cannot win the war. In the absence of a likely military solution the various players in the conflict have sought to advance their interests through other means. Over the last 30 years Northern Ireland has become the site of intense ideological dispute. Various parties have attempted to mobilise support for their specific interests both within and without the six counties. The nature of the ideological contest that has attended the troubles is scrutinised in the two chapters that close the book. The endeavours of the British state to ensure the dominance of the metropolitan reading of the 'Northern Ireland problem' are examined. The focus then shifts towards the attempts of republicans and loyalists respectively to propagate their own distinctive interpretation of the conflict in the province.

THE FORMATION OF NORTHERN IRISH SOCIETY

The purpose of this book is, therefore, to document the manner in which contemporary Northern Irish society is organised, experienced and imagined. The particular social formation that currently obtains within the six counties is the product of at least three important circumstances or processes. Each of these substantially informs the discussion that follows and hence is worth underlining at the outset.

First, and most obviously, Northern Ireland is the site of an enduring ethnonational dispute (Wright 1987). The seeming inability of Protestants and Catholics to 'get along' with one another invariably and understandably perplexes outsiders who often otherwise consider Northern Irish people to be thoroughly agreeable. The persistence of ethnic conflict within the six counties has ensured that Northern Ireland has come to be regarded in some quarters as 'a place apart' from the modern world (Rose 1982). Moreover, the preoccupation with certain ostensibly religious concerns that feed into ethnonational persuasion has meant that the people of the province are frequently portrayed as entirely immune to the counsel of reason. The conviction that Northern Irish people are the demented charges of atavistic passions has of course been articulated through conveniently crass racist stereotypes that have proved depressingly resilient.

The assumption that the conflict in Northern Ireland represents simply an expression of the irrational collapses under even the most cursory inspection. While the events of the last 30 years may well

have been abhorrent they could scarcely be considered to have
been aberrant. The tensions and divisions that simmer within the
six counties are at some level a rational expression of the manner
in which Northern Irish society has been and indeed continues to
be organised. The apparently 'sectarian' enmities that infect
Northern Ireland owe their origins largely to the rather more
temporal matters that attend the distribution of life chances in the
province. The seemingly exotic concerns of Northern Irish people
transpire to be neither unusual nor irrational. Indeed the issues
that are dear to the citizens of the province turn out to bear a close
resemblance to those that animate the members of most other
societies.

The view that the communal divisions prevalent within Northern
Ireland mark the province as 'different' has been severely
undermined by international events over the last decade. When
the troubles erupted, the political violence taking place in the six
counties genuinely appeared to be a throwback to a previous age.
In the 1970s the fact that people who were, after all, white
Europeans were willing to kill and die in the name of the
sect/ethnie/nation struck most commentators as beyond belief.
Two decades on, the notion of ethnonational violence has, unfortunately, become rather less inconceivable. The events that
heralded the end of the Cold War both articulated and accelerated
the emergence of particular political enterprises that privilege the
rights and interests of specific ethnic, national and even racial
groupings. Over the last decade ethnic and xenophobic feelings
have gained ground within European societies that previously were
presumed to have transcended such antiquated and irrational
sentiments. The rise of ethnonational longing has meant that
avowed racists have been able to assume public office, migrant
workers have been burned to death in their hostels and entire
multiethnic states have been sundered. Regarded against this
decidedly miserable backdrop, the incidence of ethnic violence
within the six counties begins to appear somewhat less peculiar
than has been conventionally assumed. Indeed viewed in the light
of recent events in other European countries the existence and
persistence of the troubles might be taken to illustrate not the back-
wardness of contemporary Northern Irish society but rather,
perversely, its essential 'modernity'.

Second, and equally evidently, Northern Ireland happens to
be a capitalist society. The particular social formation that exists
in the six counties is the product of a prolonged and complex
process of accumulation. The province exhibits all of the inequal-

ities and injustices that are associated with bourgeois society. Working class people living in the six counties suffer the same indignities as workers in every other western state. In order to capture the nature of the province we must, therefore, acknowledge the status of Northern Ireland as an example of the genus of 'capitalist society'.

At the same time though it is important to appreciate that which is specific to Northern Ireland. While the social formation that defines the six counties may be far from unique it remains particular nonetheless. The process of capitalist accumulation has bestowed upon the province a distinctly complex social order. The class relations that mark the six counties do not of course exist in an abstract or indeed pristine manner. On the contrary, the evolution of capitalism in the northeast of Ireland has created an intricate sequence of hierarchies that oversee the allocation of material and figurative resources in the province. The manner in which these seemingly distinct systems of privilege interact generates many of the nuances and dynamics of contemporary Northern Irish society. The interplay between those hierarchies associated with class and ethnicity respectively proves to be especially crucial in determining how life in the province is ordered and experienced.

The recent period of political upheaval in Northern Ireland has of course coincided with the radical reconfiguration of international capitalism. The world now looks rather different from the way it did in the summer of 1969. Certain processes at work within the global economy over the last 25 years or so have served to strengthen enormously the power of capital over labour. Increasingly mobile multinational corporations have come to operate under conditions that are ever more conducive to profit. At the same time the reconstruction of the international division of labour has lengthened dole queues throughout the western world. Those workers who have managed to remain in employment frequently enjoy little security or legal protection. The ideologues of the new world economic order seek to legitimise the shameful developments of the past quarter of a century through the threadbare imperatives of 'freedom' and 'choice'. To add insult to injury, influential voices within mainstream sociology encourage us to embrace in the name of 'reflexivity' changes that have benefited only a tiny minority of the world's population. The reordering of the global economy that has taken place since the early 1970s has buffeted Northern Ireland with considerable force. The manifold injustices associated with what are euphemistically termed 'flexible' labour markets, for instance, are readily apparent in the context of the six counties. The status of Northern Ireland as an essentially peripheral region of an increasingly changeful global economy is clearly implicated in the social life of the province. Hence in the chapters that follow efforts will be made to illustrate that the nature of contemporary Northern Irish society has been defined in part by processes and decisions that originate rather further afield.

The third and final issue worth highlighting before we move on is that of the particular – and in certain respects peculiar – constitutional status of the six counties. Commentators are prone to refer to Northern Ireland as a 'state'. This familiar characterisation is, however, factually inaccurate. Northern Ireland is not, has never been and hopefully will never be, a state. It is simply a region of one. The particular position that the six counties occupy within the United Kingdom goes some way to explaining the course that Northern Irish society has followed over recent generations. Representatives of the metropolitan interest are often keen to establish that the British state remains 'above' the 'Northern Ireland problem'. Nothing could of course be further from the truth. The British state represents in fact not merely an actor in the Northern Irish conflict but also the actual context of that conflict (O'Dowd et al. 1980).

The constitutional location of Northern Ireland remains profoundly contingent. The British political establishment looks upon the current status of the six counties within the Union with at best formal indifference and at worst explicit hostility. The conduct of Westminster since partition has been guided primarily by a concern to insulate itself from the volatile affairs of Northern Ireland. During the fifty years of Unionist misrule at Stormont the political class in London behaved as though the six counties had simply ceased to exist. Only the outbreak of the troubles would prove sufficient to persuade the metropolis to take a more active interest in the affairs of the province. In the spring of 1972, as Northern Ireland seemingly teetered on the brink of outright civil war, the sovereign parliament at Westminster reluctantly decided to dissolve the Stormont legislature and assume direct responsibility for the governance of the province. Although originally conceived as a temporary expedient, 'direct rule' has remained in place until the present day. At the moment plans are being acted upon for Westminster to transfer certain powers to the new assembly in Belfast conceived under the terms of the Good Friday Agreement. Even if the proposed devolution scheme proves successful it is likely, however, that the metropolis will continue to exercise executive authority over the province for some time to come.

The conduct of public policy since the demise of the Stormont legislature has been instrumental in defining the course that Northern Irish society has taken in recent times. The introduction of direct rule appeared to have marked a radical change in the disposition of the metropolis towards the six counties. In practice though, the British political establishment has chosen to cling to the perennial construction of Northern Ireland as 'a place apart' (Boyce 1991). The conviction that the province is irretrievably 'different' from the rest of the United Kingdom has produced rather different outcomes in different areas of public policy. The political schemes that Westminster has devised under direct rule have reflected largely the metropolitan concern to maintain a discreet distance from Northern Ireland. Over the last quarter of a century British politicians have consistently aspired towards political settlements that would allow the six counties to be consigned once more to the margins of the United Kingdom. The official understanding of Northern Ireland as 'other' has ensured that the people of the province have been forced to endure relatively poor rights of citizenship. British citizens who happen to live in Northern Ireland have been systematically excluded from the party political life of the state. Furthermore, political enterprises have been proposed for the province that would have been – until very recently at least – deemed inappropriate for the other regions of the United Kingdom.

The political policies that have been introduced under direct rule have, therefore, served merely to underscore the subaltern position of the six counties within the United Kingdom. In the realm of social and economic affairs, however, the official construction of Northern Ireland as 'a place apart' has had rather more beneficial consequences for the people of the province. Among the central concerns of London has been an anxiety to establish those social conditions that would allow the six counties to be restored to their former position in political quarantine (Cunningham 1991, pp. 134–5). Influential figures within Westminster and Whitehall would seem to have presumed an intimate connection between the relative underdevelopment of Northern Ireland and the political violence that has overtaken the province. This presumption has ensured that the level of public money flowing into the six counties has grown substantially since the demise of the Stormont legislature. The era of direct rule has been one of frequently remarkable fiscal benevolence. Levels of public provision in Northern Ireland are considerably higher than would have been the case had the Stormont regime somehow managed to remain in existence. Furthermore, the citizens of the province have been relatively cosseted from the relentless erosion of the welfare state that has occurred within the United Kingdom since the formation of the first Thatcher cabinet.

The conduct of the executive under direct rule emerges, therefore, as something of a paradox. On the one hand, the political initiatives endorsed by the metropolis have left Northern Irish people in little doubt as to their status as rather less than equal citizens of the United Kingdom. On the other hand, the social and economic measures that have been adopted since the demise of Stormont have bestowed considerable benefit upon a large swathe of the population of the province. The tensions that have defined public policy over the last quarter of a century have had an enormous bearing upon the recent direction of social and political life within the six counties. Accordingly, the dialectics of direct rule represent one of the principal themes running through the chapters to come.

SOME WORDS ABOUT WORDS

The six northeastern counties of Ireland comprise one of the most disputed territories in the western world. The conflicts that are readily associated with Northern Ireland are inevitably and vividly reflected at the level of language. Words are routinely employed both to affirm and undermine the legitimacy of the partition settlement. Given the crucial political significance of language, some mention should be made here as to the terms that are used throughout the rest of the text. The reader will notice that I have used most, and perhaps even all, of the principal words and phrases that are summoned to describe that part of the island of Ireland that remains within the British state. At various turns reference is made to 'Northern Ireland', the 'north of Ireland', the 'northeast of Ireland', the 'six counties', the 'province' and even 'Ulster'. The seemingly promiscuous manner in which language is used throughout the book reflects in part a desire for some degree of stylistic variation. It also raises a couple of rather more important concerns.

The decision to use all of the terms for Northern Ireland that are in wide circulation intimates an aversion to those ideological enterprises that have dominated discursive practice in the region. In the province words are employed, often in a disingenuous fashion, to advance interests that are invariably questionable. The myriad terms that denote Northern Ireland suggest views of the region and indeed of the wider world that are ultimately reactionary. It is often difficult to judge who precisely is the more objectionable or indeed tiresome: the northern Irish Protestant who proclaims his loyalty to 'Ulster' but who has never even considered visiting Donegal, the southern Irish champagne republican who feigns such passion that she could not possibly bring herself to issue the phrase 'Northern Ireland' but who would nonetheless never dream of setting foot in so vulgar and dreary a place, or the northern Irish nationalist who has grown comfortable under direct rule but who refuses to refer to the region of the British state in which he happens to live in terms other than 'the six counties'. The formal inclusiveness of the language that appears in the text might be read as indicative of the currently fashionable pluralist trend towards appreciating every version of political identity in Northern Ireland as equally and inherently valuable. In reality though the manner in which words are used throughout the book is intended to suggest that all of the philosophies that presently dominate the political culture of the province have similarly little to offer the beleaguered citizens of the six counties.

The adoption of multiple terms to refer to what is legally called 'Northern Ireland' underscores also an understanding of the limits of language. Words are of course essential to our appreciation of social realities. Indeed words are themselves constitutive of those very realities. While language may serve to order the social world there are clear boundaries to the facility of language to *reorder* it. An understanding of these limits is vital when approaching a society like Northern Ireland whose conflicts are produced and reproduced in part through linguistic convention. The status of the six counties as a bourgeois social formation ensures that the significance and value of words are strictly finite. Like all other capitalist societies, Northern Ireland is a place where the many are exploited and oppressed in the interests of the few. No amount of linguistic dexterity will be sufficient to alter that particular, miserable reality.

1 The Nature of Division: Ethnicity, Nationalism and Sectarianism

Clearly Northern Ireland is a deeply divided society. Within the province there are two principal communal blocs: one variously described as 'Catholic', 'nationalist' and 'Irish', the other designated as 'Protestant', 'unionist' and 'British'. The relationship between the 'two communities' that coexist within the six counties has been defined down the centuries by a profound hostility. Over the last 30 years the enmities that fester within Northern Ireland have given rise to sustained violence. A fundamental ambition of the sociologist concerned with the nature of contemporary Northern Irish society should be to characterise the divisions that have produced the troubles. An adequate understanding of that which divides people living in the six counties requires the introduction of the concepts of 'ethnicity', 'nationalism' and 'sectarianism'. These terms should, therefore, be defined at the outset.

SOME DEFINITIONS

The concepts upon which this particular chapter centres are among the most complex and disputed within the social sciences (See 1986, p. 2). Little agreement exists among sociologists and others as to the precise meaning of notions like 'ethnicity', 'nationalism' or 'sectarianism'. The specific understandings of these terms that are advanced in the discussion that follows would, therefore, be contested by other social scientists. While the definitions of 'ethnicity', 'nationalism' and 'sectarianism' that are employed throughout this chapter are inevitably open to debate, their introduction will hopefully nonetheless shed light upon the nature of the fissures that presently obtain within Northern Irish society.

Ethnicity may be understood as a feeling of belonging to a specific ethnic grouping or *ethnie* (Jenkins 1986, p. 4). An ethnie represents an aggregate of individuals who consider themselves to possess a shared ancestry and cultural identity. The distinctive cultural persona of the ethnic community typically finds expression through language, religion, custom and belief. *Nationalism* also articulates a sense of membership of a particular body of people – namely the 'nation' – who regard themselves as having a common biography and culture. There exists, therefore, a close resemblance between nationalist sentiment and ethnic feeling. Indeed, the similarity is so pronounced that commentators frequently use the notions of 'ethnicity' and 'nationalism' interchangeably. There are, however, at least two important differences between the concepts.

First, ethnicity and nationalism respectively express feelings of belonging to collectivities that are, potentially at least, rather different. The ethnie represents a remarkably homogeneous social aggregate. Those who inherit specific ethnic traditions frequently bear close physical and cultural resemblance to one another. The community that springs from the imagination of nationalism, in contrast, has the potential to be rather more varied. While members of the nation share certain essential experiences and identities they may also exhibit considerable cultural – and occasionally even racial – diversity. Many national communities are of course founded upon particular, exclusive ethnic personae. Some are able, however, to accommodate a range of individuals who look and sound radically different from one another.

Second, ethnicity and nationalism may be distinguished in terms of the political programmes which they seek to promote. James Kellas (1991, pp. 4–6) has observed that while ethnic groupings are often keenly aware of their common interests and grievances they typically do not demand to be allowed to form their own political association or state. Consequently the political strategy that arises out of ethnic feeling typically entails the pursuit of equality of citizenship within the context of existing constitutional arrangements. Nationalist sentiment, in contrast, tends to foster rather more radical political ambitions. A fundamental character-istic of nationalism is an insistence that the perceived community of descent has an inalienable right to 'self-determination'. When some or all members of the nation happen to live within the confines of a state that also plays host to other national communities, the articulation of nationalist sentiment inevitably involves calls for existing constitutional boundaries to be redrawn Hence, while ethnicity gives rise to political demands that are essentially reformist, nationalism emerges as a distinctly revolu-tionary political creed.

The divisions that exist within contemporary Northern Irish society are regularly characterised as 'sectarian'. The manner in which the notion of 'sectarianism' is often employed is arguably, however, imprecise and inaccurate. Commentators frequently use the term 'sectarian' to denote forms of belief and conduct which are clearly secular and which would be more accurately charac- terised within the categories of 'ethnicity' and 'nationalism'. The concept of sectarianism should be strictly reserved for considera- tion of the realm of religion. The term properly refers to that complex of beliefs and conduct that arises out of the conviction of the importance of religious faith, religious practice and, above all, religious difference. Faith in the value and integrity of one's own religious beliefs can often promote intolerance and hostility towards those of others. Hence, 'sectarianism' often has the pejorative connotations of an outlook shaped by religious bigotry. It is this particular meaning of the term which is typically invoked by commentators appalled at the hatred and bloodshed that have frequently defined relations between the peoples of Northern Ireland.

THE DIMENSIONS OF ETHNIC DIVISION IN NORTHERN IRELAND

Ethnicity represents a pervasive source of identity and division within contemporary Northern Irish society. The boundary that exists between nationalists and unionists living in the province assumes numerous forms. Some of the more important lines of ethnic fissure in the province are outlined below.

Religious Affiliation

Perhaps the most reliable signifier of ethnic identity in Northern Ireland is that of confessional status. The ethnic distinctions that obtain within the six counties demarcate two communities that subscribe to contrasting religious creeds. The coincidence between ethnic and religious status in the province has ensured that the competing identities that the peoples of Northern Ireland espouse are often characterised by social scientists as 'ethnoreligious'.

The ethnoreligious divide in Northern Ireland is often portrayed simply as that of a Protestant majority on the one hand and a Catholic minority on the other. While entirely accurate, this common representation fails to capture the true demographic com- plexities of the province. Protestants do indeed form the larger of the two communities in the six counties. The numerical advantage that unionists enjoy is, however, rather less substantial than often assumed. The 1991 census revealed that 51 per cent of people living in Northern Ireland were willing to identify themselves as Protestants and 38 per cent as Roman Catholics (McGarry & O'Leary 1995a, p. 179). It would appear, therefore, that there are five unionists for every four nationalists in the six counties. A closer examination of the data suggests, however, that this particular sectarian ratio in fact overstates the difference in the size of the two communities in Northern Ireland. When the 1991 census was being carried out some 115,000 people – around seven per cent of the entire population – simply refused to disclose their religious affiliation. Given the suspicion and indeed hostility that many nationalists harbour towards every limb of the British state, a disproportionate number of those citizens who declined to answer the questions on religion are likely to have been Roman Catholics. The numerical superiority of the unionist community is, therefore, in all probability rather smaller than a cursory glance at the census data would indicate.

Recent demographic trends, moreover, would suggest that the already delicate balance between the two predominant ethnoreligious blocs in Northern Ireland will become increasingly delicate with the passage of time. The era of the troubles has seen the nationalist community expand slowly but significantly nonetheless. Over the last three decades the proportion of the Northern Irish population that belongs to the Roman Catholic faith has officially increased by four per cent. In light of the reluctance of many nationalists to complete their census returns it is likely, however, that the Catholic community has grown rather more substantially than official statistics would imply.

Numerous seasoned commentators have suggested that the decades to come will witness the further enlargement of the nationalist population in Northern Ireland (McGarry & O'Leary 1995b, pp. 403–4). It is difficult to predict the precise impact that the increasingly precarious balance of ethnoreligious forces within the six counties will have upon communal relations in the province. Of crucial importance of course will be the manner in which unionists respond to the gradual erosion of their status as a majority. The seemingly inexorable expansion of the nationalist population may nurture within the unionist community that sullen intransigence that has frustrated the cause of political progress at every turn in the past. Alternatively, the prospect that they may be reduced to the status of a minority at some stage in the future may encourage unionists to negotiate a political settlement from the relative position of strength that they occupy in the present. Contemporary demographic trends are, therefore, likely to promote both reaction and revision among the ranks of Ulster unionism. The interplay between these divergent political impulses is of course already clearly apparent in the disputes that the present 'peace process' has generated within the fractious unionist family.

The familiar construction of the ethnoreligious divide in Northern Ireland as that between a Protestant majority on the one hand and a Catholic minority on the other obscures at least one further salient aspect of the balance of sectarian forces that currently obtains therein. While every Catholic living in the province belongs to one church, the same is not true of course for their Protestant counterparts. 'Protestant' is a generic term that covers literally dozens of religious denominations that vary enormously both in terms of size and theological disposition. The single largest group within Ulster Protestantism are the Presbyterians who form a congregation of 336,891 people. While the following that Presbyterianism attracts is clearly substantial it is nonetheless barely half that of the province's single largest denomination, the Roman Catholic church, which boasts a membership of 605,639. The complex denominational variety that exists within the Protestant community in Northern Ireland suggests that we should exercise caution when seeking to characterise the ethnoreligious composition of the six counties. While Ulster Protestants may justifiably be regarded as a majority, it is important to bear in mind that they are in fact a 'majority of minorities' (Boal et al. 1991).

One further important difference between the two dominant ethnoreligious traditions that inhabit the 'narrow ground' of Northern Ireland should be acknowledged. Rates of religious observance in the province are phenomenally high by western standards. Examination of patterns of church attendance would seem to suggest that the Catholic community in the six counties is especially devout. The British Social Attitudes Survey has provided information on patterns of religious practice in the province that accords with a range of other research projects. The survey has revealed that in the late 1980s 86 per cent of Northern Irish Catholics claimed to attend church at least once a week. The proportion of Ulster Protestants who were equally fastidious attenders was 44 per cent (McGarry & O'Leary 1995a, p. 174). It would appear, therefore, that Catholics living in the province are twice as likely as their Protestant counterparts to visit their place of worship on a regular basis.

Definitions of Self

Ethnicity is essentially a definition of personal and collective selfhood. Ethnic identities are assembled out of the sequence of answers that arise when we pose the questions: 'who am I?', 'who are we?'. These enquiries generate understandings which sociological jargon sometimes terms 'ontologies'. The process of ontological reflection by definition leads nationalists and unionists to starkly different conclusions. Catholics and Protestants in Northern Ireland formulate divergent understandings of who or what they are. As a result they give different names to their respective senses of peoplehood. These names are among the dominant signifiers of ethnicity in Northern Ireland.

The definition of self that has most currency among Catholics living in the six counties is one that encodes a sense of belonging to a community that encompasses the entire island (Moxon-Browne 1991, p. 25). The countless surveys that have been carried out over the course of the troubles indicate that around three out of every five nationalists in the province consider 'Irishness' to be their principal form of identity (Ruane & Todd 1996, p. 71). The replies that Northern Irish Catholics typically provide during opinion polls suggest that they identify with those who reside in the same island but not the same state. That strong feelings of Irishness have survived among the Catholic community in the province in spite of more than seven decades of partition may be attributed in part to the existence of certain networks that encourage and enable association between nationalists living either side of the Irish border. Various institutions that play an essential role in the everyday lives of Northern Irish Catholics are organised on an island wide basis. The operation of bodies such as the Roman Catholic church or the Gaelic Athletic Association engenders a sense of community among Irish nationalists who happen to be citizens of different states.

While Catholics in Northern Ireland apparently identify closely with the rest of the island, many would also seem to regard themselves as being different in certain crucial respects from those who live south of the border. In opinion polls a substantial minority of Catholic respondents, often as many as one quarter, select 'Northern Irish' as the most faithful description of who they consider themselves to be (Ruane & Todd 1996, p. 71). It is somewhat difficult to arrive at an authoritative understanding of what precisely 'Northern Irishness' means. Presumably this particular version of identity represents a subtle qualification of a broader sense of 'Irishness'. 'Northern Irishness' may express a feeling among nationalists living in the province that while they may share certain essential cultural traits in common with the residents of the Irish Republic, they possess a radically different historical experience. The inclination of many Catholics to regard themselves specifically as 'Northern Irish' may perhaps, in other words, represent an admonition of southern nationalists who have, since partition, essentially abandoned to their fate their ethnic kin stranded in the six counties.

Versions of 'Irishness' would seem to more or less exhaust the definitions of self to which Northern Irish Catholics subscribe. The ontological condition of the nationalist community would appear to make little acknowledgement of the proximity of the other island. In opinion polls only a tiny minority of northern Catholics – rather fewer than one in ten – are willing to identify 'British' as the term that most accurately captures their sense of being in the world (Ruane & Todd 1996, p. 71). Citizenship of the United Kingdom has evidently proved insufficient to nurture among nationalists strong feelings of belonging to the wider environs of these islands.

The definitions of self that Northern Irish Catholics construct contrast strongly with those of the other principal ethnoreligious community with whom they share the 'narrow ground' of the six counties (Moxon-Browne 1991, p. 25). The form of identity that proves most popular among the Protestant community in Northern Ireland is that of 'Britishness'. The data generated by surveys of public opinion intimate that a substantial majority of unionists – invariably between two thirds and three quarters – regard themselves as British (McGarry & O'Leary 1995a, pp. 110–11; Ruane & Todd 1996, p. 59). The feelings of Britishness that exist among Ulster Protestants have grown significantly since the eruption of political unrest in the late 1960s. The pioneering research that the political scientist Richard Rose (1971) carried out on the eve of the present troubles indicated that four out of every ten unionists perceived themselves primarily as British. Three decades later the proportion has become rather closer to seven out of ten.

That feelings of Britishness should have grown so seemingly dramatically among Ulster Protestants over the recent period of conflict may perhaps be explained through reference to those complex processes of social and economic change at work since the demise of the devolved parliament at Stormont. The era of direct rule has been characterised by fiscal benevolence. Westminster administrations of various ideological complexions have sustained public expenditure at rather higher levels in Northern Ireland than in the other regions of the United Kingdom. The relative generosity of the British exchequer over the last quarter of a century has led to the creation of a substantial body of relatively lucrative and secure positions within the public sector. There exists a large number of unionists, and of course nationalists, who understand that they owe their recent mobility and newfound affluence to the disposition of the province's direct rulers.

The conduct of the executive since the dissolution of Stormont has, therefore, underwritten the increasingly enviable lifestyles enjoyed by certain elements within the unionist community. The era of direct rule has further served to reconfigure the everyday life experience of a great many Protestants living in Northern Ireland. Before the outbreak of the current political crisis, Ulster unionists were essentially isolated from the broader cultural and political life of the United Kingdom. Possession of some of the essential apparatus of state during the Stormont period inevitably nurtured among unionist ranks a distinctly debilitating version of parochialism. The experience and imagination of a Protestant people who had grown complacent living in a Protestant state rarely extended beyond the boundaries of the six counties.

The operation of direct rule has, however, inexorably eroded the rather less than splendid isolation of the unionist community within the United Kingdom. Over the last quarter of a century many unionists – and more specifically the unionist middle classes – have become increasingly assimilated into the mainstream of British public life. The restructuring of the Northern Irish economy under the aegis of direct rule has bound sections of the unionist community ever more closely to the rest of the United Kingdom. The distinctly pivotal role that the state plays in the economic life of the province has meant that the organisation of work in both the public and private sectors, and especially in the upper occupational echelons, has come to be 'integrally tied to British policies and practices' (Todd 1987; 1988). As a consequence, many middle class unionists – and their nationalist counterparts also of course – have been drawn increasingly into channels of communication and career advancement that span the United Kingdom and centre upon the British state. These connections are experienced in the guise of attendance of conferences and meetings held in Great Britain, negotiation with state agencies and institutions, routine communication with fellow civil servants in other regions of the United Kingdom and so forth.

The ties that bind the unionist community to the 'mainland' have been strengthened further by recent trends in higher education. Before the onset of the troubles it was quite rare for people from the province to undertake degrees outside the island. In 1968, the year in which the modern conflict arguably began in earnest, only 326 students left Northern Ireland to take up places in British universities. Over the course of the troubles, however, the number of people from the six counties who elect to study in England, Scotland and Wales has grown enormously. It has become particularly popular among the children of the unionist middle classes to attend university 'across the water'. By the early 1990s the number of students from the province enrolled for their first year in British universities and polytechnics was approaching 3,000. The increasing popularity of Great Britain as a place to study means that there are presently in excess of 8,000 Northern Irish people undertaking degrees in institutions of higher education located throughout the other regions of the United Kingdom. The political unrest and chronic unemployment that have until recently blighted the province have frequently meant, moreover, that many of these ostensibly temporary migrants choose not to return once their courses are complete. Recent patterns in higher educational destinations have, therefore, ensured that a great many of the children of the Protestant middle classes have effectively permanently relocated to Great Britain. In the process, an enduring emotional identification with the other parts of the United Kingdom has been established among a substantial section of the unionist community in the six counties.

The growing familiarity of unionists with the 'mainland' finds further expression in recent patterns of travel. The number of residents of the six counties who visit Great Britain has increased enormously during the era of direct rule. The expansion of air travel in recent times has been especially pronounced. In the early 1980s some of the major airlines initiated 'shuttle' services connecting Northern Ireland to various locations throughout Great Britain. These routes have proved hugely and increasingly popular, not least among the province's professional and business classes. In the decade after 1984 the volume of flights between Northern

Ireland and the other regions of the state rose from 329,000 to approximately 500,000.

The operation of direct rule would seem, therefore, to have impacted profoundly upon the interests and experience of Ulster unionists. The inflection of public policy since the early 1970s has conferred considerable affluence upon a significant swathe of the unionist community. The enormous instrumental benefits that have flowed from direct rule might reasonably be expected to have encouraged unionists' sense of identification with the metropolis. Over the last quarter of a century, moreover, elements within the unionist fold have been drawn more fully into the wider environs of the United Kingdom. The present generation of unionists actually possesses rather stronger affective ties with – and indeed rather greater personal experience of – British society than their predecessors did. For certain unionists Edinburgh is the place where they saw their daughter graduate, Cardiff the city where they attended that crucial business conference, London the venue for that unforgettable shopping trip one Christmas a few years back. The period since the dissolution of Stormont would seem, therefore, to have radically altered the manner in which sections of the unionist community experience and understand the state in which they happen to live. The United Kingdom has come increasingly to represent not only a community to which unionists imagine themselves to belong, but also one to which they actually do belong.

The era of direct rule would seem, therefore, to have generated material interests and biographical details that have served to bind elements within the unionist community ever more closely to the adjacent island. Various processes at work within Northern Irish society since the early 1970s have encouraged unionists to identify more closely with the other regions of the state. The experience of direct rule has, in other words, nurtured feelings of 'Britishness' among unionists. It is this particular ontological trend that has been amply recorded in the myriad opinion polls that have been carried out during the troubles.

The unionist experience of direct rule has of course been rather less straightforward than the discussion thus far would suggest. The policies that Westminster administrations have introduced have frequently found favour within the unionist community. The conduct of the executive, however, has often also engendered alienation among unionist ranks. The formal indifference with which Westminster regards the constitutional status of Northern Ireland has inevitably and consistently raised the hackles of Ulster

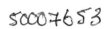

unionists. Hence, while the era of direct rule has on the one hand persuaded unionists to identify more closely still with the British state, it has on the other heightened their perennial distrust of the British government. The tensions that instruct the unionist mind find pertinent, if muted, expression perhaps in the responses that Ulster Protestants provide during surveys of political opinion.

Around one in six unionist respondents select 'Northern Irish' as the phrase that best captures their understanding of themselves (Ruane & Todd 1996, p. 60). As ever this particular ontological construction proves difficult to decipher. One possible reading is that 'Northern Irishness' possesses the same meaning for Protestants as it does for Catholics. In choosing to identify themselves as 'Northern Irish' certain unionists have, in other words, articulated a qualified sense of association with the rest of the island. It is extremely unlikely, however, that this particular interpretation would prove to be correct. Among the unionist community few feelings of kinship exist with those with whom they happen to share the island. An alternative interpretation suggests itself. The phrase 'Northern Irishness' voices perhaps the ambivalence that informs the disposition of contemporary unionism. The notion declares an identity that, although local, does not preclude a sense of belonging to the broader context of the United Kingdom. To consider oneself 'Northern Irish' does not of course mean that one does not at the same time understand oneself to be thoroughly 'British'. On the contrary, the region identified within the ontological condition of 'Northern Irishness' is one that exists strictly within the wider setting of the United Kingdom. While the notion of 'Northern Irishness' does not necessarily obliterate a sense of 'Britishness' it does, however, provide a qualification to that particular sense. In selecting the local as their principal source of identity unionists acknowledge that in certain respects they are distant – and indeed have been *distanced* – from the rest of the United Kingdom. Feelings of 'Northern Irishness' would seem, therefore, to articulate unionists' understanding that their British citizenship, while treasured, remains ultimately precarious.

Within the unionist community there is an acute awareness that in specific crucial regards Northern Ireland exists on the very margins of the United Kingdom. Realisation of the exceptional, and indeed subaltern, status which they endure within the Union has inevitably fostered disenchantment among unionist ranks. This palpable sense of grievance has, however, failed to persuade unionists to imagine themselves to belong to a community other than that delimited by the boundaries of the United Kingdom. The evidence furnished by surveys of political opinion would indicate that unionists are loth to embrace those versions of identity that imply the dissolution of the Union.

Among the numerous possible definitions available to respondents in the six counties is that designated by the term 'Ulster'. While it is tempting to regard the identity of 'Ulster' as simply an equivalent of 'Northern Irishness' it would probably be a mistake to do so. Both ontological states articulate a distinctive sense of place – an identification with those tracts of the island in which the Protestant community has tended to congregate. An Ulster identity acknowledges the local, however, in a manner that does not necessarily entail an association with the wider environs of the United Kingdom. The specific geopolitical configuration to which the term makes reference predates the Union. An Ulster identity may, therefore, be one that constructs Northern Ireland as a place that exists – or rather *should* exist – outside the context of the United Kingdom. To declare oneself as an 'Ulster' person may, in other words, be to eschew the status of Britishness.

Throughout the troubles there has been a sequence of bold predictions foretelling the inexorable rise of Ulster identity among the ranks of the unionist community (B&ICO 1977). Various commentators have insisted that the conduct of Westminster would engender disaffection on a scale that would persuade increasingly substantial numbers of unionists to regard themselves primarily as Ulster men and women. Consideration of those opinion polls carried out during the recent conflict, however, reveals these claims to have been entirely erroneous (McGarry & O'Leary 1995a, p. 110). At the beginning of the troubles there would appear to have been a strong sense of 'Ulster' identity among the unionist population. Indeed, one third of the Protestants surveyed by Richard Rose in the late 1960s elected to identify themselves as Ulster folk. Over the course of the troubles, however, the proportion of unionists who chose the term 'Ulster' as capturing best their sense of self has declined enormously (Nelson 1984, p. 9). By the early 1990s only one in ten unionist respondents were prepared to identify themselves primarily as 'Ulster' men and women.

The marked decline of Ulster identity among unionists in Northern Ireland would seem entirely consistent with the ontological trends sketched earlier. Over the last three decades many people from unionist backgrounds have come to see, and to feel, themselves as belonging principally to a community that accommodates all of the regions of the United Kingdom. Unionists have increasingly chosen to denigrate those versions of the local that promise to imperil that broader sense of being in the world. The propensity among unionists to privilege feelings of 'Britishness' explains their evident aversion to Ulster identity. The term 'Ulster' has powerful connotations that extract Northern Ireland out of the context of the United Kingdom. An 'Ulster' identity is one that challenges rather than complements a sense of Britishness. It is scarcely surprising, therefore, that it has been so thoroughly rejected by unionists whose lives and emotions have become more closely entwined than ever before with those of their fellow British citizens.

While relatively few unionists are willing to embrace an Ulster identity there exists even less enthusiasm among unionist ranks for Irishness. When unionism aligned in the closing decades of the previous century, its adherents were quite content to regard themselves as 'Irish' people subsumed within a broader community of the 'British' (Loughlin 1995). The direction that Irish nationalism subsequently took seriously questioned, however, the presumed complementary nature of these ontological forms. The nationalist enterprise insisted that 'Irishness' and 'Britishness' represented ways of being in the world that were essentially incompatible. As the demand for national autonomy gathered pace in Ireland, unionists came increasingly to accept this particular reading. Throughout the present century the unionist community has gradually demoted feelings of 'Irishness' in favour of a sense of 'Britishness'. This process of ontological distinction has inevitably gathered pace over the course of the recent conflict in Northern Ireland. The endeavours of elements within the nationalist community to break the connections between these islands has encouraged the unionist mind to regard 'Irishness' as a form of identity that is ultimately injurious to a sense of being British. As a consequence, the number of unionists willing to regard themselves as 'Irish' has dwindled significantly during the recent troubles. In the late 1960s around one in five Protestants living in the six counties considered themselves principally to be Irish. Over the last three decades, however, this particular constituency within the unionist community has all but disappeared (McGarry & O'Leary 1995a, p. 110). At the moment only a very small body of unionists – perhaps as few as one in 25 – consider 'Irish' to be the term that captures best their own sense of being in the world.

Education

Those ethnoreligious divisions that characterise the six counties find especially graphic illustration within the province's educational system. Pupils in Northern Ireland are almost entirely segregated along confessional lines. The scale of the segregation that exists within the province's schools moved the eminent political scientist John Whyte (1986, p. 230) to suggest that the educational system provides those practices that are most important in defining and reproducing the ethnoreligious divide within Northern Ireland.

With few exceptions Protestant and Catholic children growing up in Northern Ireland are educated apart from one another. Those schools that fall directly under the authority of the state are formally intended to be non-denominational and provide a broadly Christian education to pupils drawn from diverse religious traditions. In reality, however, these institutions have proved unable to attract children from Catholic families. As a result, the state or 'controlled' schools that operate in Northern Ireland are *de facto* Protestant schools.

Children from nationalist backgrounds typically receive their formal education in schools that are governed not by the state but rather by the Roman Catholic church. The evolution of the Catholic educational system in Northern Ireland has been defined largely by the conflicting ambitions of retaining independence from official agencies on the one hand and attracting greater public funding on the other. In the aftermath of partition, those schools in the six counties attended by nationalists operated effectively without reference to the institutions of the fledgling Northern Irish state. The Catholic educational system initially received only modest funding from the Unionist regime and for a time in the 1920s the salaries of nationalist teachers were provided by the Irish Free State. During the lifetime of the devolved parliament at Stormont, however, the level of public funds channelled into Catholic or 'maintained' schools gradually increased. By the late 1960s the lure of greater state funding had become sufficient to persuade the church hierarchy to concede some control over the education of Catholic children. A minority of the representatives on the Board of Governors of Catholic schools would in future be government nominees. In return the state pledged to provide all of the running costs, primarily the salaries of teachers, and 85 per cent of the capital costs – notably those expenses incurred through the construction of new buildings – of Catholic schools.

These arrangements lasted until the winter of 1992 when an important reformulation of the relationship between the Catholic school system and the state was announced (Cormack & Osborne 1995, p. 514). The Northern Ireland Office offered a commitment that henceforth all of the capital expenses of schools catering for Catholic children would be met out of the public purse. In future these institutions would be governed by newly constituted authorities comprising nine persons, only four of whom would be nominated by the church. It would appear, therefore, that the hierarchy of the church has ceded control over the governing bodies of Catholic schools. The British government has, however, agreed that those individuals it nominates for positions on school boards should be subject to the approval of the church authorities. It is entirely likely, therefore, that in practice the Catholic church will retain fundamental control over the education of the younger members of its flock.

The school constitutes of course one of the principal sites of the socialisation process. An influential study conducted in Great Britain during the 1970s estimated that pupils spend on average 15,000 hours within the educational system (Rutter et al. 1979). During the considerable period of their school careers, children are introduced to particular recurrent understandings of who they are and, equally importantly, who they are not. The education process in Northern Ireland as elsewhere plays an indispensible role in the promotion of specific forms of social being and distinction.

The segregated schools that operate within Northern Ireland inevitably tend to nurture those cultural identities associated with the particular ethnoreligious communities from which their pupils are drawn (Murray 1985). The formal and hidden curricula that characterise 'controlled' and 'maintained' schools respectively often diverge considerably. Those schools that fall within the remit of the state and cater for pupils who come overwhelmingly from Protestant families typically promote a sense of Britishness. The Union flag may be flown upon occasion and portraits of the Royal Family may be on view. The school may observe the pivotal moments of British state ritual. Pupils may be encouraged to honour the memory of those who served in the armed forces during the wars of this century. The academic curriculum of the school may exhibit a leaning towards the consideration of British history and geography. Physical education may entail the promotion of ostensibly 'English' sports such as cricket or rugby.

The culture that obtains within state schools in the province, therefore, encourages pupils to perceive themselves as 'British'. Those institutions that cater for children from nationalist backgrounds inevitably generate a rather different sense of being in the world. The Catholic educational system would seem to advance a distinctive version of Irishness. The ethos of 'controlled' schools is often, as one would expect, explicitly religious. Catholic iconography may appear frequently on the walls of the institution and school holidays may coincide with specific religious festivals. Moreover, religious instruction may feature prominently in the syllabus and pupils may undertake retreats in the company of their classmates. The formal curriculum devised within the school may reveal a preference for Irish history and geography. The sports that pupils are encouraged to pursue may be those associated with the Gaelic Athletic Association (GAA).

The divisions that define contemporary Northern Irish society are, therefore, clearly evident within the province's educational system. Almost every pupil in the six counties attends a school populated exclusively by his or her ethnoreligious kin. There are, however, two categories of exception to this general rule. First, there is a small body of Catholic children, mainly from middle class neighbourhoods, who go to schools that are in effect Protestant. The parents of these pupils are usually attracted by the exceptional academic records of certain Protestant grammar schools. Second, there are some pupils enrolled in institutions that are specifically designed to cater for more or less equal proportions of the 'two communities'. These 'integrated' schools have attracted considerable attention and enthusiasm over the last 15 years or so. Indeed supporters have occasionally asserted that educating children together represents the single greatest opportunity of ensuring that the younger generation in the six counties will be able to transcend the enmities that have consumed their predecessors. In spite of the ambitious claims made in its name, the integrated education movement in Northern Ireland remains very much in its infancy. At the moment only one out of every 43 pupils in the province is enrolled in a school that draws equally from both major ethno-religious communities (DENI 1997). In 1989 the Northern Ireland Office introduced certain financial inducements designed to encourage the formation of integrated schools in the province. Consequently the last decade has witnessed the opening of various institutions catering for children of all religious backgrounds and none, scattered throughout the six counties. In spite of these developments, however, it would seem highly unlikely that in the foreseeable future integrated schools will be able to break the mould of segregated education in Northern Ireland.

Cultural Products and Practices

Those ethnic identities and divisions that obtain within Northern Ireland are actualised through the cultural practices in which the 'two communities' engage and in the cultural products which they consume. The cultural rites and artifacts that represent the most important signifiers of ethnoreligious persuasion within the six counties are as detailed below.

Names

It is frequently the case in Northern Ireland that particular forenames and surnames indicate membership of one ethnoreligious community rather than the other. Irish names are of course more or less the exclusive preserve of the nationalist community. There are also some names that derive from the English language that suggest that the bearer belongs to one or other ethnoreligious traditions. Should one be introduced to someone called 'Billy' or 'Sammy' one might reasonably presume that person to be a Protestant. Equally, should one cross paths with 'Anthony' or 'Mickey' an educated guess would suggest that these individuals hailed from the nationalist community. One further – though rather less important – baptismal trend that may be discerned in the province is a peculiar propensity for some Protestant parents to use apparent surnames as forenames for their sons. It is far from uncommon in Northern Ireland to come across unionists with christian names such as 'Hamilton', 'Frazer' or 'Boyd'.

Language

At first glance language would seem to be one of the few cultural artifacts that Catholics and Protestants have in common. English is the first language of the overwhelming majority of people living in the six counties and is spoken fluently even by those who claim another language as their mother tongue. Nonetheless, the issue of language is one which both reflects and inflames the ethnic divisions prevalent within Northern Irish society. Considerable controversy surrounds the role and status of the Irish language. Irish speakers are drawn almost entirely from the Catholic community and the language is taught solely in those 'maintained' schools that cater exclusively for the needs of pupils from nationalist backgrounds. A substantial minority of northern nationalists would seem to possess at least some knowledge of Irish. The last census of population carried out in 1991 indicated that nine and a half per cent of the entire population of Northern Ireland claim a rudimentary, or better, understanding of the Irish language. Given that almost all of these people are likely to hail from the nationalist tradition, it would seem that around one quarter of the Catholic community in the province possess at least a working knowledge of Irish.

The significance that the Irish language possesses for Northern Irish nationalists is, of course, rather greater than suggested by the total of individuals who are actually able to converse through that medium. Even those who have merely a passing acquaintance with the language will often acknowledge Irish as an essential component of who or what they consider themselves to be. The manner in which Irish is regarded and treated – not least by the British government – has come to represent for many nationalists a ready metaphor for their status as an ethnopolitical community. Attempts from whatever quarter to disparage the language are read as a slight against self even by those Catholics who have no particular interest in becoming Irish speakers.

The disposition of the unionist community towards the Irish language tends to be rather less sympathetic. In the minds of Protestants living in the six counties, Irish constitutes the linguistic expression of a cultural tradition and a political enterprise that are both profoundly alien. Unionists have frequently articulated their hostility towards the Irish language through infantile derision (McGarry & O'Leary 1995a, p. 221). One prominent unionist politician – Sammy Wilson of the Democratic Unionist Party (DUP) – was moved to dismiss Irish as a 'leprechaun language'. Others within the Protestant community have, however, chosen to take the medium of Irish rather more seriously. For many unionists the revival of the Irish language during the troubles is emblematic of a growing cultural confidence and assertiveness among nationalists that threatens ultimately to undermine the constitutional status quo. In the unionist mind, therefore, Irish represents the linguistic form of a cultural persona that is not merely alien but hostile. The aversion that the unionist community harbours towards Irish has ensured that it is not offered as part of the curriculum in 'controlled' schools that instruct children from

Protestant households. It is hardly surprising, therefore, that the number of Protestants in Northern Ireland who are able or indeed willing to speak Irish is distinctly negligible.

The Media

The operation of the media has in general served to create interests and experiences that are common to both of the principal ethnopolitical communities within the six counties. Individuals from unionist and nationalist backgrounds have exhibited equal enthusiasm for those versions of mass culture served up by the media empires that have come increasingly to dominate the globe. Catholics are no more or no less likely than their Protestant counterparts to have cultivated a passion for the exultant melancholia of *Radiohead*, the playful millenial angst of the *X-Files* or the byzantine narratives of Italian football.

Ethnoreligious persuasion has nonetheless exercised some influence over the manner in which the citizens of Northern Ireland encounter and consume the products of the media industries. Certain elements of the media in the province have tended to cater more or less exclusively for the tastes of one or the other ethnoreligious community. These distinctions become readily apparent when we consider the two morning newspapers that are published in Belfast. The *Irish News* attracts an estimated readership of 140,000 people drawn overwhelmingly from the Catholic population (McGarry & O'Leary 1995a, p. 223). The features and editorials of the newspaper often give voice to political interests that are essentially those of constitutional nationalism. The *Irish News* devotes considerable attention, moreover, to a range of Gaelic cultural and sporting events.

The other principal morning newspaper published in the province appeals to an altogether different ethnoreligious group. An overwhelming majority of the 133,000 individuals who read the *News Letter* each day are Protestants. The particular ethnopolitical composition of its readership inevitably finds reflection in the coverage that the newspaper provides. The editorials that appear in the *News Letter* generally advance an unequivocally unionist interpretation of events. The cultural practices that are covered in the newspaper are invariably those conventionally associated with Britishness. Little or no mention of traditional Irish music or Gaelic games – or at least none of a complimentary nature – is to be found between the covers of the *News Letter*.

Sport

Among the improbable claims that have gained currency within popular discourse is that which portrays sport as an essential site of communal reconciliation. Athletic events are portrayed with some frequency as creating a space that enables peoples from diverse backgrounds to transcend their differences in the pursuit of a shared passion. While the rites associated with sport may well have the ability to heal, they also have of course the facility to wound. The role that sport can play in the production and reproduction of social division becomes painfully clear within the specific context of Northern Ireland (Sugden & Bairner 1993a).

Most of the sports that are popular within the six counties exercise an attraction for one, but not the other, ethnoreligious bloc. Those games that are administered by the Gaelic Athletic Association (GAA) are pursued solely by members of the nationalist community. Protestants living in the province invariably regard the GAA with suspicion and hostility. The antipathy that emanates from the unionist community owes a great deal to the standing orders of the association. Rule 21 of the constitution of the GAA expressly forbids members of the security forces from playing Gaelic games (Sugden & Bairner 1993b, pp. 172–5). The existence of this particular provision has inevitably fuelled the unionist conviction that the association is merely another manifestation of the republican movement. In the eyes of many unionists the function of the GAA is not simply cultural but political as well. The animosity that Protestants often feel towards the association has at times given rise to violence. In recent years loyalists have instigated numerous attacks upon the personnel and facilities of Gaelic sports clubs.

While Gaelic games are evidently the preserve of northern nationalists, there are certain sports that are more closely associated with the unionist tradition. Individuals who exhibit an enthusiasm for cricket, rugby or hockey might reasonably be presumed to have had a Protestant upbringing. These athletic pursuits offer to many unionists an important sense of who or what they are. The symbolic significance that cricket, rugby or hockey possess for the unionist community remains, however, somewhat less than that which Gaelic games hold for nationalists in the province.

The reluctance of nationalists to embrace certain sports that are central to the lives of many unionists represents of course an articulation of ethnic consciousness. Catholics living in the six counties tend to regard cricket, rugby and hockey as pastimes that are quintessentially 'English'. These particular pursuits are understood, in other words, to be expressive of a cultural identity that nationalists consider to be different from – and ultimately inimical to – their own (Sugden & Bairner 1993b, pp. 186–8). In choosing to shun 'garrison games', therefore, nationalists in the six counties advance an important definition of who they are or, more accurately perhaps, who they are not.

Hence, the segregation that pervades contemporary Northern Irish society finds pertinent expression within the realm of sport. While the 'two communities' within the six counties often incline towards different sports there is nonetheless one particular pursuit that appeals to both. Association football or soccer exercises an enormous and equal appeal for Catholics and Protestants alike. In Northern Ireland, as elsewhere, football is followed with particular passion within working class communities. Soccer regularly brings into contact Catholic and Protestant secondary school pupils who might not otherwise have the opportunity to meet (Sugden & Bairner 1991, p. 140). Given its almost universal appeal, association football represents the sport that in principle possesses the greatest potential to promote intercommunal dialogue and appreciation within the six counties. In practice though, soccer has more often provided a forum for the exhibition of the most grotesque forms of ethnopolitical prejudice. This has been true at both club and international level.

Local soccer in the province has been traditionally dominated by teams based in Belfast. Patterns of football allegiance in the regional capital have inevitably betrayed the existence of territorial and ethnopolitical loyalties. The intense competition that exists between Belfast clubs often acknowledges the divergent ethno-religious composition of their followers. Historically one of the keenest rivalries within the Irish League was that between Linfield, whose supporters are overwhelmingly loyalists, and Belfast Celtic, whose fans were almost all nationalists. The ethnopolitical animosity that the followers of both clubs harboured for one another produced numerous episodes of violence, culminating in an especially notorious incident in the late 1940s when a match had to be abandoned due to rioting during which one of the Celtic players was severely assaulted by Linfield supporters. Within a few years Belfast Celtic had folded and the club's former ground is now the site of a shopping mall (Bairner 1997).

The ethnopolitical enmities that provide one of the subtexts of local soccer in Northern Ireland have of course been exacerbated by the political upheavals of the last three decades. The shifting sectarian geography of Belfast has ensured that Cliftonville, situated in the north of the city, has come to be a club supported almost entirely by nationalists. Relations between followers of Cliftonville and those of other teams more closely associated with the unionist community are, as one might expect, often less than cordial. Fixtures between the club and the likes of Crusaders, Glentoran, Portadown and Coleraine routinely entail verbal abuse being hurled between rival supporters and occasionally descend into serious violence (Bairner 1997). Throughout the troubles the security forces have held to the view that were the followers of Linfield to be allowed to travel to Cliftonville's cramped stadium in north Belfast a major breach of the peace would almost inevitably ensue. As a result, in the years since 1970 Cliftonville have been forced to stage their 'home' matches against Linfield at the latter's ground at Windsor Park. The apparent improvement in the local political climate that has occurred over the last few years has, however, ensured that Linfield was able recently to return to 'Solitude' (Bairner & Shirlow 1998, p. 175). On 21 November 1998 Cliftonville played host to 'the Blues' for the first time in almost three decades. The advent of the fixture was inevitably greeted in many quarters as further evidence that Northern Irish society is gradually returning to normal. An alternative reading might suggest that the form that the tie assumed merely underscores the abiding fragility of political relations in the six counties. That the game had to be played in the morning, before a crowd restricted to merely a fraction of what it would otherwise have been, attests to the depth of the communal antagonism that persists in the province.

The ethnoreligious prejudice that infests association football in Northern Ireland is exemplified best perhaps in the recruitment practices of the province's most successful club side. It was until very recently customary for Linfield to select only players from Protestant backgrounds (Bairner & Shirlow 1998). Throughout the 1980s Linfield enjoyed phenomenal success in the Irish League. It was evidently a source of enormous pride for many of the Protestants who followed the fortunes of Linfield that the triumphs of the club had been secured by a side manned exclusively by their ethnoreligious kin. As Linfield swept from one championship to the next their followers would bellow from the sidelines their support for the 'eleven Protestants'. The particularism that has traditionally governed team selection at Windsor Park was made explicit during 1992 by the manager of the club at the time (Sugden & Bairner 1993b, p. 179). In an interview with a fanzine,

Eric Bowyer summoned the candour to admit that under prevailing circumstances it was highly unlikely that he would be able to sign someone from the nationalist community.

This admission surfaced in the mainstream press and in time came to the attention of a pressure group based in the United States that takes an active interest in the affairs of the province. The Irish National Caucus sought an indirect channel through which to bring financial pressure to bear upon Linfield. Companies including Coca Cola were encouraged to withdraw vital sponsorship from the Irish Football Association (IFA) which the pressure group considered guilty by association with Linfield because of its practice of staging international fixtures at the club's ground. While the Irish National Caucus was unable to persuade any corporation to withhold further patronage, the adverse publicity which it generated would seem to have had some impact upon recruitment practices at Windsor Park. Within months of the original controversial interview with Eric Bowyer, Linfield had signed a Catholic player from fierce rivals Cliftonville. While Chris Cullen made relatively few appearances in a Linfield jersey, a number of other individuals from nationalist backgrounds have subsequently made a rather greater impact at Windsor Park. Indeed arguably the best player to have represented Linfield during the 1990s has been a Catholic from the southern Irish border town of Dundalk.

Association football frequently offers a mirror to the fissures and animosities that define the social formation that obtains within the six counties. The political violence that has cursed Northern Ireland over recent generations has inevitably impacted directly upon numerous local soccer clubs. The principal victim of the civil unrest that has overtaken the province since the late 1960s has undoubtedly been Derry City (Bairner & Shirlow 1998, p. 170). The club's stadium is located in the Bogside district which was of course one of the epicentres of the upheavals that heralded the onset of the present troubles. As the political climate in Northern Ireland degenerated apace throughout the early 1970s various other Irish League clubs became increasingly reluctant to fulfil away fixtures with Derry City. The conviction that the Brandywell represented a dangerous venue seemed to have been confirmed when a busload of visiting Ballymena United supporters was attacked outside the ground. In the wake of the attack the authorities insisted that in future Derry City would have to play their home games at a neutral venue. Supporters of the club inevitably proved reluctant to travel to the Coleraine showgrounds for 'home' matches in numbers comparable to those that had regularly attended the Brandywell. Dwindling attendances, coupled with the substantial additional expenditure arising out of having to stage all of their fixtures outside the Bogside, ensured that the financial costs associated with running Derry City soon became intolerable. In 1972 the club bowed to the seemingly inevitable and offered its resignation to the Irish League (Sugden & Bairner 1993b, p. 180). At various stages during the decade that followed Derry City applied for readmission. On each occasion the club's application was refused by the local football authorities. Increasingly frustrated with the intransigence of the Irish League the custodians of the dormant Derry City began to explore the possibility of competing south of the border. The response of the authorities who administer domestic soccer in the 26 counties proved rather more enthusiastic. Consequently, since 1985 Derry City has competed in the League of Ireland, occasionally with success and frequently before packed stadia.

It is often held that sport should represent a pristine and inclusive realm of human engagement untainted by the exclusive, and frequently squalid, imperatives that arise out of political allegiance. Even a cursory acquaintance with the recent history of domestic soccer in Northern Ireland confirms that such distinctions are often impossible to maintain. Over the last few years various actors have sought to use association football as a medium through which to declare and advance their particular political interests. In recent summers certain controversial loyalist parades have led to tense and often violent confrontations which have attracted a great deal of international attention. Nationalists living in various locations within the six counties – the Garvaghy Road in Portadown, the Lower Ormeau Road in Belfast, the County Antrim village of Dunloy among others – have expressed unwillingness to allow members of the Orange Order to process along 'traditional' routes through their districts. The opposition that nationalist communities have offered to Orange parades has of course engendered outrage among substantial elements of the Protestant population. Almost inevitably loyalists have sought to mimic the tactics that nationalist demonstrators have, with varying degrees of success, come to adopt. There exists, however, a relatively meagre tradition of religious or political parades within the Catholic community. In the absence of a precise equivalent of the Orange march, loyalists intent on impeding the movement of members of the nationalist community have chosen to improvise. Throughout the winter of 1996/97 Catholics seeking to go to mass in a particular parish in Ballymena were greeted by a hostile loyalist mob. The boorish blockade of Harryville church merely confirmed the suspicion of many onlookers located on this island, and further afield, that Ulster Protestants are prone to the crudest forms of sectarian prejudice.

Those loyalists intent on retaliating against nationalist obstruction of Orange parades also chose certain soccer fixtures as convenient contexts in which to advance their aims. In the autumn of 1996 Cliftonville – a club which, as we noted earlier, attracts support mainly from the nationalist community – was scheduled to compete in the semi-finals of a local cup competition. The relevant tie was to be staged at the Oval, the home ground of Glentoran which is situated in the heart of loyalist east Belfast. As a contingent of Cliftonville supporters accompanied by a police escort approached the venue they encountered a group of local residents blocking the road. While the travelling fans eventually gained access to the ground and the match was completed, the actions of loyalists living in the vicinity of the Oval had evidently established an unfortunate precedent. In the months that followed, Cliftonville's away fixtures occasionally became the arena for demonstrations staged by loyalists. The scale of loyalist protest was inevitably greatest when the club travelled to Portadown, the north Armagh town in which the parades issues has created most animosity. On one occasion a busload of visiting supporters was badly assaulted outside Shamrock Park while the Cliftonville players considered the atmosphere within the ground to be so hostile that they refused to emerge from the dressing room after half time.

The propensity for the political divisions that prevail within Northern Ireland to intrude upon local soccer was clearly illustrated in the course of a controversy that broke during the winter of 1998. Donegal Celtic is a football club based in a strongly republican district of west Belfast. Although it currently competes in one of the province's junior divisions, the club possesses enormous potential and harbours ambitions to enter the Irish League. The progress of Donegal Celtic has, however, been impeded at various turns by the ethnopolitical tensions that brood within the six counties. In 1996 the west Belfast side was drawn in a cup competition to face a team representing the Royal Ulster Constabulary (RUC). Residents of the community in which Donegal Celtic is situated invariably look upon the police with distrust and disdain. Local feeling about the match was considered so strong that the club decided that it could not fulfil the fixture.

In October 1998 the names of Donegal Celtic and the RUC were once again drawn out of the hat together. On this occasion the two clubs were supposed to meet in the semi-final of the Steel and Son Cup which, although being a strictly junior competition, attracts considerable interest and prestige. Initially at least, Donegal Celtic seemed to believe that the political changes that had taken place in the two years since the cancellation of the previous fixture meant that the tie had become viable. Although a couple of players had indicated that they would not be available for selection, most people associated with the club seemed to be of the view that the match should go ahead. The intention of Donegal Celtic to fulfil their fixture against the RUC drew inevitable criticism from republican quarters. Relatives of those killed or injured by the RUC declared that it would be inappropriate for a club that has such close associations with the nationalist community to have sporting ties with an unreconstructed police force that has inflicted enormous suffering upon that same community. The President of Sinn Fein, Gerry Adams, sought to bring his own substantial personal influence to bear through veiled comments that implied that it would be better if the match were not to go ahead.

Under increasing pressure from republicans, the office bearers of Donegal Celtic decided to canvass opinion within the club concerning the imminent fixture with the RUC. At a subsequent meeting a large majority of the members of Donegal Celtic voted that the match should be played. This apparent declaration of popular support for competing in the semi-finals of the Steel and Son Cup served little, however, to disarm republican opposition. Allegations began to surface in the local press that certain Donegal Celtic players had been visited at home and work by republican activists who had advised them that it would be best not to participate in the forthcoming match against the RUC. With depressing inevitability, the efforts of republicans to ensure the cancellation of the offending fixture quickly came to fruition. On the eve of the semi-final a representative of Donegal Celtic announced that the club had decided reluctantly to withdraw from the competition.

The ethnopolitical tensions that routinely contaminate local soccer are equally apparent when we shift our focus towards the international scene. In principle, the Northern Irish team represents all of the people of the six counties. In practice, however, the international side appeals more or less solely to members of the unionist community. The distinctly exclusive connotations that the Northern Irish team currently possesses are largely a product of the era of the troubles. Before the onset of the modern political unrest the football side representing the province exercised an appeal that often transcended the communal divide. As late as 1950 the Irish Football Association (IFA) continued to select players from south of the border (Sugden & Bairner 1994, p. 125). Until the 1970s, moreover, the official title of the international side was in fact 'Ireland'. In the years that preceded the troubles, therefore, the IFA often seemed to engage in practices that sought to include all of the diverse peoples of the province.

The 'meaning' of the international side has, however, altered dramatically in the course of the troubles. Over the last 30 years the Northern Irish team has become increasingly closely associated with elements of the unionist community. John Sugden and Alan Bairner (1993b, p. 179; 1994, pp. 129–30) have argued persuasively that the entirely successful efforts of loyalists to appropriate the international side may be read as a response to the political crises that have unfolded during the troubles. In the 1970s Protestants were deprived of certain institutions and agencies with which they had come to identify strongly. With Stormont prorogued and the B-Specials disbanded, elements within the unionist community began to look for other emblems that could articulate and sustain their particular sense of selfhood. The international soccer side, Sugden and Bairner suggest, represented the only available agency with the potential to express adequately loyalists' sense of who they are and of course who they are not. As a consequence the Northern Irish team has come to possess huge symbolic significance for many Protestants living in the province.

The anxiety of loyalists to claim it as their own has inevitably meant that the international side has come to have profoundly exclusive ethnopolitical connotations. Over the last quarter of a century Windsor Park has become an increasingly inhospitable venue for Catholics and even for liberal Protestants. In the course of every international game sections of the crowd will chant familiar ethnopolitical slogans and songs. Visiting teams and their supporters will be subjected repeatedly to hearty renditions of 'the Sash' and 'the Billy Boys'. The ethnopolitical sentiments issued from the stands of Windsor Park during internationals are mainly directed towards abstract others who would never dream of setting foot inside the ground on such occasions. There have been times though when players representing Northern Ireland have been verbally abused by supporters supposedly there to cheer them on. One individual who was incessantly barracked was the hapless Anton Rogan, who inspired animosity among sections of the Windsor Park crowd for no other reason than he happened to be a west Belfast Catholic who for a time made a living playing for Glasgow Celtic, a club that occupies a central position within the demonology of Ulster loyalism (Sugden & Bairner 1994, pp. 129–30).

The particular ethnopolitical connotations that the Northern Irish soccer team has acquired over the course of the troubles have inevitably alienated nationalists. This process of alienation has been accelerated by the improvement in the fortunes of the other international side on the island that has taken place since the late 1980s. Over the last decade many nationalists who have an interest in soccer have switched their allegiance to the Republic of Ireland on the grounds that it enables them to follow a team that has not only been relatively successful, but has also ethnopolitical associations with which they are entirely comfortable. At international matches hosted in Dublin it has become increasingly common to see on display Irish tricolours that bear placenames originating within the six counties.

The divided football loyalties of the two principal ethnoreligious traditions within the province were brutally exposed during a notorious international fixture staged in November 1993 (Harvie 1996). Northern Ireland and the Republic of Ireland had been drawn in the same World Cup qualification group. Ill fortune further conspired to ensure that the final round of matches in the group pitched the two teams against one another at Windsor Park. While Northern Ireland had no chance of qualification, their opponents needed to take a point from the fixture in order to proceed to the World Cup finals in the USA the following summer. The particular tensions that all meetings between the two international sides on the island can be expected to generate were heightened further by the highly volatile political climate in which the match was played. The massacres at Greysteel and on the Shankill Road had taken place within the previous month. Against this particular backdrop it was always likely that on the evening of 17 November 1993 Windsor Park would provide the venue for an exhibition of the most grotesque versions of ethnopolitical prejudice that contaminate the six counties. The partisan support gathered in the ground bellowed their allegiance for the home side in the hope that a rare victory would deprive the loathed Irish Republic of a place in the World Cup finals. A sequence of loyalist anthems was delivered throughout the entire duration of the game. Elements within the crowd managed to plumb new depths through a series of songs that glorified those who had slaughtered six

Catholics in the Rising Sun bar three weeks earlier. While unionists were strongly behind the Northern Irish side, the allegiances of nationalists lay in the main with the visitors. The eventual outcome of the fixture was to prove rather more pleasing to the latter. An equaliser late in the game ensured that the Republic of Ireland would be the sole representatives from these islands to compete in the 1994 World Cup finals.

That the enmities that corrupt the province should have found expression within the realm of soccer scarcely comes as a surprise of course. Association football has after all in various locations and historical periods provided a space for some of the worst excesses of humanity. The facility of ethnopolitical distinction to pervade certain other realms of sport might be considered rather more remarkable. Even that most sedate and bourgeois of games – namely golf – has been unable to remain aloof from the communal distinctions and divisions that are part of the social fabric of Northern Ireland. This becomes apparent when we examine the ethnoreligious composition of the membership of two golf clubs located close to one another in south Belfast. The facilities of the prestigious Malone club tend to be enjoyed in the main by Protestant business and professional people. The newer club, situated at nearby Balmoral, in contrast, typically draws its members from the growing body of middle class Catholics who live in the leafy avenues of the regional capital.

Space

That which separates unionists and nationalists in Northern Ireland is often symbolic or cultural. Ethnic division in the province also, however, finds literal, physical expression through the manner in which space is organised, transformed and experienced. The ethnopolitical cleavage that exists within the six counties assumes a couple of important *spatial* forms.

Regional Distribution of the Two Communities

The two largest ethnoreligious communities that coexist within Northern Ireland are unevenly distributed throughout the six counties. Nationalists have recently assumed the status of a majority within the regional capital of Belfast. In the main though, the nationalist population tends to be concentrated in those district council areas located in the western reaches of the province

(Douglas 1998). As the number of nationalists living west of the River Bann has grown over the past couple of decades, unionists have begun to drift away from these districts and especially from certain areas situated close to the border. As a result the Protestant population in Northern Ireland has come to be concentrated increasingly in an eastern enclave that comprises parts of counties Antrim, Down and Armagh.

Residential Segregation

Members of the 'two traditions' in Northern Ireland often reside, therefore, in different regions of the province. Even when unionists and nationalists happen to reside within the same district, however, they often effectively live apart from one another. The data garnered during the 1991 census of population offers a sense of the scale of the residential segregation that exists within contemporary Northern Irish society (McKittrick 1994, pp. 40–6). The census results suggest that around half of the total population of the province lives in districts in which 90 per cent or more of the population comes from one or other ethnoreligious bloc. The residential segregation seemingly characteristic of the entire six counties would appear particularly acute in the context of the region's capital. In 35 of Belfast's 52 census wards residents are drawn more or less entirely from one or other ethnoreligious tradition. The physical separation of nationalists and unionists has found literal and symbolic expression in certain parts of the city with the erection by the authorities of walls designed to keep the feuding factions apart. While these 'environmental barriers' or 'peace lines' were originally conceived as temporary, many have assumed a distinctly permanent appearance. The process of residential segregation has become so advanced within Belfast that there now exists only a handful of areas in which substantial numbers of Protestants and Catholics live amicably side by side. The upper stretch of the Antrim Road in the north of the city and the Malone Road to the south spring readily to mind. These middle class districts are, however, presently in the midst of a prolonged process of ethnic recomposition. It remains to be seen whether the few mixed neighbourhoods that currently exist in Belfast will, over time, retain their pluralist character.

The spatial distinctions that define contemporary Northern Irish society are particularly pronounced within working class districts. The experience of living in a divided society frequently impacts dramatically upon the disposition and conduct of the working classes. The distinctive mosaic of interfaces between separate, and frequently hostile, ethnoreligious communities that often defines the landscape of Belfast and elsewhere severely inhibits the spatial mobility of people from working class backgrounds. Young working class men are particularly likely to find themselves constrained within deeply restricted 'life worlds' (Jenkins 1983). The hostility that often defines relations between the 'two communities' ensures that individuals of working class stock possess an intimate understanding of ethnopolitical geography and of those ethnographic cues that signal communal affiliation. The latter knowledge is actualised through the ritualised practices of 'telling the difference' – an intricate process that varies hugely in terms of subtlety through which one social actor seeks to ascertain the ethnic status of another. Possession of these interpretive skills is crucial in enabling a person to 'manage' everyday situations in a manner that avoids offering inadvertent offence to those with whom one comes into contact. Knowing how to 'tell' can under certain circumstances, of course, become an indispensible means of self-preservation.

Endogamy

The ethnoreligious distinctions that are a hallmark of contemporary Northern Irish society are manifested further in patterns of marriage within the six counties. In the province almost all marriages are 'endogamous', that is, they involve partners drawn from the same ethnopolitical tradition. The prevalence of endogamy within Northern Ireland means that only one in 20 marital unions that take place actually pairs individuals who come from different ethnoreligious origins (McGarry & O'Leary 1995a, p. 186). The apparent reluctance of Northern Irish people to enter into 'exogamous' or 'mixed' marriages largely represents a reflex of the numerous other forms of segregation that exist within the six counties. Individuals from divergent ethnoreligious backgrounds growing up in the province frequently attend different schools, workplaces and social venues. The experience of living in a divided society inevitably dissuades the practice of exogamy. As McGarry & O'Leary (1995b, p. 850) bluntly, though reasonably, observe, if 'Catholics do not meet Protestants, they are unlikely to want to marry them'.

Life Chances

When examining patterns of ethnic division social scientists often focus primarily upon concerns that are essentially cultural and symbolic. Sociologists tend to be concerned with what members of discrete communal blocs consider themselves to be and how these definitions of self are represented through systems of language, belief and creative expression. Those social distinctions that attend ethnic personae are, however, not only cultural but material as well. Unionists and nationalists differ not simply in terms of their understandings of who or what they are, but also with regard to the 'life chances' that they happen to enjoy or endure. The existence of significant economic disparities between the 'two communities' constitutes an essential element of the broader pattern of ethnopolitical distinction within the six counties.

Historically, Catholics and Protestants living in Northern Ireland have had radically different socioeconomic profiles. In the decades between partition and the eruption of the troubles the middle classes within the Catholic community were relatively small and engaged in a narrow range of economic activities that invariably entailed the provision of services to fellow nationalists. The typical occupations of the middle class nationalist during the Stormont period were those of doctor, teacher, priest and publican. Since the introduction of 'direct rule' in the spring of 1972 the Catholic middle classes have grown remarkably. The social mobility that many nationalists have experienced over the last quarter of a century has been facilitated largely by an expansion of both third level education and employment opportunities in the public sector. While many upwardly mobile Catholics have secured positions that involve them offering services exclusively to their co-religionists, many others have entered occupations that do not require them to associate solely with members of their own 'community'. Social mobility has in time generated interesting patterns of spatial mobility within the six counties. In Belfast nationalist members of the new middle classes have gradually migrated to particular neighbourhoods that were once the sole preserve of the unionist elite.

While middle class Catholics have secured impressive gains under direct rule they still face certain disadvantages relative to their Protestant counterparts. Nationalists still tend to be under-represented within the upper reaches of a series of occupational categories. This pattern of disadvantage becomes apparent in the composition of the 30,000 strong workforce currently employed within the Northern Ireland Civil Service (NICS). The Fifth

Report compiled by the Equal Opportunities Unit of the NICS (DFP 1994) reveals that Catholic civil servants tend to be heavily concentrated in lower occupational grades. At the moment individuals from nationalist backgrounds make up some 37.4 per cent of those employed in the non-industrial civil service. However, a mere 15.7 per cent of employees who have reached the most senior occupational band within the NICS – that of Assistant Secretary and above – are drawn from the nationalist community.

The trends that are evident among the ranks of the civil service prove to be symptomatic of a wider process of ethnoreligious exclusion within the Northern Irish labour market. In 1994 a local market research firm set out to ascertain the identities of the most influential players in the province's public and business life (Macauley 1994). The company named one thousand people whom it considered to be the most important 'movers and shakers' in Northern Ireland. Only 85 individuals of nationalist origins managed to make it on to the prestigious list.

The pattern of nationalist disadvantage that emerges when we examine the more affluent elements within Northern Irish society becomes equally apparent once the focus shifts towards the working classes. The lower orders within the Catholic community historically have suffered even greater hardship than their Protestant counterparts. The era of the troubles has merely served to confirm the especially subaltern status that working class nationalists endure. The coincidence since the early 1970s of sustained political violence and the brutal reconfiguration of the global economy has had profoundly detrimental implications for a great many workers living in the six counties. These particular processes have not, however, proved equally traumatic for all sections of the local working classes. Political upheaval and economic crisis have been unable to afford an 'equality of misery' to the poorer elements of Northern Irish society. The rapid decline of manufacturing over recent generations has impacted gravely upon working class Protestants who traditionally dominated shipbuilding and heavy engineering. The creation of thousands of relatively lucrative positions within the security forces has, however, tended to stem the rise of unemployment within loyalist districts. The nationalist working classes have been rather less fortunate. Research undertaken during the 1990s suggests that Catholic men are more than twice as likely as Protestant men to be out of work (Gallagher et al. 1994, pp. 8, 55–6; O'Hearn 1998, p. 55). The relatively high incidence of unemployment within working class nationalist neighbourhoods has inevitably led to greater rates of poverty. The deprivation that exists among the Catholic working classes was intimated in a recent study of the recipients of free school meals (McGill 1995). These are provided to the children of those who are unemployed and claiming income support from the state. The survey in question noted that 35 per cent of Catholic pupils were entitled to free meals compared to only 15 per cent of their Protestant peers.

ETHNICITY AND NATIONALISM

The discussion advanced thus far confirms that contemporary Northern Irish society bears the multiple inscriptions of ethnic feeling. People living in the region frequently give voice to starkly different identities and beliefs. An issue that remains, though, is whether the profound sense of ethnicity that people living in the province often possess gives rise to political sentiments and ambitions that might be considered *nationalist* in the precise sense of the term outlined earlier. We need to consider if the divergent ethnic personae that they claim actually encourage Catholics and Protestants to aspire to live in different states. In other words, do nationalists' feelings of Irishness prompt an ambition to become citizens of the Irish Republic and do unionists' sense of Britishness move them to wish to remain citizens of the United Kingdom?

These important questions are rather more troublesome than commentators sometimes assume. The conclusions at which we arrive will of course depend largely upon the nature of the data upon which we choose to draw. The discussion that follows centres upon three potential sources of information.

The Incidence of Political Violence

The ideological formation of nationalism spawns a range of political strategies and practices. Nationalists frequently seek to advance their particular interests through pacific means including intellectual debate, electioneering and civil disobedience. On countless occasions, however, the enterprise of nationalism has given rise to political violence. The recent history of Northern Ireland unfortunately confirms this particular lamentable trend. Since the late 1960s the antagonistic nationalisms that seem to exist within the six counties have authored a conflict that has claimed 3,500 lives. The concerns of the various combatants who have participated in the troubles have ostensibly been nationalist ones. Those who have taken up arms over the last three decades have apparently been animated by an ambition to become, or remain, part of that state which they consider to lend political expression to the existence of that national community to which they imagine themselves to belong.

In recent decades elements within the Catholic community have sustained a remarkable campaign of guerrilla warfare against the personnel and institutions of the British state. The formal purpose of the 'armed struggle' has of course been to create those conditions that would ensure that the six counties – which republicans consider to be properly part of the Irish nation – come to fall under the jurisdiction of Dublin. Members of the unionist community have sought to resist republican insurgence through force of arms. An anxiety to ensure that Northern Ireland remains within the United Kingdom, among other things, has moved numerous unionists to engage in acts of both official and unofficial violence – that is, to enrol in the security forces and various loyalist para-military factions respectively.

While support for politically motivated violence is clearly strong within Northern Ireland it remains nonetheless far from universal. Over the last couple of decades tens of thousands of Catholic voters have lent their support to a political party (Sinn Fein) that has organic associations with a military organisation (the Provisional IRA) that has claimed more lives than any other in the course of the troubles. Most nationalists have, however, proved unwilling to endorse the political wing of the republican movement. An aversion to political violence is equally apparent on the other side of the communal divide. Many within the unionist community are at best deeply ambivalent towards the frequently draconian conduct of the security forces. The recent spate of elections in Northern Ireland has, however, demonstrated that most unionists have little regard for those loyalist parties that maintain close links with groups that have engaged in unofficial acts of violence.

Political violence proves, therefore, to be a highly problematic barometer of nationalist sentiment in the context of the six counties. That many people, both Catholic and Protestant, have been willing to take up arms – both legal and illegal – to defend or subvert the constitutional status of Northern Ireland suggests the depth of feeling that nationalism frequently inspires. While acts of violence may articulate the nationalist feeling of many people living in the province they also prove to be profoundly abhorrent to many other social actors who could equally well be considered nationalists, whether of the Irish or British varieties. The profound emotions which nationalism seems to generate among the residents of the six counties do not preclude an equally vehement opposition to bloodshed. While political violence may articulate particular versions of nationalist sentiment within Northern Ireland it remains unable to capture various others. Hence, while the incidence of conflict suggests the *depth* of nationalist feeling in the province, it fails to convey its full *breadth*.

Voting Patterns

The divisions that pervade contemporary Northern Irish society inevitably become apparent when people enter the polling booth. Predictably, ethnoreligious origins provide an extremely reliable predictor of electoral preference within the six counties. Our principal concern here should be to ascertain whether the different parties that Northern Irish Catholics and Protestants support articulate versions of political discourse that may be interpreted as *nationalist*.

Almost all Protestant voters in the province endorse political parties whose fundamental reason for existence is the maintenance of the Union between Northern Ireland and Great Britain. Those parties that enjoy the allegiance of the unionist electorate are often prepared to compromise on the precise terms under which the six counties remain within the United Kingdom. All are steadfastly unwilling, however, to contemplate any constitutional settlement that would nudge the province beyond the environs of the Union. Hence, the essential rationale of the frequently bewildering array of Unionist parties that operate in the province is to ensure that the Protestants of Ulster are able to remain citizens of that state which plays host to the national community to which they feel themselves to belong. The electoral preferences of the unionist community would seem, therefore, to articulate political ambitions that are fundamentally nationalist.

Examination of voting behaviour suggests the political disposition of nationalists to be somewhat more complex than that of unionists. In the main, Northern Irish Catholics cast their votes for political parties whose principal intention is ostensibly to secure the assimilation of the six counties into a unitary Irish state. The electoral preferences of the Catholic community would seem, therefore, to emerge out of political aspirations that are essentially nationalist. Once we move beyond the noble rhetoric of manifestos to consider the actual practical goals of the parties in question, however, a rather different interpretation of the political ambitions of Northern Irish nationalists begins to offer itself.

While the Nationalist parties that operate north of the border espouse a formal aspiration towards the creation of a united Ireland, both parties would appear increasingly willing to accept a political settlement that would entail the continuation of partition. In principle the Social Democratic and Labour Party (SDLP) remains committed to the ideal of Irish unification. In practice, however, the party seems to be guided by political sentiments that are less nationalist than social democratic. The fundamental concern of the SDLP would appear to be not to ensure that nationalists living in the six counties become citizens of an Irish Republic, but rather to enhance the terms under which northern nationalists remain citizens of the United Kingdom. The abiding pragmatism of the SDLP has become increasingly apparent in the disposition of its principal competitor for the nationalist vote. The radical agenda that Sinn Fein has traditionally advanced has conventionally centred upon the imperative of building a united Ireland. For many years the party offered unequivocal support to the efforts of republicans to end partition through force. In recent times, however, the tone of republican discourse has softened appreciably. During the present decade the prospect has grown that Sinn Fein would be prepared to countenance a political settlement that would allow Northern Ireland to remain within the United Kingdom. The decision of republicans to endorse the Belfast Agreement merely confirmed the drift of Sinn Fein towards the political centre.

Examination of the priorities that animate Sinn Fein and the SDLP intimates the pragmatism that increasingly defines nationalist politics in Northern Ireland. It would seem that the foremost – or at least most immediate – concern of both nationalist parties operating within the six counties is not to end British rule in Ireland, but rather to embellish the rights of those Irish nationalists who happen to remain British citizens. The electoral preference of nationalists living in the province would seem, therefore, to be shaped by political concerns that arise out of sentiments that are more *ethnic* than *nationalist*.

Constitutional Preferences

The complex relationship that exists between ethnicity and nationalism in Northern Ireland may be traced further through the seemingly endless sequence of surveys of political opinion that has taken place over the course of the troubles. An overwhelming majority of Ulster unionists regard themselves first and foremost as British. The countless opinion polls that have been undertaken over the last three decades would suggest that the particular version of ethnic identity prevalent among unionist ranks translates readily into nationalist sentiment. Their understanding of themselves as being British finds clear expression in the constitutional preferences that unionists voice. More than nine out of ten unionists who take part in opinion polls express a desire to remain citizens of the United Kingdom (Breen & Devine 1999, p. 61). Only one in 20 unionist respondents select those constitutional options – whether a united Ireland or an independent Ulster – that would signal the end of the Union.

A preliminary examination of survey data would seem to suggest, therefore, that the ethnic sentiment predominant within the unionist community has found expression through forms of political ambition that are ostensibly nationalist. Rather closer consideration of opinion polls indicates, however, that the constitutional aspirations that unionists hold are somewhat more ambivalent than their emphatic ethnic identification would imply. It is important here to acknowledge not only whether Northern Irish Protestants aspire to remain citizens of the United Kingdom, but also the particular terms under which they would prefer to do so.

The unqualified sense of Britishness that unionists often avow might lead one to presume that most would tend towards those constitutional arrangements that promise to bind Northern Ireland most closely to the other regions of the United Kingdom. This particular presumption would seem in part to have been borne out by those opinion polls that have been conducted in the province. Since the advent of direct rule, 'integrationism' has come to exercise considerable appeal among the ranks of the unionist community. In political surveys completed over the last couple of decades as many as two out of five unionist respondents have indicated that they would prefer Northern Ireland to continue to be governed from Westminster – albeit in a rather more democratic form than hitherto (Ruane & Todd 1996, p. 58). The advances that the 'integrationist' case has made among unionists acknowledges of course the appreciable material and cultural benefits that direct rule has bestowed.

While the 'integrationist' enterprise enjoys considerable appeal within the unionist community it remains rather less than universally popular. For every unionist who would prefer that direct rule – albeit in a substantially revised form – became the permanent mode of government for Northern Ireland, there is at least another who looks forward to the day that the province is once again administered from Stormont. This ambition to see the restoration of devolution to the six counties reveals an instructive ambivalence within the unionist disposition. Most unionists in the province would seem to define themselves primarily as members of a community that accommodates all of the peoples of the United Kingdom. Nonetheless, there are a great many within the unionist fold who are simply unwilling to endorse those constitutional arrangements that promise to consummate most fully their professed sense of being in the world. The reluctance of a substantial swathe of unionist opinion to embrace the integrationist project exposes the limits of British nationalism within Northern Ireland.

The equivocation that inscribes the outlook of contemporary unionism reflects the subordinate status that the people of the province endure within the United Kingdom. While unionists are attracted to numerous elements of the British state, they are at the same time often alienated by one of its principal agencies. Within the unionist community there exists an abiding suspicion of the interests and actions of the British government. The conviction that the sovereign parliament remains at best indifferent to the welfare of Northern Ireland has prompted unionists to seek to limit the authority that Westminster exercises over the province. Anxiety concerning metropolitan intentions has engendered support for the restoration of the Stormont legislature, even among elements of the unionist community that would otherwise dismiss devolution as the political reflex of a mindless parochialism.

The data that have emerged from opinion polls suggest that the ethnic feeling prevalent among Northern Irish nationalists translates less readily into constitutional ambitions than is the case with Ulster unionists. Most of the Catholics who live in the province regard themselves as Irish in various senses of that particular term. The powerful sense of Irishness that obtains within the nationalist community does not seem, however, to have been mapped directly onto political ambition. Observers of social and political life in the six counties invariably presume that all Northern Irish Catholics would prefer to be residents of a united Ireland. Analyses of the 'Northern Ireland problem' usually rest upon the assumption, in other words, that every nationalist in the province is precisely that. The information yielded by surveys of political opinion within the six counties suggests a rather more complex state of affairs.

Polls carried out in Northern Ireland often seek to ascertain the fundamental constitutional ambitions of people living in the province. Respondents are asked simply whether they would prefer the six counties to remain within the United Kingdom or, alternatively, to become part of the Irish Republic. As one would expect, Catholics who participate in surveys are more likely to select the latter option. The proportion of nationalists who express an aspiration towards a united Ireland proves, however, to be rather less substantial than frequently assumed. Indeed, only a bare majority of respondents from nationalist backgrounds – around 55 per cent in the surveys collated by Breen and Devine (1999, pp. 59–61) state that they would prefer Irish to British citizenship. While most Catholics would seem to harbour an ambition to live in a united Ireland a significant minority apparently prefers the constitutional status quo. Around one in three nationalists who cooperate with opinion polls intimate their desire for Northern Ireland to remain within the Union. It would appear, therefore, that every third nationalist living in the six counties is not in fact a nationalist in the precise sense of the term.

The apparent reluctance of a large body of nationalists to embrace the ideal of a united Ireland may be explained in various ways. In part it may have arisen out of a reading of political possibility. The demographic advantage that unionists have enjoyed has ensured that over recent generations the prospects of Irish unification have seemed distinctly bleak. The apparent impossibility of the nationalist enterprise has inevitably come to inflect the constitutional aspirations of Catholics living north of the border. Many nationalists in the province have become unwilling to endorse the ideal of a united Ireland simply because they regard it as unattainable.

The seeming aversion of elements within the Catholic community towards the nationalist project may be interpreted further as a pragmatic expression of material interest. The period since the dissolution of Stormont has witnessed the emergence of an enlarged and more variegated Catholic middle class. The enormous instrumental benefits that have flowed from direct rule have ensured that a substantial section of the nationalist population has come to have a vested interest in the constitutional status quo. If Northern Ireland was to continue to be part of the United Kingdom for some time to come it would be unlikely that the new Catholic middle classes would be troubled deeply. It is important though to avoid reading too much into the pragmatic endorsement that more affluent nationalists seem to have extended to the Union.

While the United Kingdom may have conferred considerable benefit upon the Catholic middle classes, it possesses little real ontological value for them. Middle class nationalists who are perfectly content to be British citizens are nonetheless loth to regard themselves as British nationals. Even those Catholics who would prefer that Northern Ireland remained within the Union would in the main be unwilling to wear a poppy or to attend a function that would require them to stand to attention during 'God Save the Queen'.

The enquiries of political surveys often strive to ascertain the *ideal* constitutional arrangements of people living in Northern Ireland. Respondents are at times required to name the state to which – all other things being equal – they would choose to belong. Opinion polls carried out in the province invariably also include other more specific questions concerning political orientation. Individuals are usually invited to select the most desirable from a sequence of available political options: a united Ireland, joint authority, direct rule, power-sharing devolution and so forth. This more focused form of enquiry casts light upon a version of constitutional aspiration that is tempered by an understanding of the possible. Asking social actors to nominate the specific political arrangements they would like to see most reveals not only what they want, but also what they are willing to tolerate.

Those more finely calibrated questions that are posed during surveys intimate an important aspect of the disposition of the nationalist community in Northern Ireland. When asked to nominate the optimal political direction available to the people of the province, the number of nationalists who select options that would effect the unification of Ireland remains substantial. The proportion of nationalist respondents who articulate support for a united Ireland turns out to be rather smaller, however, than when they are required simply to state their preference for Irish or British citizenship. The data that Ruane and Todd (1996, p. 69) draw together suggests that only a minority of Catholics – between 40 and 45 per cent perhaps – who cooperate with opinion polls select those political arrangements that would signal the end of partition. The discrepancy that exists between the answers that greet the two rather different forms of political enquiry that appear in opinion polls may be of some importance. It suggests that there exists among the ranks of the nationalist community a body of individuals who aspire to a united Ireland but are nonetheless willing – at least in the immediate future – to lend their support to other political arrangements which they consider to be in the best interests of the people of Northern Ireland.

Consideration of the relationship between ethnicity and nationalism illuminates many of the complexities of social and political life in the six counties. There are numerous grounds on which Northern Ireland could be classified as an ethnically divided society. The ethnoreligious fissures evident within the province have inevitably found expression within the realm of political ambition and practice. Northern Ireland represents the site of a conflict between competing nationalist enterprises. The mutually exclusive aspirations of those who wish to undermine and underwrite the Union respectively have, over the last three decades, produced horrendous violence. The ethnoreligious identities that obtain within Northern Ireland have, however, been only partially translated into political projects that might be understood as genuinely nationalist. The British nationalism that defines the outlook of Ulster unionism proves to be highly qualified not least by an abiding distrust of the metropolis. Moreover, while many northern nationalists clearly regard the unification of Ireland as a noble and obtainable ambition, others would seem to consider it an undesirable or, more realistically, impractical objective. Realisation of the nature of the political environment that exists within these islands – of the boundaries of the possible – has served to dilute the competing nationalisms that collide within the six counties. Many, and perhaps most, unionists do not regard the integration of Northern Ireland into the United Kingdom as feasible. Equally, many and perhaps most nationalists regard the integration of the six counties into the Irish Republic as presently beyond the realm of political possibility. The pragmatism that tempers the nationalisms that compete within the province suggests that there might exist the room and appetite for compromise that may enable a genuinely durable political settlement in Northern Ireland.

A SECTARIAN CONFLICT?

A further issue that needs to be addressed is whether the divisions that exist within the six counties owe their origins to religious belief and practice. Can the conflict in Northern Ireland be conceived as 'sectarian' in the particular sense of the term outlined earlier? The role that religious sentiment has played in the recent turbulent history of the province has preoccupied a number of commentators. The relationship between religion and ethnopolitical division in Northern Ireland has frequently been understood in two entirely different ways. Each of these interpretations will be considered in turn.

The Northern Irish Conflict is a Holy War

Observers of the troubles have frequently sought to establish religious feeling as *the* fundamental cause of political division within the six counties. The view that the 'Northern Ireland problem' is essentially one of sectarianism has found considerable favour within elements of the media and not least among the authors of satirical cartoons. As a consequence there exists a popular opinion – particularly outside Northern Ireland – that the violence in the six counties represents a form of 'holy war'. In the mainstream media, the conflict in the province is frequently portrayed as savage – the reflex of a primitive religious fanaticism. The troubles are often depicted as having emerged out of beliefs and concerns that are entirely irrelevant to the contemporary world. The political violence that has marred the last three decades is held to represent a seventeenth century conflict played out in modern dress.

A somewhat more sophisticated version of the 'holy war thesis' appears in the academic literature generated by the troubles. The writings of Steve Bruce (1986) have sought to establish the significance of evangelical protestantism in defining the ideological character of contemporary unionism. Furthermore, the analysis that John Hickey (1984) has advanced suggests that religious feeling has played a vital role in producing and reproducing the tensions that have given rise to political unrest in the province. The writer whose work we shall focus upon here for the purposes of illustration is the political scientist Padraig O'Malley (1990; 1995).

O'Malley discerns an intimate connection between the theological and ethnopolitical distinctions that exist in Northern Ireland. The doctrines of Catholicism and Protestantism generate of course rather different systems of explanation and belief. The theological traditions out of which they have emerged have, therefore, bequeathed to nationalism and unionism divergent forms of political discourse. Their inheritance of distinct discursive programmes has, O'Malley insists, meant that nationalists and unionists are often unable to trust or even understand one another.

According to O'Malley the teachings of Catholicism at times appear equivocal with regard to certain aspects of morality. This ambivalence becomes particularly apparent, he suggests, in the distinction that Catholic theologians draw between mortal and venial sin. The moral equivocation that seems to characterise Catholicism finds echoes in the discursive forms that are associated with contemporary Irish nationalism. Nationalists frequently sound loquacious, ambiguous and evasive, not least to the sensitive ears of the Ulster unionist.

O'Malley moves on to suggest that the version of political discourse that Irish nationalism has adopted bears little resemblance to that favoured by the other principal ethnopolitical tradition on the island. The doctrines of Protestantism invariably entail a belief in absolute truths and particularly in those assumed to be disclosed by the gospel. Protestants find little need for those subtle distinctions that enable an intricate calibration of morality. Particular forms of conduct are either sinful or they are not. The absolute and unequivocal nature of the Protestant faith, O'Malley asserts, inevitably influences the manner in which unionists seek to articulate their political beliefs and ambitions. The discursive forms that are associated with Ulster unionism are characteristically direct and unambiguous.

The operation of two radically different versions of political discourse in the province is considered by Padraig O'Malley to have promoted and prolonged the Northern Irish conflict. Because they interpret and explain the world in ways that are distinct, nationalists and unionists have more often than not proved unable to communicate with one another. O'Malley seeks to illuminate the discursive barriers that exist in the province through examination of the debates that attended the hunger strikes initiated in 1980 and 1981 by republican prisoners seeking political status. Among the controversies that divided clerics was that which centred upon whether the conduct of the hunger strikers could be considered suicidal. Protestant ministers noted that prisoners who refused food did so in the full knowledge that they might die. The strategy of the hunger strike should, therefore, be acknowledged as an elaborate version of suicide.

The hierarchy of the Catholic church chose to adopt a rather different reading of the dispute in the prisons. Catholic theologians pointed out that while the hunger strikers were aware of the possibility of their own death, that was not the rationale that informed their actions. In the absence of intent it would be inappropriate to designate the behaviour of those involved in the prisons dispute as suicide. The distinction drawn between reason and effect enabled the Catholic hierarchy to sidestep a potentially calamitous clash of interests. Had the church deemed the prisoners' actions to be suicidal they would have been compelled to denounce the hunger strikes as a mortal sin. This judgement would of course have alienated that vast bulk of a Catholic community that had become increasingly outraged by the British government's handling of the prisons issue. The subtle distinctions that the Catholic hierarchy mobilised, therefore, enabled an approach to the hunger strikes that was both theologically plausible and politically expedient.

While the stance that the Catholic church adopted in relation to the prisons dispute broadly chimed with the sentiments prevalent within the nationalist community, it also inevitably caused outrage among unionists. In the minds of most Protestants the reluctance of priests to condemn the hunger strikes revealed a moral ambivalence which in turn betrayed clear political sympathies. The approach that the Catholic hierarchy took on the issue was assumed to have been guided, not by a sense of theological propriety, but rather by ideological conviction. In refusing to denounce the fasts as suicide Catholic theologians merely declared their role within the broader republican enterprise.

Religion Does Not Really Matter

Various writers have set out to highlight the role that religion plays in fostering division within Northern Irish society. The more dominant trend within the academic literature has, however, been to deny that the conflict in Northern Ireland is in fact sectarian. The latter approach is exemplified in the work of the American political scientist Michael MacDonald. In *Children of Wrath* (1986) MacDonald seeks to establish colonialism as the principal source of the distinctions that persist within contemporary Northern Irish society. The plantation of Ulster enabled a body of settlers to exercise colonial authority over the native population. In spite of all appearances to the contrary the distinctions between these communal blocs do not derive essentially from religious affiliation. Religious categories – as designated by the generic terms 'Protestant' and 'Catholic' – are merely markers of other rather more important forms of identity and status. The divisions that exist within Northern Ireland emerge not out of religious feeling, but rather the specific secular advantages that colonialism has offered planter over gael.

The conviction that religion exercises little real influence over the Northern Irish conflict appears with particular force in marxist commentaries. Perhaps the most influential materialist reading of the troubles is that provided in Michael Farrell's seminal text *Northern Ireland: The Orange State* (1976). The analysis that Farrell and other marxist writers advance insists that ethnoreligious divisions are more apparent than real. It is argued that the conflict in Northern Ireland does not genuinely owe its origins to religious sentiment. Ethnoreligious identities are considered to be merely distorted signifiers of other forms of division that are more fully grounded in the material realities of Northern Irish society. Ethnic or religious feeling represent little more than surrogates for other more salient personae that are associated with social class. The marxist reading of the troubles suggests that while the ethnopolitical divisions that exist within the six counties may be lamentable, they are far from accidental. The essential function of ethnic longing is to weaken the working classes by distracting their attention from those real interests which they have in common. The persistence of ethnoreligious feeling in Northern Ireland serves, therefore, to strengthen the hand of those powerful elements that derive benefit from the particular social formation that obtains therein.

How Important is Religion?

The readings of the troubles that circulate within popular discourse and the academic literature give rise, therefore, to two starkly different understandings of the relationship between religion and politics in the six counties. Neither of the distinctive interpretations outlined above manages, however, to convince entirely. Those commentaries that seek to conceive the troubles as essentially religious misunderstand and misrepresent both the substance and form of the conflict that has overtaken the province. Within the populist media in particular, the view has often been advanced that the 'Northern Ireland problem' is an ancient squabble between two fanatical tribes that cling obstinately to remarkably antediluvian views of the world. In reality, however, the conflict in the six counties centres not upon arcane theological disputes but rather more intelligible matters such as social justice, citizenship rights, physical security, cultural entitlements and so forth. The violence that has scarred the last three decades has, despite all appearances to the contrary, articulated concerns that are the very stuff of liberal democracy. The troubles should be conceived, therefore, not as an ancient quarrel but rather as a profoundly modern one (Feldman 1991, p. 5; Miller 1994).

The essential modernity of the Northern Irish conflict would seem to have been confirmed by recent political developments that have taken place beyond the six counties. The present decade has witnessed the rise throughout Europe of ethnic and nationalist feelings hitherto assumed to have been consigned to history. The resurgence of ethnic nationalism in the 1990s would suggest that the divisions that have generated political violence in Northern Ireland are rather less peculiar than has often been assumed. In the mid 1970s Tom Nairn published an influential survey of the development of the modern British state. Nairn (1977) chose to preface his observations on Northern Ireland with an enquiry as to whether the ethnic violence that had engulfed the province should be considered a relic of the past or, alternatively, a portent of the future. The kindling of ethnic feeling and prejudice that has occurred within contemporary European societies would indicate that the troubles have in fact, unfortunately, proved to be portentous.

Commentators such as Padraig O'Malley who emphasise the intimacy of religion and politics frequently seek to locate the Northern Ireland problem at the level of discourse. The divergent theological mores which they have imbibed ensure that nationalism and unionism read and explain the world in entirely different ways. Consequently, when nationalists and unionists talk they do so in a manner that merely serves to promote mutual distrust and antagonism. Perhaps the most glaring shortcoming of the interpretation that O'Malley advances is that it rests upon remarkably crude stereotypes of both religious traditions and those who follow them. In his writings Catholics appear as discursive gymnasts while Protestants are cast as straight talking literalists. Within these familiar stereotypes there exists of course at least a kernel of truth. Northern nationalists have often seemed relatively adept at playing with words and ideas. John Hume has, after all, been able to draw international acclaim for a political style that rests almost entirely upon cant and incantation. The nationalist community in the province, however, could scarcely claim a monopoly on discursive dexterity.

Over the last decade or so unionists have become increasingly willing and able to articulate their political beliefs and aspirations. The discourse of contemporary unionism centres largely upon the notion of 'citizenship' (O'Dowd 1998). A central article of faith among unionist intellectuals is that the United Kingdom does not constitute a nation but rather a multinational state (Aughey 1989; 1995; 1997). The British state is considered to transcend particular communal interests and to provide a framework of legal equality within which a diversity of personal and cultural expression can proceed. The virtue of the United Kingdom means that the Union represents the form of political association that serves best the interests of all of the people of Northern Ireland. Nationalists living north of the border are encouraged to come to terms with existing constitutional arrangements and thereby avail themselves fully of the multiple benefits that flow from British citizenship.

At first glance the counsel of contemporary unionism appears entirely liberal and reasonable. Closer examination suggests a rather different estimation. The particular manner in which unionist intellectuals choose to employ the concept of 'citizenship' turns out to be deeply disingenuous. Unionists tend to conveniently designate as civic that which might be more accurately classified as national. 'God Save the Queen' is considered to be merely a musical sequence that operates as an emblem of state and which should therefore be played at every public event in the province. Individuals from nationalist backgrounds are simply expected to summon the courtesy to listen respectfully while the anthem is recited during university graduations and other ceremonies. In reality of course these expectations are entirely unreasonable. 'God Save the Queen' represents in fact not merely a civic anthem but a national anthem also. While the strains of the song may well be comforting to unionists, they are at the same time deeply offensive to many nationalists. The manner in which figures within the unionist community have sought to reconstruct the national anthem over the last few years might be considered emblematic of a growing willingness to spin words for their own advantage. Unionists have sought to portray as neutral and civic certain institutions and practices that are actually associated more or less exclusively with their own ethnonational tradition. The concept of 'citizenship' has been mobilised in an attempt to establish as hegemonic those rites and icons with which unionists feel comfortable. A liberal and inclusive discourse has been employed, in other words, to advance a political enterprise that would appear to be reactionary and exclusive. We are left, therefore, with an impression of the Ulster unionist that is rather far from the straight talking literalist summoned from the imagination of Padraig O'Malley.

The distinctive reading of the troubles that Padraig O'Malley advances fails to convince in at least one further regard. In his writings O'Malley suggests that the Northern Irish conflict acknowledges the mutual incomprehension of nationalists and unionists. In reality, however, the 'two communities' that reside within the six counties tend to understand one another only too well. Indeed nationalists and unionists often exhibit a remarkable facility to decode the rhetoric that emerges from the other ethnopolitical tradition. Nationalists are only too aware that unionists mobilise the inclusive ideal of citizenship in order to advance their own exclusive political interests. Equally, unionists understand that when republicans play with the notion of 'consent' they do so in pursuit of political advantage. The 'Northern Ireland problem' should be considered less one of discourse than of desire. The residents of the six counties often find it difficult to get along with one another because they frequently want different things. In particular there are many people living in the province who would prefer to live in different states from one another. In order to grasp the nature of the conflict in Northern Ireland we need, therefore, to shift our focus from the form to the substance of the politics that prevails within the six counties. The enmities that simmer in the province have not arisen because nationalists and unionists are incapable of understanding one another. On the contrary in fact. Nationalists and unionists are prone to mutual distrust not because they refuse to listen to one another but rather because they invariably do not like what they hear when they do so.

Those commentaries that depict the conflict in Northern Ireland as indelibly sectarian are profoundly questionable. Alternative readings that insist that religion has no real bearing whatsoever upon the troubles also, however, turn out to be rather less than entirely persuasive. The conflict that has overtaken the six counties in recent generations does not represent a form of 'holy war'. The tensions that have given rise to political violence in Northern Ireland centre in fact upon issues and interests that are thoroughly secular and scarcely peculiar to the province. While the troubles may not be a religious conflict it is nonetheless a conflict upon which religion has exercised a palpable influence. Religious belief and practice within the six counties have served to promote those secular identities and disputes that form the basis of the 'Northern Ireland problem'. A brief illustration will hopefully suffice.

The distinctive forms of religious practice associated with the different faiths that exist within the six counties shape everyday life and experience in ways that may have some political significance. The Roman Catholic church places considerable importance upon religious observance. Catholics living in Northern Ireland attend mass with remarkable frequency. As a result, members of the nationalist community in the province tend to meet their co-religionists on a regular basis. The particular united form of the Roman Catholic church serves further to promote association between Northern Irish nationalists. Every Catholic living in the province belongs to the same religious denomination. Hence at certain crucial moments all nationalists who happen to attend church are exposed to similar sermons on critical moral and political issues. The particular forms of practice that are associated with Roman Catholicism would seem, therefore, to generate bonds – both literal and symbolic – among the otherwise diverse members of the nationalist community. These significant ties may offer one possible explanation as to why Northern Irish nationalists have been able to survive the upheavals of the last three decades comparatively unfragmented.

The forms of religious practice associated with Ulster Protestants are of course rather different. The diverse creed of Protestantism is characterised by a lesser emphasis upon religious observance and a propensity to schism. Protestants resident in the province belong to a wide range of denominations and attend services with considerably less regularity than their Catholic counterparts. When a Protestant goes to church she communes with a fraction of her wider ethnoreligious community that is dwarfed by the collectivity formed by Catholics at prayer. The experience of religion would seem, therefore, to bind Protestants together rather less strongly than Catholics. The religious disunity that exists among the Protestant community may go some way to explaining the tendency over the course of the troubles for unionists to bicker and fragment.

CONCLUSION

The foregoing discussion will hopefully have mapped out that which divides the 'two communities' in Northern Ireland. While they may have a great deal in common, unionists and nationalists tend nonetheless to understand and explain themselves in rather different ways. These differences are actualised in a series of social institutions and conventions which in turn serve to reproduce communal division in the province. Those ethnonational distinctions that produce the 'Northern Ireland question' do not of course represent the sole line of fissure within the six counties. In the chapters that follow we shall examine two other identities that are essential sources of division within Northern Irish society but which are, nonetheless, often given scant attention within academic commentaries. The salience of class and gender distinctions will be acknowledged in turn.

2 The Significance of Social Class

These are scarcely auspicious times for the left. An unfortunate confluence of recent social and political trends has conspired to question seriously the value of materialist interpretations. The reconstruction of western societies out of the debris of the economic crises of the 1970s has led to the emergence of increasingly intricate class hierarchies. Changed work practices and accelerated consumption have both served to blur the boundaries between previously distinct social strata. The increasingly complex and dynamic nature of contemporary bourgeois society has invited predictable and indeed opportunistic responses from neoliberal critics. Most famously the political scientist Francis Fukuyama (1989; 1992) has declared that we are living through the end of history. The unprecedented material wealth and optimal political freedom that global capitalism has allegedly afforded humanity have ensured, Fukuyama insists, that the notion of social class has effectively ceased to have real meaning.

Those commentators who consider the social significance of class to have declined substantially often make reference to the realm of personal and political identity. The eminent sociologists Anthony Giddens (1994; 1998) and Ulrich Beck (1992; 1994) have argued that people living in contemporary society have increasingly come to transcend the influence of social aggregates such as classes. Social actors have apparently begun to dispense with traditional collective identities in order to assemble their own distinctive personal biographies out of the plentiful resources of everyday life. For both Giddens and Beck the fluid social relations that have arisen out of the process of globalisation offer the conditions that promise to liberate the individual. The principal authors of the brave new world of flexible accumulation are no longer social classes, but rather autonomous human subjects.

The tendency among social scientists to question the salience of the role that class plays within contemporary society is reflected in one of the most important recent analyses of the 'Northern Ireland problem'. In *Explaining Northern Ireland: Broken Images* the political scientists John McGarry and Brendan O'Leary offer an impressive exploration of a range of competing interpretations of the troubles. The authors are strongly critical of those readings that have a materialist inflection. Interpretations of the troubles that centre upon the concept of social class add little to our understanding of the nature of the conflict within Northern Ireland, McGarry and O'Leary assert (1995a, pp. 152–61). People living in the province are animated principally by the cultural identities and anxieties associated with specific ethnonational communities. Preoccupation with the material concerns of social classes, therefore, merely distracts attention from the 'real' source of division inside the six counties.

The approach that McGarry and O'Leary adopt makes a great deal of sense of course. Ethnonational sentiment does after all exercise rather greater influence than class consciousness over the outlook and conduct of those who live in the province. Nonetheless the reading of the Northern Ireland problem that the political scientists provide exhibits at least two important shortcomings. First, McGarry and O'Leary would seem to regard the political culture that obtains within the six counties as essentially unidimensional. The interpretation which they advance would appear to rest upon the assumption that it is only the social identity that exercises greatest influence over the political life of the province that 'really' matters. Ethnonational status evidently represents the principal source of political allegiance within Northern Ireland. Those social identities that attend class distinctions are, therefore, afforded merely cursory acknowledgement.

The apparent unwillingness of McGarry and O'Leary to take social class seriously constitutes an important flaw in their work. While socioeconomic status clearly represents a less important source of political identity within the six counties than ethnoreligious affiliation, it remains crucially significant nonetheless. Social class exercises a palpable – if often unacknowledged – influence upon the political culture that marks the six counties. Their understandable, though ultimately debilitating, preoccupation with ethnonational distinctions blinds McGarry and O'Leary to the significance of the role that class divisions actually play in the public life of Northern Ireland.

The second criticism that may be levelled at *Explaining Northern Ireland* is rather more important. In spite of the title which they chose to give their book, McGarry and O'Leary have a propensity merely to describe that which needs to be explained. At various stages the authors attest that ethnonational affiliation represents the predominant source of political identity and division within

Northern Ireland. The reader is never provided, however, with an adequate interpretation as to why this may be so. In the absence of a persuasive explanation we are left with the impression that the prevalence of ethnonational sentiment within Northern Irish political life should be considered inevitable, reasonable, 'natural' even.

The substance of the political culture that defines the six counties is of course rather more problematic than the silence within McGarry and O'Leary's work would suggest. The predominance of ethnonational sentiment within the public life of the province is far from inevitable. Indeed there are substantial grounds for the argument that social class rather than ethnoreligious affiliation should be the principal author of political belief and practice within Northern Ireland. Socioeconomic status certainly has rather greater bearing than ethnoreligious distinction upon the distribution of essential life chances within the six counties. Given the nature of the inequalities within contemporary Northern Irish society, one would not have to be a raving reductionist to anticipate that social class might constitute the most important source of political identity in the province. In reality of course this is not the case. The political culture that prevails in Northern Ireland flies in the face of the material realities of existence there. That ethnonational allegiance manages to exercise most influence over the political life of the province should not, therefore, be accepted on face value but rather should be acknowledged as a problem that demands proper explanation.

The purpose of this particular chapter then is to resist an essentially regressive trend within contemporary social science. The discussion that follows sets out to illustrate that social class has an enormous impact upon the manner in which Northern Irish society is structured and experienced. Socioeconomic distinctions are clearly implicated in the ways in which the social actors in the province think, feel and act. An appreciation of the crucial role that social class plays in the lives of the residents of the six counties should be considered essential, therefore, to an adequate understanding of the nature of contemporary Northern Irish society (Smyth 1980).

THE DISTRIBUTION OF LIFE CHANCES

The particular form of contemporary Northern Irish society has arisen out of a specific and complex process of capitalist development that has spanned the past couple of centuries. Northern Ireland clearly exhibits all of the inequities and disparities that are the classic hallmarks of bourgeois society (Wilson 1989, p. 13). The existence of substantial class divisions within the region becomes readily apparent when we consider patterns of income distribution. Information garnered by the British Treasury reveals that the different social strata within Northern Ireland experience vastly divergent life chances (Milburn 1994). In 1994 the collective earnings of the most affluent ten per cent of Northern Irish taxpayers actually exceeded those of the least affluent 50 per cent. The disparities in earnings that have always existed within the six counties have become even more pronounced in recent decades. The accession to power of Margaret Thatcher in the spring of 1979 heralded an era of growing inequality throughout the entire United Kingdom. When the Conservatives entered office the gap between rich and poor within Northern Ireland was already enormous. During the fiscal year 1980/81 the most wealthy ten per cent of the province's economically active population received incomes that were, on average, eight times greater than those of the least wealthy 50 per cent. With the passage of time this particular ratio of inequality has grown appreciably. The social and economic policies that have been implemented by successive Conservative administrations have ensured that the void between the 'haves' and the 'have nots' within Northern Irish society has widened alarmingly over the last generation. By the tax year 1993/94 the top decile of wage earners in the province had come to enjoy incomes that were on average 13 times larger than those received by the bottom half.

The information furnished by Her Majesty's Treasury reveals Northern Ireland to be a society characterised by substantial and growing material inequalities. The fact that the distribution of income in the region has become increasingly inequitable over recent years may be attributed both to the reconfiguration of the global economy that occurred in the wake of the oil price rises of the early 1970s and to the conduct of public policy since the intro-duction of 'direct rule' from Westminster. The interplay of these two crucial processes has often impacted in radically different ways upon the various aggregates that comprise the Northern Irish class formation. The discussion that follows focuses upon the distinctly divergent experiences of the middle and working classes respec-tively. Each will be examined in turn.

The Middle Classes

The modern period of political upheaval has at one time or another proved thoroughly traumatic for almost all of the people of Northern Ireland. The era of the troubles has also ironically been one of unprecedented opportunity for many within Northern Irish society. The last three decades have witnessed the growth of prosperity among the province's middle classes. The burgeoning affluence of the professional and business classes owes much to the policies that have been introduced since Westminster dissolved the Stormont legislature and assumed responsibility for the governance of the six counties. Under the auspices of direct rule Northern Ireland has experienced spectacular increases in public expenditure (Wichert 1991, p. 161). The relative generosity of the British exchequer has enabled a significant expansion of employment in the public sector (Borooah 1993). At present the British state provides employment for around four out of every ten of those who work within the six counties. The expansion of the public sector has facilitated the enlargement of the Northern Irish middle classes (McGovern & Shirlow 1997, pp. 188–9). The province's new middle classes typically enjoy secure public employment which offers remuneration equal to that received by state employees working in the other regions of the United Kingdom. While those living in Northern Ireland who work for the state have incomes comparable to their British counterparts, they face house prices running at only two thirds of the UK average (*Social Trends* 1998, p. 183). The relatively low cost of housing in the province means that the Northern Irish middle classes enjoy rather greater purchasing power than individuals performing similar jobs who live 'across the water' (Gaffikin & Morrissey 1995; McGarry & O'Leary 1995a, pp. 295–6).

The expansion of the public sector that has taken place over the last quarter of a century has provided many people with relatively secure and reasonably lucrative positions. The conduct of public policy under direct rule has also bestowed considerable benefit upon certain individuals who are not in fact directly employed by the British state. Since the demise of the Stormont parliament Westminster has chosen to adopt a distinctly interventionist approach towards the Northern Irish economy. Official agencies such as the Local Enterprise Development Unit (LEDU) have provided substantial practical and financial assistance to private companies within Northern Ireland. The particular industrial policies that direct rule administrations have pursued have served to underwrite the affluence of the Northern Irish business classes. The generous assistance dispensed by state bodies has enabled indigenous capital to generate rates of profit which simply are not justified by corporate performance. Research carried out by the Northern Ireland Economic Research Council (NIERC) reveals that during the 1980s local manufacturing concerns declared profits that were 60 per cent greater than those registered by similarly efficient firms located in other regions of the United Kingdom (Teague 1993).

The essentially Keynesian policies that the British state has implemented since the abolition of the Stormont parliament have, therefore, conferred considerable affluence upon a broad section of Northern Irish society. The new wealth that exists within the six counties has in time given rise to increasingly conspicuous patterns of consumption (Breen 1994; Gaffikin & Morrissey 1995; MacKinnon 1993). Commentators are often quick to point out that there are more luxury cars relative to population in Northern Ireland than in any other part of the United Kingdom (Rolston 1993). The prodigious spending power of the Northern Irish middle classes becomes especially apparent when we reflect upon the recent spectacular revival of Belfast. The violence that engulfed Northern Ireland during the 1970s impacted with particular gravity upon the people and architecture of the regional capital. The bombing campaign that republicans initiated at the outset of the troubles destroyed one quarter of all commercial floorspace in the centre of Belfast (Cebulla & Smyth 1995, p. 86). Most of the larger British retail concerns understandably declined to open stores in the city. The spate of random killings that soured life in Belfast during the 1970s ensured that citizens often preferred to socialise exclusively within their own local communities. In early evening the city centre quickly came to resemble a ghost town. The baleful and oppressive atmosphere that haunted 1970s Belfast inspired local band *Stiff Little Fingers* to pen their resonant anthem of alienated youth *Alternative Ulster*.

Over the last decade or so the fortunes of Belfast have changed dramatically. The remarkable rejuvenation of the commercial and night life of the city that has taken place in recent times has been sponsored largely by the growing purchasing power of the province's professional and business classes. As the threat posed by republican bombers has diminished, and the ability and willingness of the local middle classes to consume have increased, Belfast has come to represent an ever more attractive market for retailers (McGovern & Shirlow 1997, p. 189). Most of the larger

British high street stores have in recent years opened outlets in the city and in adjacent dormitory towns. At present there are three major record chains competing for business within a few hundred yards of one another in the centre of Belfast.

The rising fortunes of Belfast are clearly evinced in the city's thriving night life. Much of the entertainment to be had in Belfast is concentrated in the approximate mile that spans the distance between the city centre and the university precinct. Since the mid 1980s a host of bars and restaurants have opened along the 'Golden Mile', many of which cater for exotic and expensive tastes (Brennock 1991). The various eateries that have opened within Belfast's entertainment district have generally prospered. The province's middle classes appear rather more willing and able than their counterparts in other regions of the United Kingdom to spend money on dining out (*Social Trends* 1996, p. 116). In the last few years the burgeoning night life in Belfast has begun to extend beyond the confines of the 'Golden Mile'. A number of restaurants and night clubs have opened recently in areas of the city centre which a generation ago no-one would have ventured into after nightfall.

A casual glance at the entertainment section of any of the local newspapers will provide ample evidence to support the familiar official line that 'Belfast is buzzing'. The remarkable renaissance that the city has experienced lately is perhaps illustrated most clearly in the recent completion of a controversial conference and concert centre funded out of central government revenue and the local rates. Located on the banks of the River Lagan the impressive Waterfront Hall promises to draw top class entertainers from around the world to Belfast. The scale and splendour of the development are often cited as emblematic of a newfound confidence among the residents of Belfast. An alternative reading might suggest that the use of fiscal resources to facilitate the completion of a venue that will stage events beyond the financial reach of many citizens offers further evidence that the institutions of state often provide conduits through which workers are enticed into subsidising the consumption and cultural habits of the rich.

The Working Classes

The processes of social and economic change that have evolved over the last quarter of a century have affected the Northern Irish working classes in complex and often contradictory ways. The era of direct rule has proved hugely beneficial for a significant minority of working class people in the province. Since the abolition of the Stormont legislature the public sector has – as we noted earlier – grown substantially. The creation of thousands of middle class jobs over a relatively short space of time has of course afforded the more ambitious and better qualified individuals from working class backgrounds unprecedented opportunities for upward social mobility.

The political violence that has cursed the province over recent generations has ironically generated enormous material benefit for a very specific element within the Northern Irish working classes. The persistence of the troubles has necessitated an expansion of those occupations concerned with the maintenance of law and order. The enlargement of the security forces has led to the creation of thousands of jobs that are often remarkably lucrative. These openings have in the main been filled by upwardly mobile Protestant men of working class origins (Brewer & Magee 1991). During the course of the troubles the existence of a large number of well paid positions within the prison service, Royal Ulster Constabulary (RUC), Royal Irish Regiment (RIR) and so forth, has become absolutely essential to the welfare of the entire Ulster Protestant community. At present approximately one in every ten Protestant men who have jobs are in fact employed in the security forces.

In the period since the devolved parliament in Belfast was prorogued, therefore, the position of a substantial element within the Northern Irish working classes would seem to have improved. The era of direct rule has also, however, spelled enormous hardship for a further, rather more substantial, body of working class people living in the six counties. The fateful coincidence of an unstable political environment and successive recessions within the world economy has at various stages lengthened the dole queues within Northern Ireland. During the 1980s mass unemployment returned with a vengeance to the six counties. When the jobless total eventually peaked, one in six of the province's labour force was out of work.

In the last few years the rate of unemployment in Northern Ireland has fallen dramatically from the enormous levels that characterised the 1980s and early 1990s. At the moment around one in 14 of those looking for work in the province has been unable to secure employment. It should be borne in mind, however, that the unemployment rates registered by state agencies substantially understate the actual level of joblessness in the region. Since the formation of Margaret Thatcher's first cabinet in 1979 more than 30 amendments have been made to the definitions used to construct the unemployment figures (O'Dowd 1995, p. 154). The effect of these changes has inevitably been to exclude from official statistics certain categories of people who cannot find work. Hence, it would seem reasonable to assume that the true level of unemployment within Northern Ireland runs rather higher than the figures that state agencies compile would suggest.

The economic crises that have overtaken the United Kingdom in recent decades have buffeted Northern Ireland with particular force. Since partition, the six counties have consistently endured exceptionally high rates of unemployment. Throughout most of the present troubles the level of joblessness in the province was greater than that of any other region of the state. Only in the last couple of years has Northern Ireland ceased to have the highest unemployment rate in the United Kingdom. At present, people living in Scotland, Wales and the northwest of England are proportionately more likely to find themselves out of work than people living in the six counties. While the recent dramatic falls in the jobless total are to be welcomed, it remains to be seen whether Northern Ireland can permanently relinquish its traditional status as the unemployment blackspot of the United Kingdom.

Those who find themselves out of work in the six counties are relatively disadvantaged in at least one important regard. Individuals who become unemployed in Northern Ireland typically have to wait rather longer for another job than their counterparts in England, Scotland and Wales (Gorecki & Keating 1995; Silver 1995). The fact that the province suffers from an unusually high incidence of long-term unemployment – that which persists for a year or more – is confirmed in the government publication *Regional Trends*. The latest edition of the statistical compendium indicates that 35 per cent of United Kingdom citizens who cannot currently find work fall into the category of the long-term unemployed. In the specific case of Northern Ireland the proportion is rather greater. Some 54 per cent of those presently unemployed in the province have been out of work for at least a year.

The high level of unemployment within Northern Ireland reflects a recomposition of the local economy which in turn echoes developments throughout the western world. Significant shifts have taken place within the international division of labour since the early 1970s. Manufacturing concerns that were traditionally centred in the advanced economies of western states have often been relocated to the fragile economies of the underdeveloped world in order, primarily, to avail themselves of relatively low labour costs. The result has been the radical transformation of first world economies. As manufacturing has declined, the service sector has become an increasingly important source of employment. These patterns of change have been particularly evident in the context of Northern Ireland (McGovern & Shirlow 1997, pp. 188–9). Since the early 1970s the manufacturing sector of the local economy has gone into calamitous decline. Over the past couple of decades around 40,000 manufacturing jobs have been lost in the city of Belfast alone (Cebulla & Smyth 1995, p. 89). The evaporation of manufacturing employment has been especially apparent in a range of industries which once represented the fulcrum of the Northern Irish economy: shipbuilding, engineering and textiles (O'Dowd 1995, p. 143). The plight of manufacturing enterprise has ensured a significant shift in the sectoral composition of employment in the province. In 1971, 45 per cent of the Northern Irish workforce were engaged in manufacturing. Two decades later only 27 per cent of those in work were employed in the secondary sector.

The transition towards a post-fordist economy has greatly eroded employment opportunities in Northern Ireland. The last quarter of a century has been particularly traumatic for that large swathe of the Northern Irish working classes that has been consigned to the hardship of unemployment. Many working class people who have managed to remain in work have also, however, endured enormous difficulties. The coincidence of mass unemployment and diminished legal protection has meant that the more vulnerable elements of the workforce have increasingly suffered poor pay and conditions (McGovern & Shirlow 1997, pp. 193–4). The position of certain sections of the working classes has been undermined further by the advance of part-time employment. Between 1971 and 1991 the proportion of occupations that were part-time rose from one tenth to one quarter (O'Dowd 1995, p. 152). Part-time jobs are often poorly regarded and rewarded. The creation of a 'flexible' labour market within Northern Ireland has proved particularly detrimental for those working class women who are heavily over-represented among the ranks of part-time workers.

The period under discussion would seem, therefore, to have been marked by a decline in the material conditions of a substantial section of the Northern Irish working classes. Many northern workers have endured unemployment, much of it of a distinctly long-term nature. Many others have come to be trapped in increasingly poorly paid and poorly protected jobs. The plight of the northern working classes is reflected in the relatively high incidence of low income and poverty in the province (McGregor & McKee 1995, pp. 42–3). Data presented in the annual *Regional Trends* (1996, p. 127) suggests that Northern Irish families are particularly likely to fall into low income categories. The survey reveals that a quarter of all households in the province are forced to survive on a weekly income of £125 or less.

The course that the local economy has followed over recent decades has proved particularly detrimental for the less affluent members of Northern Irish society. The province's working classes have also been the principal casualties of the lamentable political events that have overtaken Northern Ireland since the late 1960s. The violence that has marred recent Northern Irish history has at one stage or another touched the lives of most people resident within the six counties (Ruane 1996). The troubles have, however, impacted most gravely upon the province's lower orders. Most of those who have played a direct role in the conflict have been drawn from working class communities. The security forces, as we noted earlier, have in the main recruited from the 'respectable' elements of the Protestant working classes. The agents of unofficial forms of violence have also come overwhelmingly from working class backgrounds. Research conducted by Louise Shara (1994) reveals that a large majority of those charged with politically motivated offences were either unemployed or engaged in semi-skilled or unskilled manual work. The information presented by Shara shows that 83 per cent of defendants who came before 'Diplock courts', whose socioeconomic status could be established, fell into these particular categories. (In the 1970s the Northern Irish legal system was reformed in an attempt to stem the rising tide of political violence in the province. An official commission headed by Lord Diplock argued that the risk of intimidation meant that it was inappropriate to expect members of the public to serve on juries during cases arising out of terrorist incidents. The adoption of the commission's recommendations has ensured that for most of the recent troubles individuals charged with paramilitary offences have been tried solely by members of the judiciary. The non-jury trials that take place in Northern Ireland are sometimes referred to as 'Diplock courts' in acknowledgement of the man who devised them.)

Most of the people who have killed during the modern conflict in Northern Ireland have come from working class backgrounds. So too have most of the people who have lost their lives. The significant absence of appropriate information means that it is impossible to capture precisely the socioeconomic characteristics of those who have died during the troubles. We may nevertheless be able to construct a reasonably accurate class profile of the victims of political violence in Northern Ireland through examination of the spatial distribution of fatalities – by considering, in other words, the particular areas of the province in which people have been killed. Adopting this approach bears out anecdotal evidence that the conflict that has beset the region since the late 1960s has proved particularly lethal for the residents of working class districts.

A decade ago Michael McKeown undertook the unenviable task of analysing the 2,763 deaths that had occurred during the first 20 years of the troubles. The information that McKeown (1989, p. 50) presents clearly confirms that those areas of the province that are materially disadvantaged have also experienced disproportionately high levels of political violence. This coincidence becomes especially evident when we examine the electoral constituencies of north and west Belfast. While neither district could be characterised as universally poor, both contain some of the most extreme concentrations of poverty that exist in Northern Ireland (Gaffikin & Morrissey 1995, p. 53). The inhabitants of north and west Belfast have endured rather greater levels of political violence than those of any other part of the province (Fay et al. 1999, pp. 141–7). Over the first two decades of the troubles the death toll in each district was the strangely identical figure of 544 fatalities. The contrast with the most affluent region of the six counties could hardly be more dramatic. The residents of North Down have been relatively sheltered from the conflict that has engulfed Northern Ireland over recent generations. Between 1969 and 1989 the number of residents of the province's 'gold coast' who lost their lives to political violence was the remarkably small total of eight.

THE OTHER APARTHEID

Those who have scrutinised contemporary Northern Irish society have been preoccupied mainly with the distinctive and enduring patterns of segregation that ethnonational division has created within the six counties. Commentators have frequently expressed concern that members of the two principal ethnopolitical communities in Northern Ireland typically attend different schools and reside in different areas. Rather less attention has been afforded to the particular forms of social and spatial segregation that arise out of class distinctions.

The education system that operates in the province radically differentiates pupils along socioeconomic lines. In contrast to some other regions of the United Kingdom, Northern Ireland has retained a distinctly selective process of schooling. Northern Irish children undertake standard intelligence tests around the age of eleven which determine the mode of secondary level education that they will receive. Success in the eleven plus examinations has an enormous bearing upon future academic progress (Gallagher 1995). Those youngsters who pass are entitled to a place in one of the province's grammar schools. These prestigious institutions frequently boast impressive scholastic standards and routinely attain the best external examination results in the United Kingdom. Northern Irish grammar schools cater overwhelmingly for the children of the professional and business classes. Cormack and Osborne (1995, p. 503) note that seven out of every ten pupils enrolled in the province's grammar schools have parents engaged in non-manual employment.

The majority of children who sit the eleven plus examinations in Northern Ireland do so unsuccessfully. Those who fail the eleven plus examinations are educated in secondary intermediate schools. These institutions are intended to offer a general education to pupils deemed unsuited to academic pursuits. Most of the children who attend secondary intermediate schools are drawn from working class communities. The research of Cormack and Osborne cited above intimates that two thirds of pupils enrolled in secondary intermediate schools have parents employed in manual labour. The funds that secondary schools receive are merely a fraction of those lavished upon the province's grammar schools. In the mid 1980s the amount spent educating each pupil attending a Protestant grammar school was more than four times greater than that devoted to each child enrolled in a Protestant secondary school (ibid, p. 513). The relative and absolute underfunding that secondary schools have endured has inevitably been mirrored in patterns of scholastic attainment. While some secondary schools have attained respectable academic standards, the results of many others remain extremely poor. As a result, the proportion of Northern Irish teenagers who leave school without any formal qualifications is high compared to the United Kingdom average (ibid, pp. 505–6; Gallagher 1995; Sheehan & Tomlinson 1995).

Socioeconomic origins, therefore, exercise an important influence upon the manner in which the Northern Irish educational system is accessed and experienced. A couple of processes at work within the province's schools are perhaps worth underlining in this regard. First, the selective system of education that persists within the six counties means that children usually attend schools in which the bulk of their peers possess socioeconomic credentials similar to their own. In Northern Ireland as elsewhere children from different class backgrounds are generally educated apart from one another. Children proceeding through the province's educational system are of course less likely to be segregated in terms of class origins than in terms of ethnoreligious status. Nonetheless the former remains an important source of distinction and division within Northern Irish schools.

Second, the particular educational system that persists in Northern Ireland ensures that children from different class origins are typically allocated to different schools which provide different standards of education. Pupils from middle class backgrounds – as we have seen – mainly attend grammar schools that usually offer an excellent academic education. Working class children, in contrast, typically go to secondary intermediate schools which frequently have poor academic standards. The process of selection at work within the province's educational system clearly offers the main advantage to the children of the professional and business classes. Northern Irish schools are, therefore, instrumental in reproducing the enormous socioeconomic disparities that obtain within the six counties.

The resilient class distinctions that characterise Northern Ireland ensure that social actors from different socioeconomic backgrounds not only are educated separately but also live apart from one another. Social scientists and others have often remarked upon the propensity of Northern Irish Protestants and Catholics to live in different districts. Rather less attention has been afforded to the specific patterns of residential segregation that are associated with class distinctions. An important exception to this trend is the research undertaken at the beginning of the troubles by the social geographer Fred Boal (1971). In the early 1970s Boal surveyed two adjacent neighbourhoods located in the southern reaches of Belfast. While both districts were populated overwhelmingly by Protestants, one was predominantly middle class and the other essentially working class. In the course of his study Boal uncovered a remarkable degree of segregation between the two neighbour-hoods. People living in the respective districts tended to socialise in different venues, send their children to different schools and attend different churches, even when they belonged to the same religious denomination. While the residents of the contiguous neighbourhoods examined by Boal may have formally belonged to the same ethnopolitical community, they had clearly been consigned, on the basis of socioeconomic status, to radically different social worlds.

In Northern Ireland as elsewhere, class distinctions produce distinctive and often enduring patterns of residence. Socioeconomic status also has an important bearing upon how social actors experience those forms of spatial segregation that arise specifically out of ethnoreligious division. The trend towards ethnic homogeneity is of course especially pronounced within working class communities (Tonge 1998, p. 91). Many children born into working class households will grow up in districts where they will never have the opportunity to encounter someone from the other ethnopolitical tradition. In certain parts of Belfast in particular working class nationalist and loyalist communities exist cheek by jowl with one another. The hostility that typically defines the limited relations that exist between these neighbourhoods has often prompted residents to construct crude defences that have in time been formalised by the agencies of the state. The 'peace lines' that one encounters when travelling through particular areas of Belfast provide perhaps the clearest sense of the limits that the Northern Irish conflict has placed upon the physical mobility of the working classes. An understandable fear of violence has ensured that many working class people in the province tend to move within strictly bounded life worlds (Jenkins 1983).

The lives of the Northern Irish middle classes are, generally speaking, rather less restricted. Ethnoreligious bigotry is of course far from the exclusive preserve of those who live in working class communities. The prejudices to which middle class individuals fall prey, however, invariably appear relatively muted not least because they are frequently mediated through the charming conventions of bourgeois etiquette. Professional and business people in the six counties will often have neighbours drawn from the other side of the ethnopolitical divide. Living in suburbs that are ethnically mixed and which have been largely untouched by the troubles allows middle class social actors to move free from the omnipresent fear of political violence that stalks many working class communities. The personal mobility of the middle classes has of course been enhanced by the affluence that they have come to enjoy under the aegis of direct rule. As disposable incomes have grown, the professional and business classes have begun to take multiple holidays each year. Burgeoning affluence has gradually eroded the parochialism that once characterised the outlook of the province's middle classes. In recent times middle class northerners have developed increasingly cosmopolitan tastes in travel. Perhaps the most potent illustration of the growing physical mobility of the Northern Irish professional and business classes is that provided by the recent transformation of the North Down town often regarded as the citadel of middle class Ulster. In the early years of the troubles Bangor resembled a classic sleepy British seaside resort. Over the last decade, however, the town has changed almost beyond recognition. The somewhat dilapidated seafront that previously existed has become the site of a thriving marina. The scores of luxury yachts moored in Bangor harbour signal that the more affluent elements within Northern Irish society have come to experience a freedom of movement typically denied to working class people whose lives are often profoundly circumscribed by the boundaries that map out ethnopolitical geography.

The discussion advanced above suggests that there exists within the six counties a system of apartheid other than that associated with ethnoreligious distinction. In capitalist societies class produces boundaries between people that are both literal and symbolic. Northern Ireland is no exception. Many of the residents of the six counties in effect live apart from those with whom they share certain ethnopolitical sentiments but who occupy rather different positions within the prevailing hierarchy of class relations. The particular patterns of social distinction that arise out of socioeconomic status have an important – if often unacknowledged – bearing upon the manner in which Northern Irish people think, feel and act.

CLASS AS A SOCIAL IDENTITY

The argument advanced thus far reveals contemporary Northern Irish society to be deeply differentiated along class lines. The enormous inequalities that attend socioeconomic distinctions are clearly revealed in the patterns of academic attainment and income distribution. Class position evidently exerts an important influence over the allocation of life chances in Northern Ireland. The salience of socioeconomic status has not been lost upon the citizens of the province. There exists ample evidence that social class has considerable bearing upon the manner in which Northern Irish people define both themselves and others.

The data yielded by large scale survey research suggests that socioeconomic status impinges strongly upon the consciousness of social actors in the six counties. People in the province emerge as critically aware of the multiple significance of class background. The consciousness of the Northern Irish working classes would appear especially acute. Those annual surveys conducted under the auspices of the British Social Attitudes project have consistently shown that working class people in the province are overwhelmingly aware of the material inequalities that mark the social order under which they live (Hayes & McAllister 1997). Around three quarters of working class respondents have acknowledged that there exist iniquitous disparities in wealth among the population of Northern Ireland (O'Dowd 1991, p. 45).

Northern Irish people would seem strongly aware that class origins are deeply implicated in the distribution of life chances within the six counties. It scarcely comes as a surprise, therefore, to learn that socioeconomic status is crucial to the definitions of self that social actors in the province construct. Surveys conducted in the region have invariably revealed that people are readily familiar with the systems of classification that are associated with class distinctions. Northern Irish respondents are typically willing and able to allocate themselves to specific locations within the hierarchy of class relations. Indeed, people living in the six counties often prove more capable of assigning accurate class identities to themselves than the citizens of other countries conventionally assumed to possess more developed systems of socioeconomic distinction. The Northern Irish working classes emerge as particularly familiar with the taxonomy of bourgeois society. International data collated by Hayes and McAllister (1995, p. 356) reveal that working class residents of the six counties are more likely to identify their socioeconomic status accurately than workers living in any other western state.

The responses that have been produced by surveys conducted in Northern Ireland are perhaps significant. The apparent familiarity of Northern Irish respondents with the classifications associated with capitalist society suggests that socioeconomic status strongly informs the outlook of social actors living in the region. Social class would seem to impinge upon who and what the people of the province consider themselves to be. Socioeconomic status influences not only how Northern Irish people define themselves but also how they regard others. The information that has emerged from the annual British Social Attitudes survey intimates that class generates feelings of solidarity among the citizens of the province. Two out of every three respondents acknowledged 'feeling close' to others from similar socioeconomic origins. The sentiments of kinship that arise out of social class were of equal magnitude to those produced by ethnoreligious identity (Moxon-Browne 1991, p. 27).

The identities that people in Northern Ireland embrace clearly bear the inscription of socioeconomic status. Social class strongly influences the manner in which individuals understand both themselves and others (Bourdieu 1986). The inhabitants of the six counties possess an intimate knowledge of the specific ethnographic cues that signify socioeconomic distinction. While less extensive and exotic than the markers of ethnoreligious persuasion, the signifiers of class status constitute an important resource upon which social actors draw in everyday situations. Accent, style of dress, secondary level school attended, cultural appetites and so on will alert individuals to the socioeconomic origins of those with whom they come into contact (McAll 1990, pp. 140–1). Awareness of the class background of those one encounters may subtly alter the form of interaction. Socioeconomic distinctions frequently give rise to strong feelings of antipathy. Although less virulent than the hostility that often emerges out of ethnoreligious conviction, the prejudice associated with social class can often sour relations and prevent specific forms of personal interaction. The strength of ethnoreligious enmity within the region has served little to dilute the snobbery which Northern Ireland shares in common with other societies.

CLASS AS A POLITICAL IDENTITY

Examination of contemporary Northern Irish society attests to the enormous significance of social class. Socioeconomic location evidently serves to determine the resources and opportunities available to individuals. Social actors are keenly aware that class status regulates the distribution of life chances within the six counties. The class consciousness that informs the outlook of Northern Irish people would seem, however, to have had little effect upon the political culture of the province. The ideological formations that are prevalent within the six counties would appear to arise not out of class sentiment but rather ethnoreligious feeling.

The influence that confessional status exercises over the political life of Northern Ireland finds numerous expressions. Ethnoreligious affiliation provides the most reliable predictor of electoral preference in the province. Members of the two principal communal blocs that coexist uneasily within the six counties invariably cast their votes for different political parties. Most Northern Irish Catholics offer their support to the Social Democratic and Labour Party (SDLP) and Sinn Fein. The electoral allegiances of Northern Irish Protestants are largely the preserve of the Ulster Unionist Party (UUP) and the Democratic Unionist Party (DUP). Only one mainstream political grouping can reasonably claim to draw roughly equal support from both of the principal ethnoreligious traditions within the region. The Alliance Party remains comparatively small, however, and managed to attract only seven per cent of the votes cast during the 1998 Assembly elections. The strength of confessional status as a source of electoral preference ensures that the number of voters who opt for a party associated with an ethnoreligious tradition other than their own is distinctly negligible. While there is speculation that some middle class Catholics may vote for the UUP, it remains extremely unlikely that the particular brand of religious and political fundamentalism peddled by the DUP would appeal to members of the minority community. Those Northern Irish Protestants who are prepared to offer electoral support to either of the main nationalist parties that run for public office are probably sufficiently rare – at least under unexceptional circum- stances – as to demand no further consideration.

The ethnoreligious distinctions that generate electoral allegiance within Northern Ireland find further echoes in patterns of political interchange. While some communication does take place across the communal divide, public figures in the province often appear willing and able to enter into meaningful dialogue solely with members of the same ethnopolitical tradition. The views that unionists express invariably seem to be intended exclusively for the ears of others within the unionist fold. The political dialogue that occurs among the diverse members of the 'unionist family' tends to become more frequent – but also often more acrimonious – during times of crisis. The propensity of political players to converse primarily with others who belong to the same ethnoreli- gious tradition – even those with whom they disagree fiercely on numerous issues – is equally evident in relation to Northern Irish nationalism. In 1993 the leaders of the two largest parties that represent northern nationalists – John Hume of the SDLP and Gerry Adams of Sinn Fein – resumed a political dialogue that had been abandoned five years earlier. The outlook of the two men remained far from identical. Nevertheless they were able to find sufficient common ground to devise a joint set of proposals concerning the future political development of the province. While the actual detail of the 'Hume-Adams document' has never been fully disclosed its appearance in the autumn of 1993 provided important impetus to the 'peace process' in Northern Ireland.

The significance of ethnoreligious persuasion as a source of political conviction becomes fully apparent when we begin to consider perhaps the most dramatic form of political conduct – namely that which results in the loss of human life. We noted earlier that working class communities have borne the brunt of the political violence for which Northern Ireland has unfortunately become famous over recent generations. It should be acknowledged, however, that the fate of the victims of the troubles has been sealed more by their ethnonational identity than by their socioeconomic standing. Those persons who have been deliberately killed in the course of the troubles were targeted either indiscriminately because they were simply Protestants or Catholics, or selectively because of their association with agencies – whether legal or illegal – considered to endanger the interests of one or other ethnoreligious tradition. The Catholic lawyer who has defended a succession of republicans in court is murdered not because he or she enjoys an enviable middle class lifestyle but rather because he or she is considered to have contributed to the hostile political forces supposedly ranged against the Ulster Protestant community. Equally, the Protestant electrician murdered by republicans while returning home from carrying out repairs to a local RUC station is killed not because he is regarded as a reactionary member of the aristocracy of labour but rather because he has assisted an agency of the state engaged in the repression of the nationalist population.

Ethnoreligious sentiment clearly provides the most important source of political belief and practice within contemporary Northern Irish society. While ethnicity may represent the *principal* author of political identity within the six counties it is by no means the only one. Ethnic feeling evidently defines the parameters and contours of political life in the province. Within the ideological framework that ethnoreligious conviction has constructed, however, other forms of social identity, and most notably those that emerge out of socioeconomic position, exercise a palpable influence (Hayes & McAllister 1997; McAuley 1994, pp. 2, 52, 124–9, 181; O'Dowd 1990, p. 63). Social scientists and other commentators have often chosen to ignore the crucial role that social class plays in the political culture of the province. The particular manner in which ethnoreligious feeling and class sentiment interact to produce political identity in Northern Ireland may be illustrated through examination of the two most important ideological formations that exist within the six counties – Irish nationalism and Ulster unionism.

Irish Nationalism

Those diverse individuals who belong to the Northern Irish nationalist tradition share a profound sense of community (Todd 1990). The ideological and emotional bonds that exist between nationalists are revealed and strengthened during periods of political turmoil. The fateful hunger strikes initiated in the early 1980s managed to generate sympathy even among Northern Irish Catholics sternly opposed to the republican movement. The tense standoffs that have developed at Drumcree over the last few summers offer more recent evidence that nationalists of all backgrounds can at times find common political cause (Douds 1996).

Even after the tumultuous events of the past three decades northern nationalists still share many political interests and grievances. The era of the troubles has nonetheless seen a substantial widening of traditional divisions among nationalist ranks (Ruane & Todd, 1992a, pp. 202–9). The ideological fissures that have grown within Northern Irish nationalism have acknowledged the changing class composition of the Catholic community in the province. The operation of direct rule has amplified existing socioeconomic divisions among northern nationalists. A large section of the nationalist community has derived enormous benefit from the policies that have been introduced by various Westminster administrations (McGovern & Shirlow 1997, pp. 193, 197). The expansion of places in third level education – coupled with the growing tendency of middle class Protestants to opt for universities in Great Britain – has enhanced the academic opportunities available to nationalist youths. The creation of thousands of jobs in the public sector has meant that many of the more gifted and ambitious members of the current generation of nationalists have been able, unlike their predecessors, to translate formidable academic attainment into lucrative and secure employment (O'Connor 1993, p. 14). Some nationalists who have been recruited into state institutions have of course encountered obstacles that have impeded their career development. The advances that members of the nationalist community have secured through public employment remain significant nonetheless.

The era of direct rule has offered many within the nationalist community unprecedented opportunities for social mobility. As certain Northern Irish Catholics have ascended the class hierarchy a distance has opened up between themselves and their fellow nationalists that is both social and spatial. Over time, burgeoning affluence has enabled many upwardly mobile nationalists to move away from districts populated exclusively by their ethnopolitical kin. These changing patterns of residence have assumed an especially significant form within the regional capital. The district of south Belfast that centres upon the Malone Road was histori-cally the preserve of wealthy unionists. The few Catholics who lived in the neighbourhood were usually servants working in the sumptuous residences that characterise the area (Sharrock 1995). In recent times, however, the ethnoreligious composition of Belfast's most exclusive district has undergone remarkable change. Members of the new Catholic middle classes have begun to acquire addresses along the Malone Road and its numerous leafy arteries (Smyth 1991, p. 144). Indeed there has been some speculation that nationalists now outnumber unionists among the residents of Belfast's most prestigious neighbourhood. The decision of numerous upwardly mobile nationalists to move into the Malone district has had some important effects. The grammar school that caters for Catholic children from the area has encountered increasing difficulty each year in meeting the demand for places. Furthermore, the recent growth in its congregation has prompted the local Catholic church to undertake an impressive programme of expansion (Brennock 1991).

The shifting ethnoreligious credentials of those who live in the leafy avenues of south Belfast provide an important illustration of the gains that many Northern Irish nationalists have made over the last couple of decades. The benefits that direct rule has bestowed upon the nationalist community have, however, been far from universal. The policies that Westminster has implemented have enhanced the opportunities for wealth and social mobility of some northern nationalists. Others within the nationalist fold have proved rather less fortunate.

The series of economic and political crises that have befallen Northern Ireland over recent generations have impacted with especial severity upon sections of the nationalist working classes. Unemployment represents a particular problem for working class Catholics and, more specifically, for working class Catholic men.

The decline of the construction industry has eroded further the employment opportunities available to working class nationalists who have invariably proved either unwilling or unable to seek work within the greatly expanded security sector. As a consequence, working class Catholic men tend to be heavily over-represented among the ranks of the province's unemployed. Indeed nationalist males are presently more than twice as likely as their unionist counterparts to be out of work. This particular index of the inequalities that exist between the principal ethnoreligious communities in Northern Ireland has altered little since the early 1970s (Aunger 1975; O'Dowd 1995, pp. 154–5).

The greater likelihood that nationalists will find themselves out of work is captured in the spatial distribution of unemployment within the six counties. Those parts of Northern Ireland that exhibit exceptionally high levels of joblessness are invariably populated primarily by nationalists (Sheehan & Tomlinson 1995). The alarming unemployment rates that exist in districts such as west Belfast, Strabane, the city side of Derry and so forth ensure that the Catholic working classes are particularly likely to experience low income, poverty and reliance upon state agencies. The disadvantage and dependence that characterise the position of many working class nationalists become apparent when we consider the distribution of a specific welfare benefit. School dinners are supplied free to children whose parents are unemployed and receiving income support from the state. A report published in the mid 1990s reveals that the recipients of this particular welfare provision tend to be concentrated heavily in Catholic schools (McGill 1995). The document in question notes that some 35 per cent of Catholic pupils are entitled to receive free dinners compared to only 15 per cent of their Protestant counterparts.

The violence of the last three decades has been especially traumatic for the nationalist working classes. The enormous resources of the British military have been deployed in the main to regulate and repress working class nationalist communities. The coercive conduct of the security forces has ranged from the routinised attrition of multiple forms of surveillance to the murder of unarmed political demonstrators. Hence, while the British state may frequently appear to the nationalist middle classes as a generous benefactor, it often appears to working class nationalists as a tireless oppressor. Working class Catholics have also been the principal victims of that violence that has originated within the loyalist community. Remarkably few of the nationalists who have been murdered by loyalist paramilitaries in the course of the troubles have belonged to the republican movement. Between 1969 and 1993 loyalists murdered 64 people who could be considered republican activists. During the same period 670 nationalists who had no formal association with the republican movement lost their lives at the hands of loyalist paramilitaries (McGarry & O'Leary 1995a, p. 160). Most of the nationalists who have died as a result of unofficial violence have been drawn from working class neighbourhoods. The composition of nationalist fatalities during the troubles reveals that the principal victims of loyalist paramilitarism have been randomly selected members of the Catholic working classes. The indiscriminate nature of loyalist violence has meant that every resident of certain working class nationalist districts is – in principle at least – at risk. Consequently the strategy that loyalist paramilitary factions have adopted has tended to spread fear throughout entire working class Catholic communities.

The interests and experiences of the class fragments that comprise the 'nationalist community' have, therefore, diverged considerably since the introduction of direct rule. The process of class polarisation at work among Northern Irish nationalists has inevitably produced and reproduced ideological divisions which have come to be indexed, albeit crudely, in patterns of electoral allegiance (Ruane & Todd 1992a, pp. 206–7; 1996, pp. 71–4, 166–70). The socioeconomic profiles of those who support the two largest nationalist political parties in the province are rather different (Irvin & Moxon-Browne 1989; Ryan 1994, p. 66). While the SDLP attracts votes from many working class nationalists, the electoral strength of the party stems primarily from its enduring appeal among the Catholic middle classes (Evans & Duffy 1997, pp. 58–9). The approach that the SDLP has advocated has been that of edging towards a united Ireland through a gradual and inclusive process of political and cultural dialogue. The political strategy endorsed by the party would seem to have chimed with the interests and ambitions of middle class nationalists (Mitchell 1991, p. 346; O'Connor 1993, pp. 35, 43, 49, 52–3). The promotion of the ideal of a united Ireland clearly accords with the deep sense of Irishness that persists among upwardly mobile Catholics living in the six counties. At the same time, the pursuit of that particular ideal through a political strategy that is distinctly gradualist serves to accommodate the instrumental concerns of those nationalists who are fearful that radical change will erode the substantial material gains that have been secured under the auspices of direct rule.

The electoral constituency which Sinn Fein draws upon differs somewhat. Since it re-emerged in the early 1980s Sinn Fein has operated primarily as the voice of the more marginalised elements among the nationalist working classes (Evans & Duffy 1997, p. 72; Irvin & Moxon-Browne 1989). The political wing of the republican movement has conventionally advocated terminating the Union through force of arms. This radical strategy would seem to have appealed to many of those working class Catholics who have enjoyed few of the economic advantages that have flowed from direct rule and who have had to bear the brunt of the habitual repression meted out by agents of the state.

During the present decade the radicalism of Sinn Fein has waned demonstrably. The political goal of the republican movement remains the establishment of a unitary Irish state. In recent years, however, many republicans have come to the realisation that the creation of a united Ireland will occur neither in the immediate future nor indeed through force of arms (Shirlow & McGovern 1998). The growing circumspection of Sinn Fein would also appear to have altered the outlook of the party on social and economic matters. Through an extensive network of grassroots organisations, republicans continue to seek to represent and advance the interests of the nationalist working classes. The references to socialism that once informed the discourse of Sinn Fein have, however, all but disappeared.

The process of revision that Sinn Fein has undergone in recent years would seem to have broadened the appeal of the party considerably. The numerous elections that have punctuated the evolution of the 'peace process' have witnessed increases in the republican vote that few observers would have anticipated. The electoral advances that Sinn Fein has secured lately may perhaps reflect the growing attraction that the party exercises among middle class nationalists. Having apparently embraced at least the essence of the prevailing neoliberal orthodoxy on economic affairs, contemporary republicanism could hardly be considered a threat to the appreciable material interests of the new nationalist middle classes. The movement of Sinn Fein towards a strategy of 'unarmed struggle', moreover, has probably appealed to those upwardly mobile Catholics who consider the SDLP to be insufficiently resolute but who have been unwilling to shoulder the moral responsibility associated with political violence. The growing popularity of Sinn Fein among the nationalist middle classes was illustrated in a particular triumph during the 1997 local government elections. In north Belfast the party polled well as anticipated in the traditional fastness of the working class New Lodge district. Rather less expected were the many votes that Sinn Fein received from middle class nationalists living in the treelined avenues that branch from the lower stretches of the Antrim Road. The electoral advances that Sinn Fein made in north Belfast were crowned when the party captured a seat in the affluent Castle ward.

Ulster Unionism

The process of socioeconomic differentiation at work among Northern Irish nationalists is equally evident within the confines of the unionist community. A specific conjuncture of social and political conditions has ensured that the unionist middle classes have grown appreciably over the past quarter of a century. The expansion of both higher education and public employment under direct rule has enabled many working class Protestants to ascend the social ladder. The opportunities for social mobility available to elements of the unionist working classes have been further enhanced by the incidence of political violence in Northern Ireland. The persistence of the troubles has of course necessitated an enormous enlargement of the security forces. Those willing to accept the considerable risks that are associated with joining the RUC, UDR and RIR have been rewarded with generous salaries and benefits. In the main the security forces have recruited working class Protestant men who have managed to attain reasonable academic qualifications (Brewer & Magee 1991).

Those who have entered the swollen ranks of the unionist middle classes have invariably come to enjoy enviable standards of living. Protestants employed in the public sector benefit from relatively secure and frequently lucrative employment. The conduct of the British state since the advent of direct rule has underwritten the interests even of those middle class unionists it does not directly employ. Over the last quarter of a century the executive has offered rather greater assistance to private businesses located in Northern Ireland than to those operating in other regions of the United Kingdom. The relatively interventionist industrial policies that the state has introduced to the six counties have been beneficial primarily to those unionists who predominate within the province's shrunken bourgeoisie.

The social and economic policies introduced under direct rule have conferred considerable affluence upon the new unionist middle classes. The coincidence of substantial salaries and relatively low house prices has inflated Protestant professionals' disposable incomes. Burgeoning purchasing power has enabled the unionist middle classes to cultivate those exclusive tastes that have made luxury cars an increasingly common sight on Northern Irish roads (Tomlinson 1995, p. 8). The enviable lifestyles that the unionist professional and business classes have come to enjoy have been underwritten further by the province's elitist educational system. Middle class unionists are often able to send their children – essentially free of charge – to secondary level schools that are the equal of any within the United Kingdom. Funds that would otherwise have to be channelled into schooling can instead be spent on dining out and the occasional jaunt abroad.

The complex processes of change that have attended the era of direct rule have proved rather less advantageous for working class unionists. Over the last quarter of a century sections of the unionist working classes have experienced a harrowing process of marginalisation. Since the onset of industrialisation within the northeastern counties of Ireland Protestant males have managed largely to monopolise the more rewarding categories of manual employment. Vacancies that arose within the shipyards and engineering concerns were habitually filled with the sons and nephews of unionists already working there. The relatively privileged position that Protestant men traditionally occupied within the labour force has of course ensured that the collapse of Northern Irish manufacturing since the early 1970s has had an especially grave impact upon working class unionist communities. While jobs have been created in other areas these have been less numerous and often less lucrative than the positions that have been shed in the manufacturing sector. The outcome has been that thousands of working class Protestant men have, over the last couple of decades, been displaced from their erstwhile role as 'breadwinners'.

The hardship that spiralling unemployment has brought to working class Protestant neighbourhoods has been compounded by the urban regeneration schemes introduced after the outbreak of the troubles. Concerned in part to improve the local infrastructure and housing stock the state has, since the early 1970s, coaxed and coerced the residents of certain loyalist communities into leaving their homes. Individuals who were uprooted were dispersed to newer housing developments that were often located large distances away. One of the working class Protestant communities that has been affected most deeply by the urban planners is that which centres upon the Shankill Road. The experience of people living in the Shankill district reveals some of the problems associated with the 'redevelopment' schemes that have been implemented since the outbreak of the troubles. Over the past two decades the population of the Greater Shankill area has dwindled dramatically. In the early 1980s 76,000 people still lived in the district. Within ten years the figure had slumped to only 27,000 (O'Toole 1993). The falling population of the Greater Shankill area often seems to have been accompanied by a growing despondency within the district. Experience gained as a community planner during the 1970s prompted Ron Wiener (1980) to offer a passionate critique of the 'redevelopment' of those communities that once clustered around the Shankill Road. According to Wiener, the policies implemented by the architects of urban regeneration served to erode the communal spirit and identity of the area in ways that soon gave rise to growing criminality.

The political violence of the last three decades has touched upon the lives of working class unionists with great frequency. Most of the personnel of loyalist paramilitary factions have been drawn from poorer Protestant neighbourhoods. Working class unionists have also been particularly likely to become the *victims* of political violence. The massacres at Kingsmills and Teebane offer stark illustration of the terror that republicans have visited upon the unionist working classes in the course of the troubles. The devastation wrought by a bomb that detonated prematurely in a Shankill Road fish shop in the autumn of 1993 provides a further important reminder of the political violence that the more subaltern strata within the Protestant community have had to endure in recent generations.

The period of the troubles has seen important changes in the relationship between the unionist working classes and the repressive apparatus of the state. Most working class unionists have retained a strong sense of identification with the security forces. Some have, however, arrived at a more critical disposition. Relations between the unionist working classes and the security forces that were already fraught were strained further with the introduction of the Anglo-Irish Agreement. In the aftermath of the Hillsborough Accord many loyalists came to regard the RUC as defenders of a political scheme that injured the interests of the entire unionist community (McAuley 1994, pp. 167–71). The gnawing conviction among working class unionists that the RUC is no longer 'their' police force has generated enormous tensions. The palpable distrust between elements of the unionist working classes and the security forces has led with some frequency to violent confrontation. The apparent relish with which loyalists have over recent summers launched attacks upon RUC officers preventing their passage along the Garvaghy Road in Portadown serves to illustrate the gulf that has opened up between those working class Protestants who have attained upward social mobility through admission to the security forces and those they have left behind.

Various processes of change at work within contemporary Northern Irish society have resulted in the dispossession of a large section of the unionist working classes. The disenchantment that marks the outlook of less affluent unionists has been nurtured by the growing conviction that they are essentially voiceless (Hall 1995, 1996; Springfield Inter-Community Development Project 1994). Working class Protestants have become acutely aware of their frequent inability to air their beliefs and grievances with any real clarity. The frustration that political inarticulacy has engendered among the poorer elements of the unionist community has been amplified by the realisation that the nationalist working classes have become rather adept at expressing their concerns and interests. Working class Protestants have been embittered yet further by the conviction that should they ever develop an ability to address a political audience beyond themselves there would be few – not least within the mainstream unionist parties – who would be prepared to give them a fair hearing. These multiple anxieties have inevitably promoted disaffection among the ranks of the unionist working classes. It is hardly surprising, therefore, that in recent years many commentators should have voiced alarm at the spread of 'alienation' within poorer Protestant neighbourhoods (Bruce 1994a; McGovern & Shirlow 1997, p. 196; O'Toole 1993).

The evidence presented thus far will hopefully have illustrated that the socioeconomic distinctions that have always existed among Northern Irish Protestants have become altogether more pronounced over recent generations. In the course of the modern conflict the interests and experiences of the various social strata that comprise the unionist community have diverged enormously. The class divisions that have grown within unionist ranks have in time found pertinent expression at the level of political belief and practice.

The half century of devolved government at Stormont was characterised by remarkable political unity among the diverse membership of the 'unionist family'. Control of the apparatus of state invariably enabled the Ulster Unionist Party (UUP) to manage successfully the competing demands of numerous class interests (Ruane & Todd 1996, p. 92). Not until the 1960s did the essentially irreconcilable concerns within the Protestant community threaten to dismantle the seemingly resilient unionist class alliance. The ostensible liberalism of Prime Minister Terence O'Neill summoned the forces of unionist reaction and resistance. The terrible events that marked the onset of the troubles both acknowledged and accelerated the fragmentation of the unionist monolith. As political violence escalated, unionism imploded resulting in the creation of a plethora of smaller political groupings. A complex process of realignment that unfolded throughout the 1970s ensured, however, that by the end of the decade there were only two serious forces within unionist politics. Various elements within the previously hegemonic UUP regrouped and re-established the organisation as the single largest political party within the six counties. By the late 1970s the Democratic Unionist Party (DUP) had seen off competition from various quarters to become the sole meaningful contender for the loyalties of the unionist electorate. Formed in 1971 by the Reverend Ian Paisley the DUP brought together a complex coalition of religious and political fundamentalists dismayed at the supposedly liberal turn that the UUP had taken under the guidance of Terence O'Neill and his successors.

The prolonged process of fragmentation and realignment that unionism has undergone during the troubles has reflected the shifting interests and experiences of the various social strata that exist within the Protestant community. The two largest unionist parties operating in the province represent contrasting political constituencies (Hayes & McAllister 1995, p. 353). The UUP draws support from all sections of the unionist electorate. The electoral success of the party has nonetheless rested upon its perennial appeal among the unionist middle classes. The distinctive socioeconomic profile of UUP voters suggests that the party has been able to accommodate and articulate the particular interests of the more privileged members of the unionist community. The era of direct rule has – as we have noted many times already – proved bountiful for the unionist professional and business classes. The particular political strategy that elements within the UUP have come to advance would seem to acknowledge the specific instrumental interests that the unionist middle classes have acquired since the fall of Stormont (Coulter 1996, pp. 177–87). Influential figures within the party have, since the late 1970s, sought to promote a political enterprise often characterised as 'integrationist'. The complete integration of Northern

Ireland into the United Kingdom would mean that direct rule – albeit in a modified form – would become the stable mode of government for the province. Political arrangements that have conferred considerable affluence upon the unionist middle classes would, in other words, be made permanent. In promoting the cause of 'integration' important players within the UUP have, therefore, sought to further a political enterprise that advances the specific and indeed substantial material interests of the more privileged sections of the unionist community.

The apparent concern of the UUP to accommodate the unionist middle classes has been reflected not only in the strategies that the party has advocated but also in the tactics it has adopted. Senior figures within the UUP – and most notably former leader James Molyneaux – have tended to the view that the interests of the unionist community are served best not by radical political departures, but rather by patient diplomacy within the corridors of power in Westminster and Whitehall. The response of the party to the endless crises that have punctuated the modern period of conflict has often been characterised by circumspection (Coulter 1997, pp. 123–5). On those occasions when the political climate seems to have shifted unfavourably, the UUP has typically resisted demands for dramatic gestures and persisted with attempts to court favour among the powerful.

The relative temperance of the largest unionist party simply mirrors the political disposition of the unionist middle classes. The leaders of the UUP have invariably chosen to eschew those moves that threaten to alienate the British political establishment. The abiding conservatism of the party clearly acknowledges the economic interests that the unionist middle classes have acquired and cultivated since the demise of the legislative assembly at Stormont. Middle class unionists have simply refused to countenance any political enterprise that might lead them to be seen as biting the hand of a British state that has fed them rather generously under the auspices of direct rule.

The electoral constituency upon which the DUP draws is clearly distinct from that which the UUP attracts. Since its formation the DUP has relied largely upon the support of the more marginalised elements within the unionist community (Evans & Duffy 1997, p. 69; McGarry & O'Leary 1995a, pp. 202–5). Small farmers, rural labourers, semi-skilled and unskilled manual workers feature prominently among those who vote for the party (Hayes & McAllister 1995, p. 353). The discourse and strategy of the DUP have appealed to many unionists aggrieved by the direction of recent social and political change within the six counties. From the outset the party has adopted a distinctly populist stance with regard to social and economic affairs. Recognisable figures within the DUP have, for instance, voiced strong opposition to the erosion of public services that has taken place within Northern Ireland over the last 20 years. The seemingly radical posture that the party has at times assumed has clearly accorded with the concerns of many of those within the unionist community who have suffered most from the economic crises that have marked the era of the troubles (McAuley 1994, pp. 58–81).

The resilient electoral appeal of the DUP owes rather less, however, to its apparent social radicalism than to its renowned political fundamentalism (Finlayson 1997b, pp. 88–9). The party has consistently offered vehement opposition to any political development that offers even the slightest offence to the unionist cause. The profoundly militant position that the DUP has adopted has found favour principally among socially marginalised Protestants. The political upheavals of the last three decades have impacted with particular severity upon the subaltern strata within the unionist community. As a result, opposition to political compromise and reconciliation have often – although not always – become rooted most firmly among sections of the unionist working classes.

Although considerable, the electoral appeal of the two largest unionist parties among the Protestant working classes remains less than total. The principal challenge to the UUP and DUP for the allegiance of working class unionists comes from a couple of parties that have their origins in loyalist paramilitarism. The Ulster Democratic Party (UDP) emerged out of the Ulster Defence Association (UDA). The Progressive Unionist Party (PUP) has close links with the Ulster Volunteer Force (UVF). Neither party has managed as yet to secure a substantial electoral foothold. In the elections to the Northern Ireland Assembly convened in June 1998 the PUP and UDP attracted between them less than four per cent of voters' first preferences. Despite their relatively poor electoral performance the 'fringe' loyalist parties have become important players in the political life of the province. During the present decade the PUP and UDP have produced numerous articulate spokespersons who have made a telling contribution to the progress of the 'peace process'. The intimate association between both parties and organisations capable of sustaining campaigns of political violence has of course afforded them an influence and significance rather greater than their electoral performance would ordinarily allow.

The role that the UDP, and more particularly the PUP have assumed has been to articulate the disenchantment that exists within loyalist communities. Many working class Protestants have arrived at an understanding that the established unionist parties are indifferent to their plight. Disaffection with mainstream unionism has created the political space that has enabled the emergence of the 'fringe' loyalists. The PUP has been especially eager to promote consciousness of class issues among the beleaguered residents of loyalist housing estates (Finlayson 1997b, p. 90; McAuley 1997, pp. 164–5). Through grassroots agitation, the party has sought to encourage working class Protestants to become more aware of their material needs and cultural identities. The attempts of the PUP to promote community development within loyalist districts have hardly met with spectacular success. The efforts that the party has made to represent the interests of working class unionists have nonetheless thrown into even bolder relief the abiding indolence of the mainstream unionist parties.

The emergence of the loyalist parties may further reflect the dis-illusionment that many working class Protestants feel because of the manner in which the unionist establishment has responded to loyalists who have committed acts of political violence. Members of the two biggest unionist parties have frequently spoken and acted in a manner that could be considered inflammatory. Prominent figures within the DUP have in particular often conducted themselves in ways that have heightened political tensions within the province (Cochrane 1997). While unionist politicians have been prepared to encourage a political climate of conflict they have at the same time been quick to dissociate themselves from other unionists engaged in political violence. The apparent duplicity that characterises the behaviour of some within mainstream unionism has inevitably engendered alienation among the poorer relations of the unionist family. Many working class Protestants have grown resentful that unionist politicians who persistently talk the language of communal hatred can summon the temerity to condemn the actions of those who take them at their word.

The position that mainstream unionism has taken on the issue of prisoners has encouraged the development of the smaller loyalist parties. Unionist politicians who have readily employed the apocalyptic discourse of 'settling days' have simply abandoned to their fate those young working class men who have foolishly heeded their endless calls to arms. Moreover, the larger unionist parties have steadfastly insisted that even should a political settlement emerge within Northern Ireland, those loyalists – and of course republicans – who have been convicted of scheduled offences must complete their sentences. The stance that the fringe loyalists have adopted in relation to the prisoners issue is inevitably rather different. As one would expect of parties that have their origins within paramilitary organisations, the PUP and UDP have consistently championed the interests of loyalists imprisoned for political offences (McAuley 1997, pp. 166–7). Both parties have consistently argued that solving the Northern Ireland problem will necessarily entail the release of all political prisoners. The counsel of the fringe loyalists would seem to have become more persuasive over recent years. The political agreement that most of the province's parties endorsed on Friday 10 April 1998 allows for the staged release of those paramilitary prisoners who belong to organisations observing ceasefires.

While the loyalist parties' promotion of prisoners' rights has evidently alienated many unionists it has at the same time attracted others within the unionist community. Within working class Protestant neighbourhoods there are numerous people who have close personal associations with individuals incarcerated for scheduled offences. Although they may not themselves approve of political violence, friends and relations tend nonetheless to be disgruntled at the treatment that loyalist prisoners have received. The propensity of the larger unionist parties to discard and at times demonise those young working class men who have been jailed for scheduled offences has created resentment within the communities from which they come. This disaffection with the unionist mainstream has cleared sufficient political ground to enable parties like the PUP and UDP to take root.

The important role that the smaller loyalist parties have come to play in the public life of the province in the last few years may be attributed further to the nature of their political strategy. In the main, the troubles have been a working class war. The violence that the unionist working classes have endured has inevitably nurtured political intransigence. The experience of conflict has also, however, encouraged willingness to compromise. Personal experience of the enormous cost of war has provided many working class Protestants with a ready understanding of the value of peace. The evident desire among the unionist working classes for an end to the conflict has been channelled in part through the 'fringe' loyalist parties.

The credentials of the PUP and UDP as 'moderates' should not be overestimated of course. Both parties remain closely associated after all with paramilitary organisations that until recently terrorised nationalist communities, that continue to conduct countless punishment attacks and that may at some stage in the future resume their indiscriminate campaigns of ethno-political violence against Catholics. These associations have not, however, prevented the smaller loyalist parties becoming vociferous supporters of the 'peace process' that has made uncertain progress throughout the present decade. The various articulate figures that have emerged from within the ranks of the PUP and UDP have constantly stressed the need for political dialogue and compromise. The ostensibly reasonable tone of contemporary loyalist discourse has contrasted strongly with the frequently intransigent rhetoric of some of the more 'respectable' unionist parties. The United Kingdom Unionist Party (UKUP), which essentially expresses the outlook of middle class unionists who have been relatively unscathed by the troubles, has adopted a fundamentalist posture of opposition to those developments that promise to bring an end to the conflict in Northern Ireland. The smaller loyalist parties which articulate the views of working class unionists whose lives have been deeply touched and frequently ruined by the political violence of the last 30 years, in contrast, have consistently exhibited willingness to make those compromises and gestures that are required if a lasting peace is to prevail in the region.

WHY ETHNONATIONAL RATHER THAN CLASS POLITICS?

The political culture that obtains within Northern Ireland accommodates a range of social interests and identities. In particular the public life of the province acknowledges the complex interplay of those political personae that emerge out of socioeconomic status and ethnonational distinction respectively. The crucial interchange that conjoins class sentiment on the one hand and ethnic or national feeling on the other does not, however, represent a relationship between equals. On the contrary in fact. Within the incessant dialogue that takes place between class consciousness and ethnonational orientation, it is the latter that invariably speaks with the louder voice and that almost always has the last word.

The predominance of ethnic and national affiliation as sources of political identity within Northern Ireland is in some respects perplexing. Ethnonational status certainly has an enormous impact upon the experiences and opportunities of social actors living in the six counties. It is entirely fitting, therefore, that the political life of the province should bear the indelible inscription of ethnic and national sentiment. While ethnonational affiliation profoundly affects the lives of people in Northern Ireland, its significance remains nonetheless subordinate to that of social class. Socioeconomic status exercises rather greater influence than ethnic or national identity over the distribution of life chances within the six counties. Whether people are working class or middle class is simply more important than whether they are Protestants or Catholics when it comes to whether they will secure employment, the nature of the job they will get, the standard of education they will receive, the type of schools their children will attend, how long they will live (Kilbane 1995), whether or not they will be killed or injured as a result of politically motivated violence and so on.

Examination of the massive inequalities that blight contemporary Northern Irish society suggests that social class possesses rather greater material significance than ethnicity or nationality. In most respects the Protestant and Catholic working classes have substantially more in common with one another than with their more privileged ethnonational kin. Moreover, the survey data presented earlier would indicate that working class people who come from different ethnoreligious backgrounds often have a strong appreciation of their mutual material interests. The class consciousness seemingly prevalent in Northern Ireland has, however, found only limited expression within the realm of politics. Socioeconomic status represents a strictly secondary source of political identity in the six counties. While the political alliances forged within the province routinely transcend class barriers, only rarely do they supersede ethnoreligious distinctions. The inability of social class to displace ethnonational affiliation as the principal author of political belief and practice within Northern Ireland may be explained in at least two ways.

First, the pre-eminence of ethnoreligious sentiment within the political culture of the province may be attributed to the machinations of certain influential players. Those resilient ethnic divisions that characterise the region have often served handsomely the particular interests of the more elevated strata within Northern Irish society. Preoccupation with the 'imagined communities' of the ethnie or nation has typically ensured that the working classes within the six counties have failed to act upon their critical understanding of the interests and grievances that they share. The prevalence of ethnic sentiment within the province has, therefore, served to dissipate the forces of social radicalism. Those who have derived greatest benefit from the bourgeois social formation that exists in Northern Ireland have inevitably – and with some success – sought to encourage ethnoreligious feeling. The more privileged elements of the unionist community have proved particularly adept at fomenting ethnic division among the working classes.

For most of this century Ulster unionism was under the control of capitalists and large landowners. Those powerful interests that dominated unionist politics until the outbreak of the present troubles were evidently concerned to retain the allegiance of the Protestant working classes. Prominent unionist politicians routinely employed a populist discourse that centred upon Protestant supremacism. Furthermore, the leadership of the UUP was anxious to be seen to be taking on board the interests and grievances of working class loyalists. As World War I came to a close many Protestant workers became heavily involved in a spate of important industrial disputes. Those wealthy men at the helm of Ulster unionism quickly moved to stem the seemingly rising tide of proletarian radicalism. In 1918 the Ulster Unionist Labour Association (UULA) was formed (Collins 1994, pp. 145–6). Over the next half century the UULA provided a channel through which representatives of the unionist working classes were assigned to the lesser positions within successive Stormont administrations (Bew et al. 1979, pp. 48–9). The association would appear to have performed the role for which it was designed with considerable success. During the period of devolved government at Stormont there were a few occasions when the unionist working classes sought to pursue those substantial interests held in common with Catholic workers. In the main, however, working class Protestants proved content to exist as subordinates within the unionist class alliance. When the unionist working classes eventually did turn resolutely against the Stormont regime they did so for reasons that owed more to ethnoreligious prejudice than proletarian solidarity.

The concern of the leaders of unionism to maintain the support of working class Protestants has found a further, more contemporary, illustration. In 1995 various individuals who were broadly sympathetic to the British Labour Party and who belonged mainly to the UUP came together to form a political pressure group. The formal purpose behind the establishment of this Labour grouping was to offer a voice to those who did not share the conventional conservatism of mainstream unionism with regard to social and economic matters. The creation of the pressure group may also be interpreted as an attempt to fend off growing competition for the electoral allegiance of the unionist working classes. In recent years the smaller loyalist parties – and in particular the PUP – have begun to highlight and promote the particular and abundant concerns of working class Protestants. The formation of a Labour grouping broadly within the orbit of the UUP constitutes a measure designed to prevent support haemorrhaging to the 'fringe' loyalists. The existence of the coalition suggests that the interests of the Protestant lower orders are being advanced within the unionist mainstream. In reality, however, the creation of a Labour chapter represents merely another empty cynical gesture on the part of a political party that has consistently abused and ignored the unionist working classes.

Examination of pertinent developments within unionism over the course of the twentieth century reveals the ability of a social and political elite to regulate and reproduce ethnonational division. Those privileged men who have traditionally run unionism have consistently sought to encourage the Protestant lower orders to believe that their true interests lie with their ethnoreligious kin rather than their nationalist fellow workers. Their efforts have clearly borne fruit. The enmities that consume the province's working classes offer lucid testimony to the machiavellian skill of the most elevated strata within Northern Irish society.

Second, the substance of the political culture that prevails within Northern Ireland may be attributed to the particular discursive forms that arise out of ethnic feeling and class sentiment respectively. Those ideological formations that emerge from ethnic and national identities often have a merely tenuous relationship with historical and contemporary realities. Intellectuals, artists and others who strive to promote the interests of ethnonational communities are at times economical with the truth. Those stories that testify to the glory of the nation or ethnie frequently have little or no basis in fact. That the dominant narratives of the ethnonational tradition may be erroneous does not of course diminish their appeal. Social actors have consistently proved willing and able to cling to tales and beliefs long since debunked by the academe. The emotional power that defines ethnic and national identities derives largely from the rich figurative systems that they produce. The existence and value of the ethnonational community are vividly articulated through anthems, flags and emblems that stir the blood of those within and without the laager.

The distinctive symbolic systems that actualise the nation and ethnie are routinely able to reduce people to tears or move them to violence. Socioeconomic status rarely seems capable of generating a comparable emotional charge. In part this is because of the particular form of political discourse that arises out of social class. Those social actors who seek to advance specific class interests – or at least those of the lower orders – tend to possess a relatively faithful disposition to the 'truth'. Representatives of the working classes will typically be concerned to outline the 'simple facts' concerning the inequities and divisions that are the hallmark of capitalist society. Statistics that illustrate unemployment, low income and poor housing will often produce feelings of outrage. The narratives of working class existence that these data advance simply cannot, however, match the frequently altogether more fantastic tales that delineate the supposed experience of the nation or ethnie.

Socioeconomic status rarely enjoys an affective power comparable to that of ethnicity or nationalism largely because it fails to produce an equally potent symbolic programme. All social classes as a matter of course construct distinctive systems of cultural representation and distinction (Sennett & Cobb 1972; Steedman 1986). Working class communities constantly produce and reproduce a collection of stories, songs and images that recount their specific experience. The cultural texts that are generated by social classes tend, however, to exercise a lesser appeal than those that originate within the nation or ethnie. It is 'the Sash' or 'the Soldiers' Song' rather than 'the Internationale' that brings tears to the eyes of working class men as the end of licensing hours beckons.

The nation and ethnie have, therefore, come to represent the principal authors of political allegiance within the six counties due largely to their ability to produce particularly persuasive discursive forms. Ethnonational distinctions provide the essence of the province's political culture not because they are the most important source of inequality in Northern Ireland. Socioeconomic status has an altogether more substantial bearing upon the iniquitous distri-bution of life chances within the six counties. Ethnonational communities have managed to lay stronger claims than social classes to the political loyalties of people living in Northern Ireland not because they have greater material significance, but rather because they tell better stories.

CONCLUSION

Evidently class represents one of the most important sources of inequality and division within contemporary Northern Irish society. Socioeconomic status generates distinctions within the six counties that are both material and figurative. In Northern Ireland as elsewhere social class strongly influences the meanings that people ascribe to their lives. These critical understandings are clearly inscribed in the political culture of the province. The class consciousness that animates social actors living in the region tends, however, to be articulated and ultimately refracted through political ideologies that owe their existence primarily to ethnic and national feeling. The enduring ability of ethnonational identity to accommodate and thereby disarm those radical sentiments that arise out of socioeconomic location merely underscores its status as arguably the most successful ideological formation of our time.

3 The Status and Position of Women

Women have been all but invisible within the enormous literature that has emerged to document the recent turbulent history of Northern Ireland (Rooney 1997, p. 535; Sales 1997b, p. 141; Shannon 1989, p. 235). The myriad texts devoted to the social and political upheavals that have seized the province over the last 30 years have been in the main written about men, by men and for men. The propensity of commentators to overlook the particular manner in which women have experienced the conflict in Northern Ireland is exemplified in an important recent text that we have encountered already. McGarry and O'Leary's (1995a) *Explaining Northern Ireland* provides an invaluable guide to the multiple competing interpretations of the enmities that fester within the six counties. At various turns the authors offer significant insights into the origins and nature of the 'Northern Ireland problem'. The readings that are advanced between the covers of *Explaining Northern Ireland* fail, however, to acknowledge the salience of gender as a source of distinction and division in the province. There is little appreciation within the text that the traumatic events of the last 30 years might have affected women in ways that are palpably different from men. Like most male academics who have chosen to scrutinise the province, McGarry and O'Leary appear to be content simply to map the lives of Northern Irish men onto those of Northern Irish women.

The decidedly scant attention that mainstream analyses have afforded to the gender distinctions that exist within Northern Ireland represents an important shortcoming. The radical processes of social and political change at work within the six counties over recent generations have often impacted differently upon the lives of women from those of men. An adequate depiction of the nature of contemporary Northern Irish society demands, therefore, an understanding of the complex ways in which experience, practice and belief are *gendered* within the particular context of the province. In acknowledging the importance of the gender divisions that obtain within the six counties we should not, however, reduce Northern Irish women to membership of a

101

unitary, homogeneous aggregate. Women in the province have numerous experiences and interests in common. They are nonetheless divided along various lines – not least those defined by social class and ethnoreligious status. Consequently, the discussion that follows will seek to highlight both the community *and* division that exist among women living in contemporary Northern Irish society.

THE DOMESTIC SPHERE

The Domestic Division of Labour

The successful reproduction of even the most complex social orders requires that certain mundane tasks must be performed. Homes must be cleaned, meals cooked, clothes laundered and the needs of children catered for. In western societies the performance of these myriad tasks of domestic labour has been conventionally designated as the responsibility primarily of women. The organisation of households within Northern Ireland merely confirms the prevalence of this particular trend.

In 1990 the Equal Opportunities Commission initiated a programme of research designed to ascertain how women living in Northern Ireland experience work. The *Women's Working Lives Survey* (WWLS) sought the views of a representative sample of one thousand local women (Kremer & Montgomery 1993). The data generated by the survey suggest that there exists a marked division of labour within most Northern Irish households. In seven out of every ten families women are solely or overwhelmingly responsible for routine household chores (Montgomery 1993, pp. 27–8). In only one of every four dwellings was housework shared equally between partners. Men exhibit rather greater aversion to some forms of domestic labour than to others. While three quarters of men have cooked a meal at some stage only one quarter have managed to unravel the mysteries of the washing machine (ibid, p. 31).

The data furnished by the WWLS reveal further that within Northern Irish households women typically assume the role of 'nurturers' of the young. In three out of every five households women are charged with all or most of the responsibility for cleaning, feeding and minding the children (ibid, p. 34). A substantial minority of men would appear to have refused to perform even the most rudimentary tasks that attend paternity. One third of Northern Irish fathers have never accompanied their children to school while a quarter have never changed a nappy (ibid, p. 37).

The contemporary Northern Irish family emerges, therefore, as a profoundly patriarchal institution. Recent generations of women have inherited from their predecessors primary responsibility for those endless functions that are indispensable to the reproduction of the domestic unit (Leonard 1997, p. 115; Sales 1997a, p. 104). The rigid division of labour that has operated traditionally in the province has proved resilient in the face of radical forces of contemporary social and economic change. During the process of industrialisation men within western societies typically sought to exclude women from important swathes of the public realm of economic life. This practice inevitably found reflection in the particular context of the northeast of Ireland. The contribution of women to the development of the Northern Irish economy should not of course be diminished or overlooked. It remains true, nevertheless, that until recently at least, women played a less substantial role in the formal economic life of the province. The limited employment opportunities available compelled many women to remain at home performing unpaid acts of domestic labour while husbands assumed the role of 'breadwinner'. The assumption of responsibility for the welfare of other family members inevitably constrained opportunities to work outside the home. The rigid division of domestic labour that would appear a perennial feature of Northern Irish society could perhaps, therefore, be regarded as both symptom and cause of the exclusion of women from the formal economic life that defined significant passages of the development of the six counties.

Over the past three decades the employment opportunities available to Northern Irish women have expanded considerably. At present women outnumber men within the local labour force (EOCNI 1997). The assimilation of women into the formal economy has failed, however, to erode substantially the inequalities that have traditionally characterised Northern Irish households. Those women who have secured employment outside the home spend fewer hours performing domestic chores than those who have not. The majority of female employees have nonetheless retained principal responsibility for keeping house and minding the children. The persistence of traditional gender roles in the face of radically altered labour market experiences is confirmed by the data yielded by the Women's Working Lives Survey. The survey reveals that even those women who work full-time outside the home typically receive little assistance with housework. Three out of every five women living in households where both partners have secured full-time employment report that they perform all or most domestic chores alone (Montgomery 1993, p. 28).

The persistence of a distinctly unequal division of domestic labour is illuminated further when we turn to consider those households in which women are the prime income earners. In recent decades employment opportunities for men have declined sharply while those available to women have grown apace. As a consequence, there are many households in which wives have replaced husbands as the family 'breadwinner'. This significant inversion of traditional gender roles has had only a limited impact, however, upon the allocation of housework (Leonard 1997, p. 116). Almost half of the women who work outside the home and whose partners are unemployed state that they conduct all or most of the multiple tasks associated with running a household. In only one of every five households in which women represent the principal wage earner do men assume primary responsibility for domestic chores (Montgomery 1993, p. 28). The reluctance of jobless men to pull their weight around the house, moreover, becomes more pronounced with the passage of time. As the period of unemployment lengthens the domestic tasks that men are willing to do tend to diminish appreciably (ibid, p. 34).

Consideration of the relevant data would suggest, therefore, that traditional gender roles persist within many Northern Irish households (Montgomery & Davies 1991, pp. 77–8; Morgan 1992, pp. 145–6). Those myriad functions associated with the reproduction of the domestic unit would appear to remain widely regarded as 'women's work'. The unequal division of labour that operates within many Northern Irish homes diminishes the lives of women in various respects. Most women selflessly devote a considerable proportion of their adult lives to maintaining the existence of other family members. The various roles associated with running a household are substantial, monotonous and physically demanding. Consequently, the unpunctuated performance of seemingly endless domestic roles can often generate feelings of alienation among women. Indeed, the pathbreaking research that Ann Oakley (1976) conducted in England during the 1970s intimated that 'housewives' typically experience and describe domestic labour in terms strongly reminiscent of the accounts that men operating production lines use to describe their working lives.

The gendered allocation of roles within Northern Irish households ensures that women expend considerable energy performing tasks that are invariably menial and ultimately alienating. Although domestic labour makes enormous demands of both body and spirit women receive no payment for carrying out those manifold chores that are essential to the reproduction of the family unit. Housework fails to attract not only financial reward but also social prestige. The importance of domestic labour invariably remains unacknowledged. In Northern Ireland as elsewhere, housework is often dismissed as not quite being 'real work'. The unequal division of labour that operates within most households serves to ensure, therefore, that the talents and energies of many Northern Irish women are consumed largely by roles for which they receive no financial recompense and from which they derive frequently insufficient spiritual reward.

The patriarchal nature of the contemporary Northern Irish family impedes the participation of women in the labour market in various ways. The role of homemaker that society confers often burdens women with responsibilities which prevent them from pursuing a career. As a result, many women are deprived of the intellectual stimulation, emotional enrichment and financial autonomy that employment can sometimes provide. The unequal distribution of household duties has not only persuaded many women to remain outside the workforce but has also hindered that increasingly substantial body of women that has actually secured formal employment. The working lives of women often have to be organised to accommodate the demands of childrearing and various other domestic responsibilities. Accordingly women have often found it convenient to secure purely part-time employment. Many of the part-time jobs taken by Northern Irish women in recent times have – as we shall see later – been poorly paid and poorly protected.

The allocation of roles within the household tends to handicap further those women who have secured full-time employment. When women go out to work full-time the volume of domestic labour that they perform tends to diminish. The decrease in the number of hours devoted to domestic labour tends, however, to be rather smaller than the length of the typical working week. Hence, a woman who enters full-time employment can expect a substantial increase in the total amount of time required to satisfy the demands of the various roles that she performs – whether as unpaid labourer within the home or as paid worker outside it. The home and office make competing demands for the time of working women that generate frequently intolerable emotional and physical pressures. The onerous roles of wife and mother tend to frustrate the ambitions that many women harbour within the world of work. The demands of home may make it particularly difficult for women to progress within the frenetically competitive environment of professional and business life. Male professionals typically have comparatively few domestic responsibilities and can therefore devote their entire energies to the development of their careers.

Domestic Violence

The modern western nuclear family has been frequently represented in distinctly glowing terms. The domestic scene has been depicted often as a realm of comfort and love, a refuge of human warmth from the perils, vagaries and indifference of the wider social world. The notion that the family constitutes a discrete social institution that should be allowed to operate in splendid isolation enjoys wide currency. Social actors are invariably loth to violate the presumed sacred privacy of the home.

Social scientists – and especially those writing from a feminist perspective – have sought to contest the highly idealised understanding of the nuclear family frequently disseminated. Sociologists have endeavoured to establish that families are patriarchal institutions. The family may well offer an environment that enables the articulation of human affection and meaning. It should also be acknowledged, however, as a site of power and oppression. The exercise of male power within the domestic sphere produces manifold detrimental repercussions for women.

The patriarchal nature of the modern family is ruthlessly exposed when we turn to examine the practice of domestic violence. The exercise of male authority within the home finds its most brutal expression in the guise of physical assault. The representations of the nuclear family prevalent throughout western societies ensured that – until recently perhaps – the violence that women endured behind closed doors was essentially overlooked. The construction of the home as sanctum prevented an understanding that the practice of domestic violence was in fact widespread. Those individuals aware of the suffering of particular women typically proved reluctant to intervene in what were regarded as the private affairs of others. Reluctance to acknowledge and address the social problem of domestic violence has not of course disappeared. There are signs nonetheless that tolerance of the violence that women endure at the hands of their partners has begun to dissolve.

The advance of social intolerance of domestic violence has both reflected and facilitated the emergence of a substantial fund of research on the issue. The data garnered in a range of countries suggest that violence against women represents a universal problem of rather greater magnitude than acknowledged hitherto (O'Connor 1995). Each year in the United States 4,000 women are battered to death by their male partners. A quarter of the women who responded to a survey conducted in Great Britain stated that they had been assaulted by a current or former lover. Sweden constitutes a state that invariably scores impressively on the various indices of the progressive, liberal society. Yet a Swedish woman dies at the hands of her male partner on average every ten days (McWilliams & McKiernan 1993, p. 15). During recent years concerns about domestic violence have gathered pace within the Republic of Ireland (Meade 1997, p. 347; Smyth 1995, pp. 206–7). The prevalence of violence against southern Irish women was suggested by the findings of pilot survey carried out in St James' Hospital during 1993 (O'Connor 1995). In the twelve months that the study lasted the Dublin hospital admitted 119 women – on average one every third day – with injuries inflicted by their partners.

The contagion of domestic violence that has been identified by a host of international surveys also of course infects contemporary Northern Irish society. Over the past three decades the people of the six counties have had to endure sustained political unrest. The preoccupation of academics and policy makers with the troubles has tended to distract attention from other important forms of violence that are rather less public and visible. As a result there has been a dearth of research devoted to the violence that women suffer in the privacy of their own homes. A pathbreaking survey published by two sociologists in 1993, however, began to address this significant lacuna in our understanding of the nature of contemporary society in Northern Ireland.

In *Bringing it out in the Open* Monica McWilliams and Joan McKiernan seek to challenge the dominant misconceptions that surround the issue of domestic violence. According to McWilliams and McKiernan (1993, pp. vii, 123), the genuine scale of the violence that women face behind closed doors remains unacknowledged. Frequently people in Northern Ireland – as elsewhere – have been content to cling to the comforting notion that assaults perpetrated against women represent merely a 'rare occurrence' (ibid, p. 31). In reality, however, domestic violence is not aberrant but rather systematic. Violence against women, McWilliams and McKiernan insist, constitutes a problem that is endemic within Northern Irish society and must be acknowledged accordingly. The suffering that women endure at the hands of their male partners must be 'brought out in the open'.

McWilliams and McKiernan (ibid, p. 5) endeavour to illustrate the scale of domestic violence in Northern Ireland through reference to official statistics. The data upon which the authors draw pertain to incidents reported during a twelve month period that spanned 1991 and 1992. It should be acknowledged that the information that McWilliams and McKiernan collated acknowledges only those cases of assault that were registered with official agencies. Most incidents of domestic violence are never reported by victims or registered by the relevant limbs of the state. Hence, official statistics tend to understate considerably the level of violence directed towards women. The data presented by McWilliams and McKiernan make harrowing reading nonetheless. Over the twelve month period scrutinised by the authors' domestic violence resulted in the deaths of ten women; 2,500 personal protection orders and 2,300 exclusion orders being issued; 416 women being made homeless and 2,800 disputes being recorded by the Royal Ulster Constabulary (RUC).

Reference to official statistics enables McWilliams and McKiernan to offer an approximation of the general incidence of domestic violence in Northern Ireland. The authors subsequently shift focus in order to examine the particular experiences of individual women who have been physically abused by their male partners. The principal resources upon which *Bringing it out in the Open* draws is a series of interviews with 56 women who have been involved in abusive relationships. The biographies that emerge from these interviews shed important light upon the manner in which domestic violence is experienced, regarded and administered in the specific context of Northern Ireland.

The women interviewed by McWilliams and McKiernan typically reported that the abuse to which they had been subjected had begun at an early stage of the relationship. More than half of the interviewees reported that they had been beaten within the first year of having become involved with their partner (ibid, p. 34). The violence directed towards the women had frequently been sustained over a considerable period of time. Some male partners remained violent even during the course of pregnancy. Nineteen women reported that they had been assaulted while carrying a child. The abuse meted out by men often resulted in severe physical injury. Thirty women had been forced to seek medical attention. The injuries suffered by 22 members of the sample had been sufficiently grave to warrant hospital treatment (ibid; McKiernan & McWilliams 1997, p. 331).

The women who spoke to McWilliams and McKiernan had been the victims of repeated, vicious physical and psychological abuse. Yet they had been decidedly reluctant to leave their violent partners. The reluctance of women to terminate an abusive relationship articulates a range of concerns (McWilliams & McKiernan 1993, pp. 45–7, 122). Women are often fearful of the shame and embarrassment that can often attend the public disintegration of a relationship – particularly a marriage – in a conservative society like Northern Ireland (ibid, p. 53). The prospect that an enraged husband might visit even greater violence upon herself and her children should she leave often persuades a woman to remain within a violent relationship. Moreover, women are often anxious that those significant others whose support is essential if they are to leave an abusive partner may not understand or support their actions. The experience of the women interviewed by McWilliams and McKiernan suggests such fears are scarcely without foundation.

Almost all of the women featured in *Bringing it out in the Open* had eventually taken the reluctant decision to leave their violent husbands. Only six remained in an abusive relationship (ibid, p. 33). Those women who had severed ties with their partners encountered numerous difficulties. In general women who had left an abusive husband had received complete support from their immediate family. This was not always the case however. Some women reported that relatives were unwilling to believe that a man who had been accepted as one of their own could be capable of heinous acts behind closed doors. Occasionally parents proved unprepared to support their daughter's ambition to terminate a relationship on the grounds that it would bring shame on the family.

While immediate families generally proved supportive those women who had left a violent husband derived little assistance from various other important institutions and agencies. The churches provide an important point of reference for many people in Northern Ireland. The salience of religious affiliation served to ensure almost half – 23 out of 50 – of the women who had taken the difficult decision to end an abusive relationship had turned to the church for support and guidance (ibid, pp. 50–1). Most of the women who had sought clerical advice, however, felt that it had been of little value. Only seven of the interviewees considered that the churches had actually helped to guide them through an especially traumatic period of their lives (McKiernan & McWilliams 1997, pp. 333–4). The advice that had been typically dispensed by clerical figures had been that victims of domestic violence should go back to their partners. Representatives of the Roman Catholic church which frowns with particular severity upon divorce were especially prone to encourage women to return to abusive relationships. The approach which they adopted frequently ensured that the churches were of rather greater assistance to the perpetrators than the victims of domestic violence. Abusive men often proved quick to enlist the support of the clergy to persuade estranged wives to return home.

The institutions of state were frequently of little more assistance to abused women than those of the church. The political tensions that fester within Northern Ireland have ensured that many citizens are deeply hostile towards the repressive apparatus of the state. The disaffection that defines the relationship between many citizens and the security forces was inevitably reflected in the outlook and conduct of those women whose biographies appear in *Bringing it out in the Open*. Some of the individuals interviewed by McWilliams and McKiernan (ibid, pp. 55–7) had been unwilling to report the assaults that they had suffered to the RUC. These women sought instead to eradicate the violence that blighted their lives through alternative channels. On a few occasions the services of local paramilitary organisations were engaged. While many women were reluctant to involve the police, most did so at some stage. The 35 women who contacted the RUC were invariably disillusioned with the response of the agency. Frequently the police simply refused to respond to the pleas of abused women for assistance. When the RUC did actually consent to attend a scene of reported domestic violence they tended not to take meaningful action. Incidents often went unregistered and charges against violent husbands were rarely pressed.

The conduct of the police proved emblematic of a broader inability or unwillingness on the part of state institutions to deal adequately with the social problem of domestic violence. Those women who had been abused by their partners came into contact with a range of official agencies on numerous occasions. The various statutory bodies that oversee crucial areas of social provision had rarely, however, established structures that would have enabled them to respond adequately to the plight and needs of battered women (ibid, pp. 65–79, 103). That official agencies have failed to create procedures that would enable them to deal with the practice of domestic violence is of course highly significant. It acts to underscore the conviction that the state affords little importance to the systematic violence to which many Northern Irish women are subjected within their own homes.

THE REGULATION OF FERTILITY

Since the 1960s there have been important advances in methods of contraception. Consequently recent generations of women have been able to regulate their own fertility with rather greater efficiency than their predecessors. The opportunity to decide the number and timing of the children to which they give birth has allowed many younger women both to raise families and forge careers. Northern Irish women are able to exercise considerably less control over their fertility than their counterparts in most other western societies. The established means of birth control are in principle as freely available within the six counties as the other regions of the United Kingdom. In practice though younger people often find it difficult to obtain adequate means of contraception (Sales 1997a, pp. 129–30). The current of moral conservatism that courses through Northern Ireland ensures that many forms of sexual activity – especially those that occur outside wedlock and between partners of the same sex – are strongly censured. Doctors have at times refused to prescribe contraceptives for younger women. Moreover, the moral sanctions that attend sexual practice have often ensured that younger people are too bashful to purchase condoms from outlets where they are openly on sale.

The legislation that defines the status of abortion within Northern Ireland differs radically from that operating throughout the remainder of the United Kingdom. The provisions of the 1967 Abortion Act ensured that henceforth women living in Great Britain could legally secure a termination. Inevitably the conservative Unionist administration at Stormont stoutly refused to extend the 1967 Act to cover the six counties. As a result the standing of abortion within the province remains determined by legislation that dates back to the middle of the last century. The terms of the 1861 Offences Against the Person Act – which have been amended slightly by subsequent legal rulings – stipulate that it is illegal for an abortion to be carried out in Northern Ireland in all but a few very particular circumstances. A pregnancy can be terminated legally if the mother has been raped or if her life is considered to be in danger. The final say on whether such an abortion is conducted rests, however, not with the woman concerned but rather with her doctor. One estimate suggests that there are between 250 and 500 legal abortions performed within Northern Irish hospitals every year. The powerful stigma that attaches to the issue of abortion ensures, however, that these terminations are not officially registered as such (Sales 1997a, p. 131).

While it may be illegal for women to have abortions in Northern Ireland, Northern Irish women do of course have abortions. A constant flow of women travel from the province to the other regions of the United Kingdom to terminate unwanted pregnancies (Davanna 1999). According to the Northern Ireland Abortion Law Reform Association (NIALRA 1992), ten Northern Irish women secure abortions in British clinics every day. The same organisation has estimated that around 15 per cent of women living in the six counties will at some stage of their lives have a termination. The social and political climate that prevails within Northern Ireland would suggest that the province will continue to 'export' the problem of abortion for some time to come. The citizens of the six counties would seem to frown upon abortion with greater severity than the peoples of most other western European states. The essential conservatism of the general populace appears to be shared by the leading players within the political life of Northern Ireland. None of the mainstream political parties based in the six counties has proved willing to offer consistent support to the principle of a woman's right to choose.

The Labour administration that swept to power on an apparent wave of popular fervour in the early summer of 1997 has a formal commitment to extend the 1967 Abortion Act to Northern Ireland. It is highly likely, however, that this will become one of the many election pledges that the British Labour Party breaks while in office (Sales 1997a, p. 134). Abortion represents one of the few issues capable of generating common cause among the diverse ethno-political factions that compete within Northern Ireland (Sales 1997b, p. 141). Any attempt on the part of a direct rule adminis-tration to make it legal for terminations to be carried out within the six counties would be greeted with fierce resistance. The prospect of widespread opposition will probably prove sufficient to dissuade Westminster from seeking to liberalise the province's currently antiquated abortion laws. The main objective of the present Labour administration in relation to the region is – like its predecessors – to create enough agreement among the various existing strands of opinion to enable political progress. The Secretary of State for Northern Ireland is rather unlikely to persist with a policy such as the extension of the 1967 Abortion Act, which is deemed to be of essentially secondary importance and which may inflame local political sensitivities in a manner which threatens yet further the prospect of a durable settlement. The rights of women living in the province will in all probability be sacrificed in the pursuit of the presumed greater good of a resolution to the Northern Ireland problem.

THE PUBLIC SPHERE: WORK

Female Participation in the Workforce

The course of development that the northeast of Ireland has followed over the past couple of hundred years has been defined largely by the process of industrialisation. At the turn of the century the city of Belfast and its environs represented one of the epicentres of the industrial world. The region has since of course experienced prolonged and traumatic industrial decline. The various manufacturing concerns that once thrived within Northern Ireland were frequently dominated by male workers. The contribution of women to the former industrial life of the province should not, however, be understated. Women played an especially important role in the production of linen (Sales 1997a, p. 33). In the period between the two world wars there were two women employed in the linen mills for every man working in the shipyards (Morrissey 1991, p. 103). The ability of women to perform with equal competence manufacturing tasks hitherto socially defined as 'masculine' was confirmed during World War II. With many men enrolled in the armed forces women came to excel at occupations – traindriving, riveting, the production of munitions and so forth – that had previously been the preserve of men. With the advent of peace, however, women were gradually displaced from many industrial concerns.

During the couple of decades that followed the carnage of World War I the number of occupational opportunities available to women in Northern Ireland dwindled. The rapid decline of the indigenous linen industry deprived a substantial body of women of employment. The arrival of multinational corporations engaged in the production of synthetic fibres replaced some of the jobs that had been lost within the once vibrant linen sector. The branch plants that opened during the 1960s tended primarily, however, to employ men.

The gradual exclusion of women from the formal economic life of Northern Ireland that occurred in the decades immediately after World War II has been arrested during the period of the troubles. Over the past quarter of a century women in the province have become increasingly likely to enter the labour force (EOCNI 1997). The census of population revealed that in 1971 43 per cent of women were 'economically active' – in other words, employed or seeking employment. During the 1970s and 1980s the number of women entering the world of work grew steadily. At the time of the 1991 census 56 per cent of women identified themselves as economically active. The growing tendency to participate in the labour force has been particularly pronounced among married women. In 1971 only one in three women who were married were employed or seeking employment outside the home. Two decades later more than half of married women had become economically active.

The burgeoning economic activity of women has gradually transformed the gender composition of the Northern Irish labour force. Data collated by the Equal Opportunities Commission for Northern Ireland (EOCNI 1997) reveal that in 1971 only 39 per cent of employees in the province were women. Over the quarter of a century since, the number of women who have entered the workforce has grown consistently. In 1996 there were more female than male employees. The numerical supremacy of women within the labour force is likely, moreover, to become more pronounced with the passage of time. The EOCNI present forecasts which predict that by 2003 women will have come to constitute 53 per cent of employees.

The prominence of women within the workforce may be attributed largely to the transformation of the Northern Irish economy that has occurred during recent times. Since the 1950s services have replaced manufacturing as the most important source of employment in the six counties. The expansion of the tertiary sector has involved the creation of jobs that require individuals to cater for the needs of others. The forms of employment generated within the service sector have, in other words, required skills and attributes that are often defined socially as 'feminine' (Sales 1997b, p. 149). As a consequence the expansion of service occupations that has occurred over the last few generations has been of particular benefit to women. The especial importance of the tertiary sector for women finds reflection in the data that Liam O'Dowd (1995, p. 151) presents. In 1993 85 per cent of female employees were engaged in the provision of services. In the same year the tertiary sector provided employment to a rather smaller proportion – 61 per cent to be precise – of the male workforce.

The growing economic activity of Northern Irish women may be attributed more specifically to the expansion of *public* services. The imposition of direct rule in the spring of 1972 heralded the enlargement of the public sector. The expansion of public employment within the six counties has been particularly beneficial for women (Morrissey 1991, p. 106; O'Dowd 1995, p. 153). 83,000 Northern Irish women were employed by the state in 1974. Over the next 20 years the number of female public employees in the province rose to 114,000. In contrast, during the same period the employment opportunities available to men within the public sector actually fell. Between 1974 and 1994 the number of men employed by the state declined from 90,000 to 79,000.

The Problems of Female Labour

It might be reasonable perhaps to assume that greater participation in the labour market has enhanced the position of women within Northern Ireland. The subordination of women within bourgeois society has often been attributed to their exclusion from the public domain. Restriction to the domestic scene has denied many women access to those public roles that can confer social status and financial autonomy. It might be anticipated, therefore, that growing economic activity has augmented the lives of women in the province.

Scrutiny of pertinent trends within contemporary Northern Irish society suggests a rather more complex and contradictory reality. The shifting composition of the labour force that has happened over the last three decades has conferred considerable benefit upon many women. Opportunities have become available to younger women in the province that would have been beyond the reach of their predecessors. The benefits that have flowed from the feminisation of the labour force have, however, been far from universal. Acquisition of employment has frequently served merely to compound the subordination that women endure. The growing participation of women in the labour market should be acknowledged, therefore, as profoundly problematic. The principal problems associated with the manner in which Northern Irish women work may be characterised as follows.

Horizontal Segregation

Those women who have secured employment in recent times have not of course been distributed evenly throughout the workforce. On the contrary, women tend to be concentrated heavily within a narrow range of economic activities. Various commentators (EOCNI 1997; Morrissey 1991, p. 105; Sales 1997b, p. 147) have discerned that most female employees are clustered within the following occupational categories: professional and related in education, welfare and health; clerical and related; catering, cleaning, hairdressing and other professional services. Hence, there exist within Northern Ireland certain forms of employment that have been designated principally the domain of women (Carey 1997, p. 99). The concentration of women within a narrow band of economic activity is usually characterised as 'horizontal segregation'. The horizontal segregation of the Northern Irish labour market has proved disadvantageous for women in at least two respects.

First, we need to consider the particular roles that women typically perform within the formal economic life of the province. Women who enter the labour force are frequently required to provide services to others and, more specifically, to care for the young. The tasks for which female employees are responsible are, in other words, often remarkably similar to those which they are expected to complete within the home. Increased participation in the workforce would not, therefore, appear to have altered radically the functions which women serve within Northern Irish society. On the contrary, growing economic activity would seem merely to have confirmed the incarceration of many women in ascribed roles that preclude their acknowledgement as equals.

Second, the horizontal segregation that defines the Northern Irish labour market has important financial consequences for women. Those occupations that are dominated by women tend to be poorly regarded and rewarded. Nurses, shop assistants, secretaries, cleaners and so on receive incomes that could scarcely be regarded as lavish. The poor rates of pay invariably associated with forms of employment classified as essentially 'female' has ensured that growing economic activity has often not afforded women financial autonomy. Rather, increased participation in the workforce would appear frequently to have merely confirmed the economic subordination of women.

Vertical Segregation

While many women have entered the labour market over the past three decades, comparatively few have managed to attain positions of status or power. Women tend to congregate on the lower rungs of those career ladders that calibrate all occupational categories. The 'vertical segregation' of female employees may be illustrated through reference to trends within the Northern Ireland Civil Service (NICS). At present within the non-industrial civil service women slightly outnumber men (Department of Finance & Personnel 1994). Female civil servants are, however, heavily concentrated among the junior ranks. Seven out of every ten civil servants located within the lowest occupational grade are women. As we ascend the occupational hierarchy that operates within the NICS the proportion of employees who are female begins to tumble. Of the 268 individuals who fall within the most senior grade of the NICS only 16 are women. The proportion of senior positions occupied by women is only around one eighth of what we would expect were female employees distributed evenly throughout the ranks of the civil service.

The vertical segregation at work within the local labour market operates even within those occupations that are dominated by women. Consider, for instance, patterns of career advancement within the primary sector of the educational system. Approximately three quarters of Northern Irish primary school teachers are women. Comparatively few women are to be found, however, among the ranks of the senior staff of the province's primary schools. The limits that exist to the career advancement of female primary school teachers are suggested by data presented by the public body responsible for the provision of educational services within the capital of the region. In 1989 there were 96 principals in charge of primary schools under the jurisdiction of the Belfast Education and Library Board (BELB). Only 37 were women (Morgan & Lynch 1995, p. 553).

The processes of gender segregation that shape the Northern Irish economy have ensured that women often fail to attain positions of prominence and influence. The media play an important role in the public life of the province. Senior figures within the media industries can at times exercise real influence over public discourse, popular opinion, the conduct of government even. The power that the media possess, however, rests only rarely with women. A recent report published jointly by the Northern Ireland Women's Rights Movement (NIWRM) and the Downtown Women's Centre (DWC) suggests there are clear limits to the advancement of female journalists and broadcasters. The information presented in *Who's Making the News?* reveals the extent of the vertical segregation that exists within the three newspapers published daily in Belfast (NIWRM & DWC 1996, pp. 12–19). Women make up 40 per cent of the workforce of the Belfast dailies. Female employees tend, however, to be concentrated heavily within the least lucrative and prestigious occupational categories (Breen 1999). Four out of every five administrators are women. As we move up the occupational hierarchies that obtain within the regional daily newspapers the representation of women dwindles noticeably. Less than a quarter of editorial positions within the Belfast dailies are filled by women. The exclusion of women from positions of authority within the print media becomes especially apparent when we examine senior management posts. A mere 13 per cent of the senior managers of the three daily newspapers that enjoy widest circulation throughout the six counties are women. The gendered iniquities that exist within the print media are equally apparent within the broadcast media. The British Broadcasting Corporation (BBC) plays a pervasive role in the everyday lives of the people of Northern Ireland. Research undertaken by a former employee suggests that women seeking to progress within the BBC have frequently encountered a 'glass ceiling'. Comparatively few women have managed to attain positions of influence within the BBC. Indeed, according to Liz Fawcett (1996, p. 22), only one of the five most senior figures operating out of Corporation House in Belfast happens to be a woman.

The notable dearth of women holding senior posts within the Northern Irish media should be acknowledged as expressive of a wider exclusion from positions of influence. During 1993 a local management consultancy agency completed a survey of those considered to be the most important players in the public, professional and business life of Northern Ireland. The relevant agency compiled a list of 1,000 bureaucrats, professionals and entrepreneurs. Of the 1,000 'movers and shakers' identified in the course of the survey only 27 turned out to be women (Macauley 1994). This statistic offers striking confirmation of the exclusion of women from the multiple sites of power that exist within contemporary Northern Irish society.

Part-time Employment

Perhaps the most recurrent euphemism that has been employed to characterise the transformation of global capitalism over the past quarter of a century has been that of 'flexibility'. The advent of the supposedly 'flexible' economy has heralded the fragmentation of biographies of work. In the decades that immediately followed World War II employees could often reasonably assume to have secured a 'job for life'. The experience of those generations that have entered the labour market since the oil price hikes of the early 1970s has been altogether different. Employment has become increasingly insecure and impermanent. Individuals are frequently required to reconstruct their lives periodically from the *bric a brac* of an increasingly hostile and fragmented labour market. Many people will enter a wide range of occupations at different stages of their careers. Increasingly the forms of employment available within western societies are merely part-time.

The processes that have transformed the global economy have inevitably found expression within the particular context of the six counties. The Northern Irish labour market has become increasingly 'flexible'. In particular there has been a dramatic rise in the number of part-time jobs that are available within the province. At the outset of the current troubles approximately one in ten employees worked on a part-time basis. By the early 1990s this proportion had grown to one in four. The majority of part-time posts that have been created during the period of the present political unrest have been filled mainly by women (Miller et al. 1996, p. 19). It has been calculated that 40 per cent of women who work are employed part-time. In contrast, only 12 per cent of male employees are engaged in part-time work (O'Dowd 1995, p. 152).

The particular appeal of part-time employment to women may be attributed largely to the gendered division of labour that characterises many Northern Irish households. Responsibility for essential domestic tasks and in particular for minding children falls – as we witnessed earlier – invariably upon the shoulders of women. In the absence of adequate public childcare provision many women are simply unable to enter full-time employment (Miller et al. 1996, p. 20). Working part-time represents a viable alternative. A comparatively short working day can often enable women to supplement household income while retaining sufficient time to cater for the needs of children. This particular attribute of part-time employment may serve to explain its especial popularity among women who are married. It has been estimated that two out of every three married women who work outside the home have part-time jobs (Courtney 1995, p. 56; O'Dowd 1995, p. 152).

The 'flexibilisation' of the Northern Irish economy has provided opportunities for women – and in particular married women – to enter the workforce in ever greater numbers. The experiences of these women have, however, often been rather less than rewarding. The growing body of individuals in the province who work part-time frequently receive risible rates of pay and typically have few career prospects (Carey 1997, p. 99; Sales 1997a, p. 104; 1997b, p. 150). Part-time workers often do not enjoy the protection of the labour movement. Moreover, there are relatively few statutory rights arising out of part-time employment. Individuals who work less than 16 hours a week are especially vulnerable (Montgomery & Davies 1991, p. 75). These workers are not entitled to compensation for redundancy, maternity leave or minimum periods of notice. The legal protections that actually do cover part-time employment often prove to be of little value. Frequently, part-time workers are reluctant to exercise the few rights that they possess for fear that they might find themselves out of a job (Sales 1997a, p. 104).

Low Pay

The position that women have come to occupy within the Northern Irish labour force has often been one of acute disadvantage. Women frequently work part-time, are typically to be found within the least prestigious and lucrative occupational categories and tend to congregate on the lower rungs of the career ladder. It should hardly come as a surprise, therefore, that women's earnings lag considerably behind those of men. Rosemary Sales (1997a, p. 152) presents information concerning the rates of pay – excluding overtime – received by full-time employees during 1994. In that year women's earnings were only 85 per cent of men's.

The disparity between the incomes of the sexes becomes more pronounced when we include overtime in our calculations. The resilient construction of men as the principal 'breadwinner' frequently ensures that male employees are often more likely to be offered overtime. That men can often rely on their partners to perform essential domestic tasks – most importantly minding the children – means that they are often more likely to be in a position to accept such offers. Consequently, overtime provides a rather more substantial proportion of the incomes of men than those of women. In 1996 overtime added eight per cent to men's earnings but only two per cent to women's (EOCNI 1997). When overtime is taken into consideration the earnings of women fall even further behind those of men. The data provided by the EOCNI reveal that in 1996 women's total incomes were on average only 76 per cent of men's.

The differences in the earning power of women and men ensure that the former tend to be over-represented within low income groups. The official definition of low pay is that which falls below two thirds of median male earnings. The *New Earnings Survey* would suggest that women are twice as likely as men to fall within the category of the low paid (EOCNI 1997). In 1996 36 per cent of women working full-time received incomes of less than two thirds of the median male. In contrast, the figure for men was 17 per cent.

The processes of segregation that define the Northern Irish labour market have ensured that the sexes often play different roles in the economic life of the province. Women earn less than men because they perform tasks that are considered to be less valuable. The designation of female labour as being of lesser value should not of course be considered an equitable estimation of the inherent worth of the economic roles that women perform. Rather, the denigration of women's work should be acknowledged as indicative of a broader process of subordination that reveals the existence and operation of a patriarchal society. Women receive lower wages not only when they perform roles that are different from those of men but also when they undertake tasks that are essentially the same. Within many fields and places of work frequently arbitrary distinctions are drawn between seemingly similar forms of labour. The existence of demarcations invariably ensures that those tasks performed overwhelmingly by men are afforded greater reward. These practices have come under challenge during recent years (Sales 1997a, p. 104). In 1985 a group of five women employed as domestic assistants by a Belfast hospital initiated proceedings to establish that their work should be acknowledged as of equal value to that of male porters and groundsmen who received higher rates of pay. The strategy adopted by the women was supported both by their trade union and by the men with whom they had drawn comparison. Legal proceedings spanning a decade eventually resulted in a verdict in favour of the domestic assistants.

The Informal Economy

Many tasks that are performed for financial reward remain undetected by the agencies of the state. These undisclosed activities are conducted within the realm of the 'hidden' or 'informal' economy. Women would seem to play an important role in the informal economy of Northern Ireland. Informal economic exchange, however, would appear to have conferred upon women no more benefit than participation in the formal economic life of the province.

The research of Madeleine Leonard (1994; 1995) sheds light upon the informal economic networks that exist within a nationalist estate situated in west Belfast. Many of the men living on the estate were out of work. Had the wives of unemployed men secured employment through the conventional channels the welfare benefits to which the household was entitled would have been reduced. As a result married women often had little incentive to enter the realm of the formal economy. Many of the female residents of the estate preferred instead to supplement the family income through forms of economic activity that could be concealed from the surveillance of state agencies. Operating within the informal economy typically involved making clothes, cutting hair and acting as an agent for mail order catalogues. The recipients of these goods and services were usually friends, relatives and neighbours.

Women living on the estate would also often offer their labour power informally to employers who were actually operating within the formal economy. This particular practice is usually identified within local parlance as 'doing the double'. In the course of her research Madeleine Leonard encountered 24 women engaged in informal wage labour. Two thirds were employed by various private companies that had secured contracts to clean offices located in the centre of Belfast. The women who worked as cleaners often had to endure poor conditions and occasionally even had to supply their own cleaning materials. The rate of pay which the cleaners received was often low and some earned as little as £1 an hour. The research undertaken by Madeleine Leonard would suggest, therefore, that women working within the informal economy are particularly vulnerable to exploitation. Financial necessity demands, however, that many working class women continue to offer their labour power informally to unscrupulous employers.

The Diversity of Women's Experience of Work

The considerable body of evidence presented above would seem to bear out the contention that the position that women have held within the Northern Irish labour market has often been subaltern. The experiences of those women who have entered the labour market over recent generations have, however, been far from homogeneous. The distinctions that exist between female employees have invariably borne the inscription of two important sources of social identity: ethnicity and class.

The controversies that have embroiled the people of Northern Ireland over the last three decades have often centred on issues of social justice. A particular concern has been the distribution of economic 'life chances' within the six counties. Commentators have regularly expressed anxiety that since the beginning of the troubles Catholic men have remained twice as likely as their Protestant counterparts to be out of work. The preoccupation with unemployment differentials among men has been understandable. It has unfortunately, however, obscured the existence of comparable trends among women. Unemployment would seem to represent an especial problem for Catholic women. At the time of the 1991 census women from nationalist backgrounds were almost twice as likely as their unionist counterparts to be out of work (Sales 1997a, p. 139). The problems faced by Catholic women seeking employment would appear to be a resilient feature of life in the six counties. The ratio between the unemployment rates of Catholic and Protestant women respectively has remained essentially unchanged since the census of 1971 (ibid).

Women from the two communities differ further with regard to the types of employment which they typically enter. Analysis of recent census reports indicates that Catholic and Protestant women often feature within different occupational categories (Sales 1997a, pp. 146–7). Women from nationalist backgrounds are especially likely to be involved in 'caring labour'. Catholic women tend to be heavily represented within those occupations which provide health and education. In contrast, women from unionist backgrounds are more likely to be engaged in the provision of financial services. The banks and insurance houses offer employment to a substantial number of Protestant women.

That women from different ethnoreligious backgrounds frequently secure different forms of employment has considerable significance. Those occupations that draw disproportionately upon the labour of women from nationalist communities are often especially poorly regarded, protected and rewarded. Consequently, the earnings of Catholic women tend to fall short of those received by their Protestant counterparts. Women from nationalist backgrounds are particularly likely to be represented among the poorly paid. A survey conducted during 1990 by the EOCNI established that 61 per cent of Catholic women earned less than £100 per week (Sales 1997a, p. 152). The proportion of women from the unionist community in receipt of comparably meagre wages was rather smaller – 53 per cent – in spite of the fact that Protestant women are more likely to work part-time.

Ethnoreligious origins have, therefore, had an important influence upon the manner in which Northern Irish women have entered the realm of formal economic activity. The experiences of working women have also been differentiated along lines of social class. Entering the labour force has often merely compounded the exploitation endured by women from working class backgrounds. Working class women have frequently had to accept jobs that offer poor wages and few statutory rights. Moreover, financial circumstances have regularly compelled the female residents of the province's most deprived communities to inhabit the particularly perilous environment of the informal economy. The working lives of women drawn from the more affluent strata of Northern Irish society, in contrast, would appear to have often proved rather more rewarding. Clearly there are fewer female occupants of the higher echelons of professional and business life in the province than social justice would require. Nonetheless we should not overlook the fact that over the last few decades many women have secured influential occupations. Women who have progressed within the professions have of course encountered those multiple obstacles that attend working in a predominantly male environment. The experience of female professionals has nevertheless often proved hugely beneficial. Those women who have managed to advance within the more prestigious occupations frequently enjoy status, autonomy and influence. Moreover, the earnings of female professionals working in Northern Ireland enable a lifestyle that would be the envy of many of those who enjoy comparable incomes but happen to live in another region of the archipelago.

The experience of women within the Northern Irish labour market has, therefore, varied enormously. While for some economic activity has entailed misery and exploitation, for others it has meant opportunity and affluence. The class divisions that exist among women in the region have widened greatly during the period of the troubles. This process of polarisation has been particularly pronounced within the environs of the nationalist community. Catholic women, as we witnessed earlier, tend to be over-represented among poorly paid workers. Women from nationalist backgrounds are also more likely, however, to feature among the ranks of the relatively affluent. The survey conducted by the EOCNI that was mentioned earlier discovered that 13 per cent of Catholic women received weekly wages greater than £200, compared to nine per cent of Protestants (Sales 1997a, p. 152). The predominance of Catholics within the category of comparatively affluent female employees could be attributed in part perhaps to the welfarist stance that Westminster has assumed since the introduction of direct rule. Over the past quarter of a century the number of jobs that the state provides in Northern Ireland has grown significantly. The positions that have been created within the public sector have – as Hazel Morrissey (1991, p. 106) points out – been filled with particular regularity by women who come from nationalist backgrounds.

THE PUBLIC SPHERE: EDUCATION

The educational system plays an important, if sometimes overstated, role in the functioning of modern societies. Acquisition of appropriate academic qualifications can often exert a significant bearing upon the roles that are allocated to individuals within the prevailing social order. The performance of girls within the educational system will frequently influence the future positions that women come to assume within the wider social formation. It is important, therefore, that we examine the impression that gender leaves upon the experience of education in Northern Ireland.

Academic Performance

In general, the academic performance of girls outstrips that of boys. The academic superiority that female pupils enjoy tends to be especially pronounced during the years of primary school. The organisation of the Northern Irish schooling system would suggest that the timing of girls' academic advantage may be particularly beneficial. Primary school children in the province still have to undertake at the age of eleven intelligence tests that were abandoned in some other regions of the United Kingdom over 30 years ago. Performance in the 'eleven plus' examination largely determines which pupils are selected for admission to one of Northern Ireland's often prestigious and academically formidable grammar schools. The relatively advanced intellectual development of girls aged eleven ensured that they traditionally performed better than boys during the selection procedure. For many years, however, the educational authorities conspired to overlook the academic superiority of female pupils (Morgan &

Lynch 1995, pp. 534, 545). Rather than allocate grammar school places purely on grounds of merit the educational authorities chose to confer them upon equal proportions of girls and boys who had sat the eleven plus examination. The adoption of gender quotas inevitably discriminated against female pupils. The strategy employed by educational bureaucrats ensured that many bright girls were denied a place in grammar schools while boys with lower test scores were actually admitted.

Growing awareness that the procedures governing the transfer of children between primary and secondary school discriminated against female pupils generated understandable indignation. The Equal Opportunities Commission for Northern Ireland (EOCNI) initiated a legal challenge to the practice of allocating grammar school places to equal proportions of boys and girls. In 1988 the courts ruled in favour of the Commission. The legal judgement established that in future the educational authorities would have to select grammar school pupils on the basis solely of merit and without regard to gender. In the years that immediately followed the court ruling appreciably more girls than boys gained places in the grammar school of their choice.

The advances that the 1988 legal judgement enabled female pupils to secure were, however, to be shortlived. During the 1993/94 school year the format of the transfer procedure was altered. The eleven plus examination ceased to assume the guise of a verbal reasoning test and centred instead upon the content of the school curriculum. The revised format would appear to have been relatively amenable to the particular attributes of male pupils. In three of the four years since the transfer test was altered boys have attained better results than girls (EOCNI 1997).

The academic advantage that girls typically enjoy at the age of eleven persists throughout the remainder of their secondary level education. Female pupils generally perform better than their male peers in the General Certificate of Secondary Education (GCSE) examinations that are usually taken at the age of sixteen (Morgan & Lynch 1995, p. 547). A recent report of the EOCNI provides information on the performance of pupils taking seven of the more common subjects examined at GCSE level – biology, chemistry, physics, mathematics, French, English and home economics. In 1996 girls attained more passes than boys in all of the subject areas mentioned (EOCNI 1997).

Until quite recently the significantly superior performance that girls typically recorded during their school lives failed to survive those examinations taken at the age of 16. In the crucial final couple of years of secondary school the prevailing pattern of gender advantage came to be inverted as the attainment of boys began suddenly to move beyond that of girls. This apparently dramatic reversal of academic fortunes reflected the differences in the importance that Northern Irish society ascribes to the education of members of the respective sexes. The presumption that the future roles of female pupils are to be found within the home rather than workplace has often ensured that the schooling of girls has been afforded rather less significance than that of their male peers. As a result many academically capable female pupils have been dissuaded from pursuing their studies beyond the minimum school leaving age.

The pattern of decline in the performance of girls remaining at school beyond 16 has, however, been arrested in recent years. The advantage that female pupils had enjoyed hitherto certainly dwindles in sixth form. Nonetheless the academic attainment of late teenage girls remains superior to that of their male contemporaries. The data collated by Cormack & Osborne (1995, p. 507) attest to the relative scholastic strength of sixth form girls. Twenty seven per cent of female Protestant pupils who left school during the summer of 1991 secured three passes in the 'Advanced Level' examinations. The proportion of Protestant schoolboys who achieved comparable distinction at A level was 22 per cent. Similar trends are at work within the province's Roman Catholic schools. While 24 per cent of female Catholic school-leavers registered three passes at A level, only 18 per cent of their male counterparts performed equally well.

The increasingly impressive performance of girls at A level has gradually altered the composition of entrants to the province's institutions of higher education. Only a quarter of those who began university courses in Northern Ireland during the academic year 1966/67 were women (Morgan & Lynch 1995, p. 535). Over the three decades that have elapsed since, the proportion of university entrants who are female has risen sharply. In 1995/96 55 per cent of undergraduates enrolled in Northern Irish universities were women (EOCNI 1997). In recent generations female students have become not only more numerous but also more successful. During 1966/67 women secured only one in seven of those first and upper second class honours degrees conferred upon Northern Irish graduates. By the late 1980s, however, the proportion had risen to half. Although women perform as well as men at undergraduate level, they remain less likely to pursue their studies further. Research conducted by educationalists suggests that a smaller proportion of female undergraduates manage to secure admission to postgraduate programmes (EOCNI 1997; Morgan & Lynch 1995, p. 535)

Subject Choice

Information garnered from a range of cultures suggests that girls and boys are often introduced to different subjects. The particular subject areas to which children lean largely reflect the distinctive assumptions that attend gender distinctions. Social orders typically operate upon the presumption that girls and boys possess different abilities and interests. The characteristics that are socially ascribed to girls invariably portray them as prone less to rational calculation than intuition, emotion and empathy. As a consequence, schoolgirls are often steered away from the positivist environs of the 'hard' sciences and towards the arts and humanities which are deemed more conducive to the female intellect. Among the dominant attributes that emerge out of the social construction of 'femininity' are an ability and willingness to tend to the countless needs of others. In the classroom girls are often nudged towards those subjects which provide initiation into their allocated social roles as carers and homemakers. Home economics sets out to offer female pupils competence in a range of essential domestic tasks. In addition, the discipline of biology, the only natural science studied predominantly by females, prepares girls for one of the most important 'caring' professions – that of nursing.

The seemingly universal tendency for girls and boys to lean towards different elements of the school curriculum is confirmed when we turn to consider patterns of subject choice in the particular context of Northern Ireland. Schoolgirls in the province, as elsewhere, tend towards the arts and languages. Three quarters of those who sat the A level French examinations held in the summer of 1996, for instance, were female (EOCNI 1997). The subject area which is dominated most by girls is of course that of home economics. Only one in eight of the candidates entered for the 1996 GCSE home economics examination was male (EOCNI 1997).

Northern Irish schoolgirls are less likely than their male peers to study science. There were considerably fewer girls than boys among those entered for the GCSE examinations in biology, chemistry and physics held during the summer of 1996 (EOCNI 1997). The under-representation of female pupils is especially pronounced within the most prestigious of the scientific disciplines

– that of physics. Only 28 per cent of the candidates who sat the 1996 A level physics examinations were in fact girls (EOCNI 1997). Female pupils attending Northern Irish schools are also appreciably less likely than their male counterparts to have the opportunity to undertake technical courses. Eight times more boys than girls were entered for the 1991 examinations in GCSE technology (Morgan & Lynch 1995, p. 538). The under-representation of females in relation to technical courses that is apparent within local secondary schools is also evident within the province's third level institutions. A mere twelve per cent of students who took engineering and technology degrees in Northern Irish universities during 1995/96 were women (EOCNI 1997).

The gendered pattern of subject choice that obtains within schools and universities in Northern Ireland has some bearing upon the distribution of life chances in the region. Scientific and technical courses often prepare individuals for occupations which attract greater status and remuneration than those that are conventionally associated with the humanities. Hence, many female pupils and students are being dissuaded from pursuing academic interests that often yield considerable material and symbolic reward. The processes of subject choice that operate within the province's educational institutions contribute, therefore, to the reproduction of the economic subordination that women endure within contemporary Northern Irish society.

Although girls and boys still tend towards different areas of the curriculum, the pattern of subject choice at work within Northern Irish schools has become less pronounced over time. In recent years, the number of girls choosing to undertake courses in the natural sciences has grown appreciably. This trend has been particularly marked within the discipline of chemistry. In the mid 1970s less than one third of those sitting the examinations in A level chemistry were female. Within two decades, however, girls had come to slightly outnumber boys among the candidates for A level chemistry (EOCNI 1997). Northern Irish schoolgirls have come increasingly not only to undertake scientific courses but also to excel at them. The performance of girls who take science subjects is almost always superior to that of their male peers. In the 1996 examinations female candidates were proportionately more likely than boys to secure passes in GCSE and A level chemistry, GCSE and A level physics and GCSE biology. Only in the case of A level biology was the performance of girls inferior to that of boys (EOCNI 1997).

THE PUBLIC SPHERE: POLITICS

Political Violence

The ethnoreligious enmities that define Northern Irish society have
over recent generations degenerated into prolonged communal
violence. The political upheavals that mark the recent history of
Northern Ireland have touched the lives of almost everyone living
in the province. The impact of the troubles has, however, been far
from uniform. The violence of the last three decades has affected
different people in different ways. More specifically, the experience
of political conflict in the six counties has been heavily gendered.
The intercommunal violence that has engulfed Northern Ireland
in recent times has often impacted upon the lives of women in a
different way from those of men.

The violence that occurs within all social formations provides
the substance of sustained ideological dispute. Particular forms of
violence are widely portrayed and accepted as being abhorrent.
The brutality that members of different ethnic communities visit
upon one another is often regarded as especially odious – as the
outpouring of primordial passions that expose the essential frailty
of modernity. Certain other versions of violence, in contrast, tend
to be viewed as positively valorous. Those violent acts that attract
the endorsement of the state are particularly venerated. The citizen
who excels during times of war is invariably cherished – held up
as the embodiment of the genuine character and virtue of the
nation. The battlefield constitutes an important site wherein the
state variously confers and denies status and honour. In common
with all other public spaces that generate kudos, the zone of war
is one from which women are largely excluded.

The exclusion of women from many of the sites and processes
of warfare articulates a particular, prevalent construction of
'femininity'. In most cultures women are portrayed as essentially
passive and maternal. There exists a pervasive social presumption
that the feminine prompts a profound concern to care for others.
Women are often venerated as the bringers and preservers of life.
The dominant traits of femininity ensure that women are ill suited
to the practice of warfare. For women to visit violence and
ultimately death upon others would represent a violation of their
essential 'nature'.

The social assumption that the realm of the military is alien to
women has defined the political conflict that has consumed

Northern Ireland since the late 1960s. It has been comparatively rare for women to have directly assumed the role of combatants during the troubles. While the role that women have played in the political violence of the last three decades has been strictly secondary, their participation nonetheless should not be overlooked. There exists within the republican movement a long tradition of women playing an active part in the 'armed struggle'. The womens' section of the Irish Volunteers – *Cumann na mBan* – performed an important role in the revolutionary upheavals that seized Ireland during the early decades of this century. The tradition of militancy among republican women has persisted into the recent period of political unrest (WIRM 1991). Numerous women have participated in the campaign of insurgence orchestrated by republicans since the early 1970s. Some have secured a certain renown. The likes of the Price sisters, Mairead Farrell and Evelyn Glenholmes spring more readily to mind than many men who have made comparable contributions to the republican movement (Sales 1997b, p. 148).

The militant tradition that exists among republican women would seem to have no equivalent within loyalist circles. The campaign of political violence associated with a cluster of loyalist paramilitary organisations has been sustained more or less exclusively by men (Miller et al. 1996, p. 13). During the initial years of its existence a women's branch operated within the largest of the loyalist paramilitary bodies – the Ulster Defence Association (UDA). In 1974 some members of the branch tortured and eventually murdered another Protestant woman – Ann Ogilby – who happened to be married and to have taken to visiting an unmarried loyalist prisoner. The killing produced widespread revulsion within the loyalist community and immediately led to the women's section of the UDA being disbanded (Sales 1997a, p. 71; 1997b, p. 148).

The political crisis of the last three decades has necessitated an enormous expansion of the repressive apparatus of the state in Northern Ireland. Comparatively few of those who have joined the swollen ranks of the Royal Ulster Constabulary (RUC), the Ulster Defence Regiment (UDR) and the Royal Irish Regiment (RIR) have been women. The experience of women who have entered the security forces has often differed markedly from that of their male colleagues. The hierarchy of the province's police force has appeared to embrace the conventional assumption that women are fundamentally unsuited to situations of combat. Female RUC officers are less likely than their male counterparts to find themselves on the 'front line' of the 'war against terrorism'. The roles that are assigned to policewomen in the province frequently acknowledge the stereotypes that arise out of prevailing gender distinctions. The energies of female officers are often devoted not to the pursuit of paramilitary operatives but rather to caring for children and other women who have fallen upon misfortune. The apparent concern of senior figures within the RUC to insulate policewomen from the dangers associated with the political conflict in the six counties ensured that for most of the current troubles the force refused to issue firearms to female officers. The fact that policewomen were prevented from carrying weapons meant that they were unable to perform certain roles essential to career development. Convinced that the hierarchy of the force was discriminating against them, a number of women initiated legal proceedings against the RUC. The resultant court ruling ensured that since 1 April 1994 female RUC officers have been entitled to bear arms in the same way as their male colleagues.

The conflict that has gripped Northern Ireland since the late 1960s would appear, therefore, to have observed certain dominant gender conventions. It has been comparatively rare for women to have been the perpetrators of the violence that has scarred the lives of recent generations in the six counties. Those relatively few women who actually have assumed the status of combatant have of course infringed powerful cultural mores. Anyone who commits – or offers ideological support to – acts of violence directed against the state will be demonised by powerful forces within the prevailing social order. A woman who does so, however, will be portrayed as *especially* abhorrent. The propensity for women associated with political violence to be particularly vilified has found numerous illustrations. One of the more important arose out of media coverage of one of the few women to have reached a position of seniority within Northern Irish political life. In the mid 1970s Maire Drumm occupied the post of Vice President of Sinn Fein. Her prominence within the political wing of the republican movement would ultimately cost Drumm her life. In October 1976 she was murdered while a patient in Belfast's Mater Hospital. It was alleged that loyalists had carried out the assassination although suspicion persists as to the real identity of the killers.

The response of the British media to the murder of Maire Drumm mobilised conventional gendered assumptions and centred primarily upon her status as a grandmother. Journalists repeatedly expressed bewilderment that Drumm could have been involved in bringing two generations of children into the world and yet support a republican strategy that had resulted in numerous deaths. The political stance that Drumm had adopted was considered to offend the role of benign nurturer conferred by the status of grandmother. Journalists seeking to encapsulate the presumed paradox of Maire Drumm – the doting grandmother who advocated political violence – did so through coining phrases like 'hate granny', 'granny of hate' and 'granma venom' (Curtis 1984, pp. 99–100). The ambition of elements within the British media to condemn Drumm as the essential embodiment of evil took a distinctly puerile turn in the pages of *The Sunday Times*. In one article readers of the paper were informed that should they wish to genuinely understand Maire Drumm they should delete the final 'm' of her surname and then spell her entire name backwards, thereby revealing the declaration: 'MURDER I AM' (ibid, p. 100).

The constructions of gender prevalent within Northern Irish society have ensured that women have been comparatively insulated from the violence that has defined the public life of the province in recent times. The belief that war is inimical to the nature of woman has produced the conviction that women should not be the *agents* of political violence. The same social prescription has also of course sponsored an insistence that women should not be the *targets* of political violence. During the present conflict in Northern Ireland this particular convention of war has in the main been respected. The troubles have primarily entailed (working class) men attempting with varying degrees of success to kill other (working class) men. It has been only occasionally that women have been the intended targets of the multiple military agencies that operate within the six counties. As a result, a remarkably small proportion of the fatalities that have resulted from the conflict in Northern Ireland have been female (McWilliams 1995, p. 16). The individuals engaged in 'The Cost of the Troubles Study' note that of the 3,601 lives lost to political violence over the last 30 years 322 – around nine per cent – have been those of women (Fay et al. 1999, p. 161).

The murders of women that have occurred during the current conflict have been particularly likely to prompt waves of revulsion throughout Northern Irish society. Those who take the life of a woman are deemed to have infringed a sacred moral code and are, therefore, denounced with especial fervour in many quarters. The killing of women within the public space of political conflict frequently generates moral panics that articulate an unease that there are, among the citizens of Northern Ireland, individuals capable of reaching hitherto uncharted depths of depravity. The equally frequent murders of women within the private space of the family home have rarely, if indeed ever, produced a comparable propensity to moral introspection (McWilliams 1995, p. 15).

Women have been considerably less likely than men to die during the modern political conflict in Northern Ireland. This should not, however, be taken or allowed to diminish the agonies that the troubles have forced women to endure. Women have not suffered any less than men as a result of the traumatic events that have consumed the six counties over the last 30 years. Rather they have simply suffered in ways that have often differed from those of men. The countless acts of violence that have punctuated the modern history of the province have impacted with particular force upon the lives of women. The thousands of murders that have occurred during the troubles have taken an especially heavy emotional toll upon women. Frequently women have had to deal not only with their own bereavement but also that of friends and relatives. In particular women have often had to face the harrowing prospect of comforting and counselling children who have lost their fathers.

The era of the troubles has also imposed enormous material costs upon the lives of women. Since the late 1960s tens of thousands of Northern Irish men have been killed, incarcerated and incapacitated. The wives and girlfriends of these men have often had to shoulder the burden of holding entire families together. Women have frequently had to raise children alone and on minuscule incomes. Inevitably, many have had to endure acute and sustained financial hardship.

The various emotional and material costs associated with the troubles have evidently taken their toll upon the minds and bodies of many women. The upheavals that recent generations have endured have encouraged nervous disorders that would appear to afflict women with particular regularity. The interventions of the medical profession have inevitably ensured that many Northern Irish women pass through life in a state of advanced sedation (O'Connor 1993, p. 12). One estimate suggests that around 35 million tranquillisers are prescribed every year in Northern Ireland. Approximately two thirds of these are taken by women (Ward & McGivern 1982).

The political violence that women have endured has been not only less frequent than that suffered by men but also qualitatively different (McWilliams 1994). Those assaults which men have issued against women drawn from the other ethnoreligious tradition have at times assumed an explicitly sexual form. As has been the case in other contexts of political upheaval, rape has been employed as a political weapon in the Northern Irish conflict. The precise scale and role of the sexual violence that has occurred during the troubles remains unclear. Our ignorance in this particular regard is of course far from coincidental (Smyth 1995, pp. 195–6). Over the course of the present political crisis an enormous body of researchers has scrutinised myriad aspects of Northern Irish society. The research that has been conducted in the six counties has invariably reflected the concerns and interests of men. Many social practices and processes that impinge especially upon the lives of Northern Irish women have been afforded little importance. The dearth of information on the role of sexual violence in the troubles may be regarded as representative, therefore, of a broader tendency on the part of social scientists to overlook women's issues.

Over the period of the troubles, Northern Irish women have of course also faced violence from *within* their own community. The physical abuse that women have endured at the hands of their ethnoreligious kin has often articulated a communal concern to maintain boundaries and regulate sexual conduct. When British troops arrived on the streets of Belfast and Derry during the summer of 1969 they were greeted with enthusiasm by many within the nationalist community. Numerous younger nationalist women inevitably forged romances with soldiers. In the 18 months or so that followed the arrival of the British army, however, relations with the nationalist community degenerated rapidly. Catholic women who were involved with British soldiers were advised and encouraged to terminate their relationships. Those who refused were often subjected to persuasive communal sanctions. Some women who persisted in dating British soldiers were tied to lampposts, their heads shaved and covered in tar and feathers. These public rituals of humiliation represented an attempt on the part of the wider community to intervene in the private lives of younger nationalist women. The practice of 'tarring and feathering' in Northern Ireland should, therefore, be acknowledged as an especially dramatic example of the broader processes through which every society seeks to regulate women's sexual lives.

Political Power

The operation of patriarchal society hinges fundamentally upon the propensity and ability of men to monopolise political power.

In most western societies women have proved unable to appropriate meaningful political authority. One of the most important points of access to power within bourgeois society is that offered by political parties. Women have been essentially marginalised within the formal realm of party politics. The Commission on the Status of Women, convened under the auspices of the United Nations, examined the gendered distribution of power within the party political process across the globe (Gray & Heenan 1996, p. 42). The Commission disclosed that in 1993 only one in eight of those elected to lower houses of parliament worldwide were women. There were eleven countries in which no women whatsoever sat in the national parliament. Moreover, in only five states did women comprise a third or more of parliamentarians.

The process of exclusion of women from formal political life that seemingly operates at a global level is evinced with especial clarity within the more specific context of Northern Ireland. The role that women have played historically within the party politics of the six counties has been distinctly minor. The voices raised during the sectarian squabbles that characterised parliamentary life during the era of devolved government in Northern Ireland were rarely those of women. In the course of the 50 years of its existence only nine women were elected to the Stormont legislature. The largest contingent of women nominated to sit through a single session of the 52 seat devolved parliament was four. In light of this, Miller et al. (1996, p. 9) would appear justified in their assertion that the political authority articulated through the legislative assembly at Stormont represented a 'virtual male monopoly'.

The marginalisation of women that was evident within the former devolved assembly in Belfast has been even more pronounced within the sovereign parliament in London. During the 75 years that have elapsed since the creation of the constitutional entity of Northern Ireland only one woman has ever been elected to represent the people of the province at Westminster (Fearon 1996a, p. 5). In April 1969 the civil rights activist Bernadette Devlin captured the seat of Mid Ulster in a by-election and managed to retain the constituency during the general election of the following year (Flackes & Elliott 1989, p. 176). Devlin was deposed as a Member of Parliament in the course of the fateful Westminster election of February 1974. The spectacular success of the youthful Bernadette Devlin at the outset of the present troubles almost inevitably proved a mere aberration. In the period since she captured Mid Ulster no other woman has been elected to represent a Northern Irish constituency within the corridors of Westminster.

The exclusion of women from the formal realm of party political life that defined the historical development of Northern Ireland has of course persisted into the present day. Women continue to exercise little influence over the party political culture of the six counties (Rooney 1997, p. 536). There has only ever been one female leader of a political party in Northern Ireland. Anne Dickson assumed control of the minuscule Unionist Party of Northern Ireland after the resignation of Brian Faulkner in 1976 and headed the party until its demise in the early 1980s (Bew & Gillespie 1993, p. 113). At present all of the leaders of the principal political parties that operate within Northern Ireland – and indeed their apparent successors – are men. The prospect of a woman taking the reins of one of the province's parties in the near future would appear rather remote.

The alienation of women from mainstream political life was illustrated graphically during the elections held in May 1996 to select representatives to attend a convention ostensibly designed to debate the constitutional future of the six counties. The electoral procedures that were devised to determine the composition of the Northern Ireland Forum were peculiar and complex. It was intended that a total of 110 delegates would attend discussions convened at the Forum. Ninety representatives would be selected from the province's 18 Westminster constituencies. Parties running in particular constituencies were required to rank their candidates in preferred order of selection. The chances of an individual being elected depended, therefore, upon the number of votes that his or her party gained and by his or her position within the rank order of candidates. Thus, should a political party attract sufficient votes to secure three of the five seats available within a given constituency then those candidates ranked one to three by the relevant party would be returned. The remaining 20 seats available within the Forum were divided equally between those ten political groupings that attracted most votes.

The results of the elections to the Northern Ireland Forum merely underscored that women occupy a marginal location within the party political life of the province. Women constituted a minority of the candidates offered by every major political party. The under representation of women was more pronounced in some political quarters than others. There was a broad tendency for Nationalist parties to run proportionately more female candidates than Unionist parties. The isolation of women was especially pronounced in the case of the Democratic Unionist Party (DUP) which represents the fourth largest political configuration within the province. Of the 54 candidates that the DUP advanced during the campaign only eight were female (Fearon 1996b, p. 14).

Women were, therefore, altogether less likely than men to run for election to the Northern Ireland Forum. Those female candidates who actually did stand, moreover, enjoyed rather less prospect than their male counterparts of being successful. In the main women appeared low on the rank order of candidates that parties devised for constituencies in which they were standing (Walker 1997, pp. 10, 41). Individuals who appeared outside the top couple of ranks faced comparatively little chance of election. The reluctance of the local parties to designate women as their strongest candidates was confirmed in the rank orders favoured by the Social Democratic & Labour Party (SDLP). The SDLP fielded a higher proportion of female candidates than many other political parties. More than one quarter of those running on a SDLP ticket were women. Nonetheless those whom the SDLP identified as their foremost candidates were invariably men. Of the 18 people that the SDLP ranked first in the various constituencies only one happened to be a woman (Fearon 1996b, p. 15). The reticence of the SDLP to champion female candidates proved symptomatic of a wider political trend. All of the parties that contested the Forum elections – even those with comparatively respectable records with regard to selecting female candidates – seemed reluctant to acknowledge women as their principal representatives. The political party most likely to rank women first was the Progressive Unionist Party (PUP). Only four, however, of the 18 people who were afforded star billing by the PUP were women (ibid).

The elections held during May 1996 offered ample confirmation of the subaltern position that women occupy within the mainstream political life of the six counties. Women were less likely than men to seek nomination to the Northern Ireland Forum and even more unlikely to run successfully. As a result only a small minority of the delegates who were elected were women. Of the 110 people designated to attend the assembly a mere 15 were women (Fearon 1996b, p. 16; Rooney 1997, p. 548). The scant representation of women within the Northern Ireland Forum underlined the patriarchal nature of the political culture that exists in the region. The composition of the body confirmed that the current tortuous political process that promises – in principle at least – to shape the futures of all of the peoples of Northern Ireland is being defined almost exclusively by the disposition and interests of men.

While the elections convened during the early summer of 1996 clearly underlined the male domination of Northern Irish political life they also, paradoxically, provided women in the province with a unique opportunity to articulate their particular concerns and grievances (Hinds 1999, pp. 121–3). Among the various distinctive features of the somewhat peculiar electoral procedures that the British government devised to select delegates to the Northern Ireland Forum was that the ten political groupings that garnered most votes would be afforded two seats each in addition to those which they may have happened to have secured within the 18 constituencies. This particular provision meant that even minuscule political associations stood some chance of securing seats at the Forum and thereby gaining admission to the unfolding process of political dialogue. The hitherto inconceivable prospect of electoral gain and political influence prompted the formation of various impromptu political alliances. The most important of these provided a vigorous feminist reading of the talks' process.

The Northern Ireland Women's Coalition (NIWC) has drawn upon the energies of a diverse range of political activists. Those women who have found common cause within the NIWC have been both 'Protestant and Catholic, unionist and nationalist, republican and loyalist' (NIWC 1997). In their literature and public pronouncements the members of the coalition have advanced a searing critique of Northern Irish political life. The NIWC have denounced the political culture that defines the six counties as antiquated and stagnant. The established political parties are held to have been unwilling or unable to think their way beyond those conventional shibboleths and nostrums that have condemned the province to murderous stalemate. The feminists operating under the umbrella of the NIWC have further condemned Northern Irish political life as narrow and exclusive. The larger political forces aligned within the six counties have typically failed to incorporate an entire range of interests, ambitions and identities. In particular, the mainstream political culture of the province has all but failed to accommodate the concerns and aspirations of women.

The ambition of those who have joined forces within the women's coalition has been to assist the transformation of Northern Irish political life. The political culture that the members of the NIWC aspire to nurture would be shaped by the principle of inclusion (Hinds 1999, pp. 124–6). The advance of pluralism would serve to enfranchise those various elements of Northern Irish society that have hitherto been marginal to the political affairs of the province. In particular, the creation of a more inclusive political culture would enable women to assume their rightful place at the very heart of the public life of the six counties.

The feminist reading tendered by the NIWC insists that the incorporation of women would transform the political process. The women's coalition hold to the view that the male domination of the public affairs of the province has undermined the prospects of a meaningful political settlement. The conduct of male politicians has invariably been marked by conservatism and intransigence. Men have proved regularly unwilling to countenance those compromises and leaps of intellectual faith that are required if the troubles are ever to end permanently. In contrast, women are regarded as possessing attributes that are eminently suited to the resolution of political conflict. Women have often proved rather more willing to listen and afford respect to the views of others. In the main it has been the female members of both major ethno-religious traditions that have sustained that vital though fragile ideological space that facilitated intercommunal dialogue. Those women drawn into the political process would – the NIWC assert – be more willing and able than their male peers to enter negotiations and make concessions. The assimilation of women into the political life of the province would, therefore, enhance the prospects of a solution to the Northern Ireland problem.

The unexpected emergence of the NIWC in the spring of 1996 articulated an ambitious enterprise geared to the transformation of the political landscape of the province (Wilford & Galligan 1999, p. 180). The formation of the women's coalition was also prompted, however, by a rather more prosaic and particular concern. The specific target that the NIWC adopted was to garner enough votes to ensure that two feminists would secure places within the proposed forum at which the future of Northern Ireland would be discussed (NIWC 1998). This objective was duly realised. Although the NIWC attracted only 8,000 votes it emerged as the ninth largest political faction within the six counties (Rooney 1997, p. 548). This status was sufficient to entitle the women's coalition to be included within the unfolding 'peace process'. Representatives of the NIWC offered a feminist perspective both at the Northern Ireland Forum situated in the centre of Belfast and at the multiparty negotiations convened in the eastern outskirts of the city.

The interventions of the NIWC have inevitably invoked the ire of established political interests. The critique of Northern Irish political culture that the women's coalition has advanced has created some strange bedfellows. Both unionists and nationalists have rallied to the defence of local political life. The distinctive interpretation that the activists within the NIWC have advanced has been frequently denounced as frivolous. Representatives of the mainstream parties have taken it in turns to dismiss the concerns that the women's coalition have raised as worthless distractions from the 'real' issues that face the people of Northern Ireland. The interrogation of the presumed priorities and verities of local political culture provided by the NIWC produced a resentment that became brutally apparent during the often farcical proceedings of the thankfully shortlived Northern Ireland Forum (McWilliams 1996). Unionist delegates to the Forum routinely greeted members of the women's coalition with sustained sexist derision. Observers were astonished and appalled that democratically elected individuals could be subjected to tireless verbal abuse within a setting allegedly designed to promote constructive and civilised political dialogue (Walker 1997, pp. 25–6).

The creation of the Northern Ireland Forum represented an essentially cosmetic exercise. The real focus of political activity within the province would in fact be elsewhere. In the autumn of 1996 a series of political negotiations began at the traditional seat of Unionist power at Stormont. As one of the ten largest political groupings in Northern Ireland the NIWC were entitled to send delegates to the multiparty talks. Over the next 18 months the women's coalition would make an important contribution to the frequently agonising deliberations that would eventually produce the Good Friday Agreement. At various crucial stages NIWC delegates acted as intermediaries between larger political factions that refused to negotiate directly with one another. The role that the women's coalition played during the multiparty talks at Stormont drew praise from various political quarters. In addition, the prominence of the NIWC throughout the peace process raised considerably the public profile of the organisation. The enormous effort that the women's coalition put into the multiparty talks was to yield an unexpected if modest reward in the summer of 1998. In the elections to the Northern Ireland Assembly two represen- tatives of the NIWC were returned. The success of Monica McWilliams and Jane Morrice raised the number of women elected to the 108 seat legislature to a miserly 14 (Galligan & Wilford 1999, p. 135).

While the NIWC has made a telling contribution to the recent political past of Northern Ireland, the influence that the organi- sation will be able to exericise over the uncertain political future of the province is likely to be distinctly negligible. The women's coalition was among the principle beneficiaries of the somewhat idiosyncratic procedures devised to govern elections to the Northern Ireland Forum. It strains credulity that equally favourable electoral circumstances would ever materialise again. Moreover, the constituency from which the NIWC can expect to draw support would appear strictly limited. Indeed the women's coalition cannot rely upon the undivided allegiance even of that limited body of feminists active within the six counties (Sales 1997a, p. 201). It would seem unlikely, therefore, that those who have joined forces within the NIWC will prove able to fulfil their ambition to alter radically the political landscape of Northern Ireland. Nonetheless the contribution of the women's coalition to local public life should not be overlooked. While it may not serve ultimately to transform the political culture of the six counties, the feminist reading tendered by the NIWC has at least cast light upon many of its iniquities. In particular, the interventions of the women's coalition have exposed more fully than hitherto the patriarchal presumptions and practices that corrupt Northern Irish politics.

Public Agencies

The discussion developed thus far has illustrated that Northern Irish women are typically dispossessed of that influence that happens to be wielded by political parties. It should be remembered, however, that power within the six counties often exists beyond the realm of the democratic process. Since the dissolution of the Stormont legislature the province has been governed in a manner that is singularly autocratic. Those individuals who have been endorsed by the Northern Irish electorate possess only notoriously menial powers. The decisions that affect the everyday lives of the residents of the six counties are taken invariably by politicians returned by British parliamentary constituencies who have been passed the poisoned chalice of selection for positions within the Northern Ireland Office (NIO). Those who have wielded the substantial executive authority available under direct rule have invariably been men (Sales 1997a, p. 171). The recent accession of a Labour administration within the United Kingdom has, however, heralded an important departure from the prevailing pattern of male domination within the NIO. In May 1997 Dr Marjorie Mowlam was selected as the new Secretary of State for Northern Ireland. Dr Mowlam may be considered exceptional both as the first woman to assume the most senior position within the NIO and as the first person of either sex to fill the post who actually wanted to do so (O'Faolain 1997).

The enormous powers available to the executive under the terms of direct rule are administered largely through a range of public agencies (Walker 1997, p. 24). Those functionaries who serve on bodies responsible for the provision of crucial public services such as health and education are often nominated by figures within the NIO. Relatively few nominees have been women. Indeed, 21 of the 142 area boards that administer the region have no female members whatsoever. While the number of women serving on the various area boards remains unacceptably low, it has, however, grown significantly over recent years. In 1986 only 18 per cent of those selected to serve on area boards were women. Over the following decade the proportion almost doubled and presently stands at 32 per cent (Gray & Heenan 1996, p. 45; Heenan & Gray 1999, p. 189; Miller et al. 1996, p. 11).

It would appear, therefore, that women have managed to secure more influence without the democratic process than within. Women are rather more likely to be nominated to one of the frequently powerful public bodies that administer the affairs of Northern Ireland than to be selected by the electorate as delegates to one of the often ineffectual political assemblies that materialise from time to time (Sales 1997a, p. 171). Hence, the argument could be made that the patently undemocratic manner in which the province has been governed since the introduction of direct rule has created certain advantages for women. In view of this, the prospect of democratisation would appear to represent a threat to women's interests. Were the powers presently appropriated by various unaccountable public bodies to be transferred to new elected institutions, the already inadequate political influence that Northern Irish women possess would be diminished yet further. The advent of genuinely democratic practice would, therefore, edge women even closer to the margins of the political process. It is with this particular dilemma that the political scientist Rick Wilford (1996, p. 52) grapples when he comments:

If the nominated bodies were to be displaced by democratically elected alternatives, would women be decanted back into the margins of public life? Patronage has, numerically, proved advantageous for women, whereas electoral competition has not. Unless candidate selection procedures are changed, women may be better served through appointment than by relying on the parties to gender-proof selection.

Civil Society

When considering the nature and distribution of power, social scientists typically adopt a narrow focus that concentrates upon the conduct of states and political parties. It should be remembered, however, that there exists an entire range of other social aggregates that seek with varying degrees of success to exercise political influence. Agencies such as social movements, pressure groups and community organisations operate within a realm of social engagement usually characterised as 'civil society'. Over the course of the present troubles elements of the civic life of the province have flourished. The persistence of political violence, the existence of widespread poverty and the circulation of enormous amounts of public largesse have sponsored the emergence of myriad organisations which often work independently of established political parties. Women have played an especially important role in the regeneration of civil society that has occurred in the six counties over recent generations (Rooney 1997, p. 537; Sales 1997b, p. 152).

The political violence that has become synonymous with Northern Ireland has led to the formation of numerous associations demanding an end to the conflict. Perhaps the most significant peace movement to have emerged during the troubles arose out of a particularly tragic event that occurred during the summer of 1976. In August of that year an injured republican gunman fleeing the security forces knocked down and fatally injured three infants. The outcry that resulted from the deaths of the Maguire children quickly led to the foundation of a social movement calling for the cessation of all acts of political violence. The 'Peace People' appeared initially to have caught a popular mood of disgust at the carnage that had overtaken Northern Ireland. For a brief period the organisation came to play an important role in the public life of the six counties. Advancing an outlook which they claimed was 'political but not party political' the Peace People convened rallies that drew enormous gatherings. The movement attracted considerable attention and admiration beyond the six counties. The international accolades that were conferred upon the Peace People culminated with the Nobel Peace Prize being awarded to two of the group's founding members (Curtis 1984, pp. 201–2; Flackes & Elliott 1989, p. 220).

A distinctive feature of the Peace People was that the movement relied primarily upon the talents and energies of women. The two figures within the organisation who became most widely known were both women – Mairead Corrigan and Betty Williams. Moreover, the enormous public rallies that the Peace People orchestrated for a time in the mid 1970s appeared to attract rather more women than men (Sales 1997b, p. 156). The gender composition of the Peace People may be read as emblematic of a wider political trend. Women have enjoyed a prominence within the peace movement which they have not managed to attain within other forms of political association. Female peace activists have at times appeared to endorse elements of prevailing social construc- tions of gender. Women working for peace have contested with some regularity that acts of violence are deeply inimical to the ideals of the feminine. A supposed innate aversion to conflict is held to have ensured that women have viewed the troubles as especially abhorrent. Activists within the peace movement have argued further that women possess certain traits that are eminently suited to the resolution of the conflict in Northern Ireland. An ability both to talk and to listen suggests that women possess attributes that will enable them to create a peace that has proved consistently to be beyond the capabilities of men (Sales 1997a, pp. 195–6).

The regeneration of the civil society of Northern Ireland over recent generations has been signalled by the proliferation of groupings operating at a local level. In working class districts throughout the six counties numerous associations have emerged to promote the interests of residents. The flowering of community politics in Northern Ireland has been due largely to the enduring commitment of women. The roles to which women have been consigned within community groups have tended, however, to be subordinate (McDonough 1996, pp. 26–7). Positions of leadership within local associations tend to be assumed mainly by men. The functions that women perform within community groups are frequently rather more mundane. The marginalisation of women evident within the party political life of Northern Ireland finds echoes, therefore, at the level of community politics.

Those women who have participated in the civic life of the six counties have often sought to promote their own particular interests as women. Over the course of the present troubles there has been a remarkable proliferation of women's groups. Indeed, conservative estimates suggest that there exist at present within Northern Ireland around 1,000 separate organisations designed to advance the cause of women (Fearon 1996c, p. 57). The women's movement has at times proved able to transcend the ethnoreligious divisions that corrode the civic and political life of the province. One especially celebrated incident of feminist solidarity occurred in response to a controversial decision taken by certain members of Belfast City Council. In 1989 it was announced that council funds would henceforth be withheld from the Falls Women's Centre because various members of the organisation were believed to have close associations with the republican movement. The announcement provoked outrage among the multifarious women's groups that operate throughout the province. Feminists and others expressed their disgust that a collection of predominantly male politicians should have decided to withdraw essential resources from an organisation that provides vital services for women. The Falls Women's Centre attracted support from what might usually be regarded as unlikely sources. Women providing similar services on the Shankill Road expressed with especial vigour the view that the decision taken by the council should be overturned. The principled and courageous stance that the members of the Shankill Women's Centre adopted inevitably produced resentment among elements of the wider unionist community. This hostility may serve to explain the announcement made during 1996 by Belfast City Council that funding of the Centre was to come to an abrupt end (Sales 1997a, p. 194).

Although there have been some memorable moments of inter-communal solidarity the Northern Irish women's movement has more often been compelled to acknowledge the contours of eth-nopolitical distinction existent within the six counties. Most of the women's groups that operate in Northern Ireland are small and based in specific local communities. The distinctive pattern of residential segregation that characterises the province inevitably means that individual women's centres are often able only to provide services to members of one particular ethnoreligious tradition (Rooney 1997, p. 546). There also exist a few larger organisations that seek to promote the views and interests of all women. These umbrella associations have, however, frequently been plagued by the 'national question'. Issues like the status and treatment of female republican prisoners have stoked ethnoreli-gious sentiments that have often fractured feelings of sisterhood. In 1975 the Northern Ireland Women's Rights Movement (NIWRM) was established with the intention of drawing together feminists from 'all political traditions and none' (Sales 1997a, p. 186). The movement would soon prove unable, however, to fulfil its noble intentions. Feminists of a broadly republican disposition felt aggrieved that the NIWRM had refused to take a radical position on the political conflict that had engulfed Northern Ireland. In particular, the organisation was felt to have abdicated its moral responsibility to denounce the repression visited upon nationalists by the British state. The dissidents within the NIWRM would soon break away to form the Socialist Women's Group which stressed that the cause of women could only be advanced within the new political environment of a united Ireland (Sales 1997b, p. 153).

The propensity for the women's movement to fragment along ethnopolitical lines has found further illustration in recent years with the emergence of two groupings which advance republican and unionist perspectives respectively. It has been primarily men who have shaped the direction of modern Irish republicanism. The most prominent and recognisable figures within the political wing of the republican movement have invariably been men. While the role that women play within Sinn Fein remains subordinate their influence has increased substantially nonetheless (Wilford & Galligan 1999, pp. 171–2, 179–80). The growing prominence of women within the republican movement has found expression in the composition of various Sinn Fein delegations. Half of those chosen to represent the party at the Forum for Peace and Reconciliation convened in Dublin were women. Moreover, there were two women among the five Sinn Fein delegates who held preliminary talks with British officials in the wake of the first ill-fated IRA ceasefire.

The burgeoning importance and confidence of the female voice within contemporary republicanism found pertinent expression during 1992. In that year a number of women possessed of a broadly republican disposition came together to discuss political developments. These impromptu discussions led to the creation of the pressure group *Clar na mBan* (Ward 1995). Since its formation *Clar na mBan* has made a number of political interventions. In the course of 1994 the grouping both convened a successful conference and made a submission to the Forum for Peace and Reconciliation. In many regards the political analysis that *Clar na mBan* (1994a, 1994b) advance adheres to the tenets of orthodox republicanism. Among the assumptions shared by the members of the organisation is that the Irish nation has the inviolable right to self-determination. The disposition of *Clar na mBan* should also be read, however, as a critique of conventional republicanism. The feminists active within the pressure group contest that there has been an historic tendency for the republican movement to demote the views and interests of women. The emergence of *Clar na mBan* may be seen, therefore, as an expression of the determination of republican feminists that women will be able to play a full and equal part in those political developments which they hope will lead to the foundation of a united Irish state.

The emergence of *Clar na mBan* has almost inevitably produced a response from the other side of the ethnoreligious divide. The formation of the *Protestant Women's Group* articulated an ambition to promote the interests of women within the existing constitutional framework of the United Kingdom (Rooney 1995a). Thus far unionist women would appear to have been less able to construct a coherent political vision or make a political impression than their counterparts within the republican tradition.

CONCLUSION

The position that women hold within contemporary Northern Irish society remains an essentially subaltern one. The thousands of books and articles that have appeared to document the troubles have made remarkably little reference to the multiple forms of discrimination and violence suffered by women living in the province. Indeed commentators on Northern Irish affairs have invariably been content to write as though women simply do not exist. The propensity to marginalise or exclude women represents one of the fundamental shortcomings of most coverage of the six counties. If we are to arrive at a more faithful understanding of the nature of Northern Irish society then observers must begin to bring to the centre of their analysis those issues and identities that arise out of gender distinctions. The problem of gender blindness is of course one that afflicts not only academic writing but also the political process (Fagan & Munck 1997). The poverty and reaction that define the public life of Northern Ireland may be attributed not least to its oppressively patriarchal character. The cause of progress in the six counties demands the promotion of a political culture that will take seriously the particular interests and inclinations of women.

4 Official Representations of the Conflict in Northern Ireland: The British State and the Media

Since the late 1960s the people of Northern Ireland have been forced to endure sustained political unrest. The conflict that has ensnared the province in recent times has been not merely military, but also ideological. The various players in the troubles have sought to advance their interests through recourse not only to guns and bombs but also to words and images. The various agencies that have collided in the six counties over recent generations have striven to claim the moral high ground. The British state, Irish republicans and Ulster loyalists alike have struggled to establish the moral authority of their own actions and ambitions and to discredit those of others. The conflict that has defined contemporary Northern Irish society should, therefore, be understood not only as a contest for military supremacy but also as – to employ a phrase that has enjoyed enduring popularity among observers of the province – a 'battle for hearts and minds' (Miller 1994, p. 12).

The 'propaganda war' (Curtis 1984) that has raged during the modern troubles could hardly be considered a contest of equals. The various parties to the Northern Irish conflict possess vastly different material and figurative resources. The agency that occupies the strongest position from which to disseminate its own particular perspective on the troubles is of course that of the British state. The various bodies that are charged with the task of articulating the metropolitan outlook receive distinctly generous funding. The comparative profligacy of the state has served to ensure that the official version of the Northern Irish conflict is the one heard with greatest regularity. Furthermore, those Westminster administrations that have been formed during the present troubles have inherited and devised various statutory provisions designed to constrain the freedom of the media. Possession of these substantial legal powers has enabled the metropolis to marginalise alternative, dissenting perspectives on the Northern Irish problem.

THE MEDIA AND THE OUTBREAK OF THE TROUBLES

Among the enduring concerns of the political establishment of the United Kingdom has been an anxiety to marginalise the troublesome territory of Northern Ireland. The ambition of the metropolis to maintain Northern Ireland 'at arm's length' found reflection in the indifference of the British media towards the province during the 50 years of devolved government that followed partition (Butler 1995, pp. 12, 38). Throughout the lifetime of the Stormont parliament journalists and broadcasters based in other regions of the United Kingdom exhibited little interest in the affairs of the province. The few media personnel who ventured across the Irish sea invariably found Northern Ireland a difficult environment in which to operate. Broadcasters seeking to examine the ethnoreligious tensions simmering within the province encountered considerable political pressure (Maloney 1991, p. 11). Even the most cursory acknowledgement of the ethnic divisions that prevail within Northern Ireland was likely to provoke Unionist politicians to demand that the relevant broadcasts be radically revised or abandoned (Smith 1996, p. 26).

Those broadcasters based *within* Northern Ireland proved even more reluctant than their British counterparts to address the particular tensions and inequities characteristic of the six counties. In 1924 the British Broadcasting Corporation (BBC) established a regional station in Belfast. In the decades that followed BBC Northern Ireland would provide distinctly sanitised coverage of the frequently unsavoury public life of the six counties. The programmes that were produced in Belfast invariably articulated an assumption that Northern Ireland represented merely another region of the United Kingdom. Broadcasters frequently sought to transcend the 'narrow ground' of the six counties and to look towards the rather wider environs of the British state, British Empire and, eventually, British Commonwealth (Cathcart 1996, pp. 5–8, 11). The particular cultural and linguistic traits characteristic of the region were systematically understated. The cultural milieu constructed and celebrated within the transmissions of BBC Northern Ireland was essentially that defined by the hegemonic ritual and stylistic practices of the more privileged elements of metropolitan society. The regional station in Belfast, moreover, frequently chose to turn a blind eye to the ethnoreligious fissures that run through the six counties. For many years BBC Northern Ireland simply refused to acknowledge those manifold rites and practices that articulate the communal divisions pervasive within the province. Not until after World War II would the Corporation cover the annual Twelfth of July Orange parades or broadcast the results of sports fixtures organised under the auspices of the Gaelic Athletic Association (GAA) (Smith 1996, pp. 25–6).

The perennial circumspection that marked the conduct of important elements within the media during the Stormont era served to insulate successive Unionist administrations from sustained critical attention. Broadcasters invariably proved reluctant to cast light upon the various injustices and frailties associated with the particular mode of devolved government introduced to the six counties at partition. The insulation of the Unionist regime would be brought to an abrupt halt, however, by the frenetic sequence of events that heralded the onset of the present troubles. During the 1960s the alienation long since latent within the nationalist community came to the fore. Resentful of their subordinate position within Northern Irish society, national-ists organised to articulate the demand for equality of citizenship. As the campaign for civil rights gathered pace communal relations in the province deteriorated. The partition settlement had finally begun to unravel. Significantly, it had done so at a time when the television set had become a standard feature within homes throughout the western world. As the political climate in Northern Ireland degenerated apace in the late 1960s the province became a focus for the world's media. Journalists and broadcasters flocked to the six counties to cover a burgeoning conflict which appeared to owe its origins to antagonisms more appropriate to the seventeenth century than to our own. As the end of the 1960s beckoned, an increasingly vulnerable Unionist administration in Belfast came for the first time to be exposed to the critical glare of an international audience. The scrutiny of the world's media would have some bearing upon the course of the political crisis about to break over Northern Ireland.

The significance of the media in times of political upheaval had been clearly demonstrated by an event that both chronicled and accelerated the seemingly inexorable descent of Northern Ireland into communal unrest. As the civil rights movement gained momentum throughout the late 1960s coalitions of nationalists and socialists joined forces to organise a series of marches designed to articulate a range of grievances and demands. One of these was scheduled to pass through Derry on 5 October 1968 (O'Dochartaigh 1997, pp. 19–21). Although declared illegal by the Unionist government the organisers decided to proceed with the march. The 2,000 demonstrators had marched 200 yards when they found their path blocked by a large contingent of the Royal Ulster Constabulary (RUC). The demonstration had until that point been entirely peaceful. Nevertheless, RUC officers began to attack the marchers indiscriminately, initially with batons and subsequently with water cannon. A government commission later established to investigate the disturbances in Derry and associated unrest elsewhere would offer stern criticism of police conduct (Farrell 1976, pp. 246–7).

The violence that police officers visited upon civil rights demonstrators in Derry defined one of the undisputed watersheds in the recent turbulent history of Northern Ireland. Indeed, some commentators have suggested that the events of 5 October 1968 were so momentous that that date should be acknowledged as marking the beginning of the present troubles (Butler 1995, p. 1). The significance that the clashes on the streets of Derry assumed may be attributed at least in part to the fact that they were captured by various television crews. The grainy images that were broadcast of RUC officers instigating random assaults upon peaceful demonstrators exercised a resonance both within and without Northern Ireland (Butler 1991, p. 99). Footage of police brutality merely served to fuel yet further the already considerable disaffection simmering among the ranks of northern nationalists. More importantly perhaps, images of the dramatic developments on the streets of Derry were beamed around the globe. Television viewers in many countries – and not least those living in Great Britain and the Irish Republic – found themselves for the first time cast in the role of eyewitnesses to the oppressive and iniquitous nature of the Unionist regime. The presence of television crews in Derry on the fateful day of 5 October 1968, therefore, nurtured sentiments that acted to erode the legitimacy and stability of the Stormont administration. In previous times the conduct of the media had ensured that the draconian excesses of state agencies and institutions were concealed or at least understated. In the age of television, however, the sectarianism that infected successive Unionist administrations was ruthlessly exposed to the critical gaze of both a domestic and international audience.

PUBLIC RELATIONS AND DIRTY TRICKS

The dramatic events that unfolded during the late 1960s acted to frustrate the perennial ambition of the British political establishment to keep Northern Ireland 'at arm's length'. As the province teetered from one political crisis to the next Westminster was compelled to adopt a rather more interventionist approach. In the course of the summer of 1969 ethnoreligious tensions that had been brewing for some time eventually erupted into sustained communal violence. Fearful that Northern Ireland was on the verge of civil war the Labour administration in London reluctantly took the decision to despatch troops to restore order to the six counties.

The intervention of the British military seemed to mark an important shift in the approach of Westminster towards the fractious affairs of Northern Ireland. In reality, however, the conduct of the metropolis continued to be guided by an ambition to insulate itself from the political life of the province. In the three years that followed the arrival of soldiers on the streets of Derry and Belfast, successive Westminster governments sought to implement reforms that were intended to allow a substantially revised version of the Stormont regime to remain in operation and thereby enable the British political establishment to once again retire a discreet distance from the six counties. The strategy adopted by the sovereign parliament would ultimately prove catastrophic. An anxiety to underwrite the credibility of the Stormont regime moved the military to seek to stem the growing tide of republican insurgence within the province. The increasingly draconian measures adopted by the security forces inevitably engendered alienation within nationalist districts and produced a steady stream of recruits to the republican movement. Those troops who had been greeted with tea and sandwiches by nationalists in the summer of 1969 had within 18 months become targets of gunfire originating from the same community. By the spring of 1972 the political crisis that had come to engulf Northern Ireland appeared to have escalated out of control. Realising that the original partition settlement had ceased to be tenable the sovereign parliament at Westminster exercised its constitutional prerogative by dissolving the devolved legislature and assuming direct responsibility for the governance of the province.

The seemingly inexorable descent of Northern Ireland into communal strife, therefore, forced a decidedly reticent political establishment in London to intervene in the affairs of the province. As the metropolis became an ever more central player in the political life of Northern Ireland, those functionaries operating within the various agencies of the state became keen to legitimise the roles that they had recently acquired within the region. In the months that opened the 1970s British soldiers increasingly came to assume the status of combatants. Influential figures within

Westminster and Whitehall were inevitably anxious to explain and ultimately justify the actions of military personnel operating within the fraught conditions of the six counties. During the same period, moreover, the metropolis sponsored a series of initiatives geared to resolve the political crisis that had engulfed Northern Ireland. Conscious of the prospect of censure from the international community the executive in London was careful to establish the rationale of those political enterprises which it sought to encourage.

The realisation that the crisis unfolding within Northern Ireland would be played out before the critical gaze of the increasingly ubiquitous media ensured that Westminster appreciated the significance of public relations from the very beginning of the troubles. The British state mobilised considerable resources in an attempt to ensure that the metropolitan reading of the Northern Ireland problem would secure precedence. At the outset of the conflict the official interpretation of the troubles was articulated principally through the agency of the military. During the early 1970s the public relations department of the British army grew rather larger than those associated with various other state institutions (Hoggart 1996, pp. 153–7). By 1976 the army press office had come to employ 40 members of staff who worked around the clock. The public relations activities of the military subsequently, however, declined substantially. From the mid 1970s onwards the British state pursued a strategy designed to 'Ulsterise' the conflict in Northern Ireland (Bew & Patterson 1985, pp. 75–110). The most important aspect of the process of 'Ulsterisation' was that British soldiers were gradually replaced by other members of the security forces who had been recruited from within the six counties. RUC officers came to occupy the front line of the campaign to resist republican insurgence. The sight of police officers rather than soldiers patrolling the streets of the province was intended to lend credence to the official contention that Northern Ireland was a society returning to 'normal' (Miller 1994, pp. 80–6).

The advance of Ulsterisation inevitably diminished the significance of the military within the public relations strategy of the British state. As the army press office was scaled down those other agencies charged with the task of disseminating the official construction of the Northern Irish conflict grew considerably. The introduction of direct rule in the spring of 1972 necessitated the creation of a government department – the Northern Ireland Office (NIO) – with specific responsibility for administering the affairs of the province. One of the numerous divisions that operates within the parameters of the NIO is the Northern Ireland Information

Service (NIIS). It is the explicit function of the NIIS to propagate the official version of the political developments that unfold within the six counties. The desire of the British state to emerge victorious from the 'propaganda war' that attends the Northern Irish conflict has ensured that the NIIS enjoys generous resources.

In the fiscal year 1997/98 the NIIS received funding to the tune of £2.6 million (NIDFP 1998, p. 28). The enormous budget that the service attracts allows it to maintain a substantial workforce. At present there are around 50 people employed by the NIIS. The scale of its workforce enables the service to generate a constant stream of information and interpretation. In the first three months of 1998 alone the NIIS produced no fewer than 330 press releases. Although the division within the NIO with specific responsibility for airing the outlook of the British state, the NIIS is not the only one that does so. Agencies such as the Northern Ireland Tourist Board (NITB) and the Industrial Development Board (IDB) also spend large sums in part advancing the official position on Northern Ireland. Consequently, the total figure that the British state spends seeking to promote its own interpretation of the conflict actually substantially exceeds the budget of the NIIS (Miller 1994, pp. 292–3).

The various departments that fall within the orbit of the NIO strive to ensure that the troubles are reported within the media in a manner that is conducive to the interests and reputation of the British state. Official agencies set out to influence the coverage provided by formally independent journalists and broadcasters through numerous means. The practice of unattributable briefings of media personnel affords civil servants an important and clandestine opportunity to place a distinctive inflection upon events. The countless press releases that are issued seek to portray the actions and intentions of the state in a flattering light and to discredit those of the various other parties to the Northern Irish conflict. Official bodies also produce rather more substantial texts that are designed to explain the Northern Ireland problem to journalists who have only recently arrived in the province and hence are unfamiliar with the nature of the troubles. These detailed documents invariably advance interpretations that are conducive to the interests of the metropolis. In the period between 1980 and 1993 alone, 123 of these 'background papers' were circulated by civil servants working within the NIO (Miller 1994, pp. 123–4).

Those institutions of the British state engaged in the 'battle for hearts and minds' have often employed their considerable resources to court figures within the media. The excursions of

journalists and broadcasters to the province have often been
financed by the NIO. In the course of 1988 the state covered the
expenses of no fewer than 172 journalists who visited Northern
Ireland. Foreign journalists are especially likely to be afforded the
lavish hospitality of the NIO (Thomas 1991, p. 125). During their
time in the province the employees of overseas media corporations are generally provided with rather distorted accounts of the
social and political life of contemporary Northern Ireland. The
readings of the troubles to which foreign journalists are exposed
are principally those articulated by government ministers, senior
civil servants and members of the security forces. The guided
tours of the province on which they are escorted are often
designed to accentuate the positive features of Northern Ireland
and to conceal some of the more unsavoury facets of life therein
(Miller 1994, p. 119).

The hospitality that has been afforded to some visiting
journalists intimates that certain state agencies possess an
appreciable capacity for charm. The efforts of official agents to
exercise influence over the media have frequently, however,
assumed an altogether less pleasant form. During the early 1970s
arguably the most significant participants in the ideological conflict
that burgeoned within Northern Ireland were representatives of
the British army. In the aftermath of the introduction of
internment without trial in the summer of 1971 elements within
the military grew anxious that republicans had begun to gain the
upper hand in the 'propaganda war'. These anxieties led to the
formation of the Information Policy Unit (IPU) towards the end
of 1971. The ostensible purpose of the IPU was to supplement
the army press office in furnishing information to the media (Foot
1996; Miller 1994, pp. 77–80). The actual function of the unit,
however, was to engage in 'psychological operations' or 'psyops'
(Campbell 1996). Inspired by the writings of counter-insurgency
theorists such as Frank Kitson (Kitson 1971), a select group of
army personnel set out to disseminate 'disinformation' designed
to erode the resolve of the community that had spawned the
republican movement. The IPU attempted with some success to
'plant' bogus news stories in the columns of the press. One of the
most common themes of these features was the contention that
the materials being used by republican bombers were volatile and
likely to detonate prematurely. Although those clandestine figures
engaged in psyops could claim the occasional success, the strategy
adopted by the IPU ultimately proved deeply damaging to the
propaganda effort of the military. Over time it became increasingly

apparent to journalists that elements within the army were disseminating untruths. Growing awareness of this strategy of
'disinformation' destroyed media confidence in the integrity of the
army press office. Journalists began to shun the military and often
came to regard republicans as a more reliable source of information
(Miller 1994, p. 79).

ADVERTISING FOR PEACE

Official agencies have sought through various means to influence
the ways in which journalists and broadcasters regard and report
the conflict in Northern Ireland. The institutions of the state have
not, however, been content to allow others to provide exclusive
coverage of the crises that chart the recent history of Northern
Ireland. On the contrary, the metropolis has down the years
produced numerous broadcasts and advertisements which have
articulated an ideologically convenient reading of the troubles. The
official version of the conflict in the province has been disseminated often through the medium of radio. The London Radio
Service (LRS) receives public funding to propagate the British
perspective on the troubles in the guise of seemingly objective news
reports and features (Miller 1994, pp. 125–8). The service has
encountered relatively few difficulties when attempting to 'place'
stories among radio stations around the world. The various wares
of the LRS are typically offered to foreign radio companies for
free or for a merely nominal fee. Financial constraints frequently
ensure that stations are only too keen to acquire the programmes
that the LRS produces. The clandestine activities of the LRS have
meant that over the years the official reading of the Northern Irish
conflict has been introduced to an international audience operating
on the not entirely unreasonable assumption that they are listening
to a balanced account of the violence that has gripped the six
counties.
    Over the past quarter of a century the British state has sought
to contest the propaganda war occasioned by the troubles through
the production of advertisements featured in the press as well as
on radio and television. The quality of the advertisements funded
by the NIO has improved remarkably over time. In particular,
those broadcast on Northern Irish television have become increasingly slick and impressive. The television advertisements
commissioned by the NIO in recent years are made by the public
relations agency McCann Erickson which has its headquarters in

New York. The company recently produced an impressively glossy compilation of 15 advertisements which appeared on local television screens between 1988 and 1995 entitled *Advertising for Peace: The Role of Psychological Creativity in Northern Ireland*. Since the promotional video was released a couple of further advertisements have been commissioned and transmitted. The title which McCann Erickson chose for the compilation tape suggests the purpose of the short films contained therein. The various advertisements commissioned by the NIO represent perhaps the most explicit and vigorous attempt on the part of the British state to win the hearts and minds of the people of Northern Ireland. These brief films combine to provide a lucid exposition of the official interpretation of the troubles. The narratives contained within the advertisements pose and respond to a series of six related questions.

What is the 'Northern Ireland Problem'?

A central function of official discourse on the troubles is to absolve the state entirely of responsibility for the upheavals that recent generations of Northern Irish society have been forced to undergo. This concern for absolution is clearly articulated within the expensive advertisements commissioned by the NIO. As one would anticipate, none of the short films broadcast on local television suggests that the political or military policies adopted by Westminster might be responsible for some of the miseries that have been visited upon the province over the last three decades. On the contrary, the advertisements seek to attribute blame for the advent and persistence of the troubles exclusively to agencies other than those that operate within the orbit of the state.

The narratives embedded within the television advertisements construct the Northern Ireland problem simply as one of 'terrorism' (Miller 1993a, pp. 78–9). The conflict in the region arises out of the existence of a small band of men – and all the 'terrorists' portrayed are male – who are given to acts of extreme violence (Butler 1991, p. 111). Those who fill the ranks of paramilitary organisations are held to enjoy little or no support within the communities which they claim to represent. Paramilitaries are depicted as parasites who control the wider population through a reign of terror (Curtis 1984, pp. 128–30). The campaign of violence waged by elements within northern society represents an assault upon the most elementary principles of democratic practice (Miller 1994, p. 88).

The ambition to depict the members of paramilitary organisations as marginal and unrepresentative figures finds expression in
the language that features within the advertisements. Many centre
upon an opposition between 'them' and 'us'. Those who belong
to paramilitary groupings are often dismissed as 'they'. 'We' on the
other hand are identified as the silent/silenced majority of the
Northern Irish people who long for peace but nonetheless continue
to suffer at the hands of the 'men of violence'. The distinctions
that are activated within the advertisements crafted by McCann
Erickson are clearly intended to discredit those who seek to
challenge the state's formal monopoly on the use of force. The
designation of republican and loyalist combatants as 'them' casts
paramilitaries in the pejorative role of other, outsider or pariah.

Commentators have observed with some frequency that the
denunciations of 'terrorism' that have been issued by the political
establishment have tended to focus disproportionately upon those
acts of violence committed by republicans (Butler 1991, pp.
113–14; 1995, pp. 84–5; Kirkaldy 1984, pp. 184–6; Thomas
1991, p. 126). This preoccupation with republican paramilitarism
acknowledges the particular strategic interests of the metropolis.
The victims of loyalist violence have overwhelmingly been
Catholics who have had no formal association with the republican
movement. Only rarely have loyalists channelled their energies into
military operations directed against the state. The strategy that
republicans have pursued during the troubles has of course
assumed a rather different form. The explicit ambition of the
republican movement has been to sunder that constitutional
arrangement that conjoins Northern Ireland and the other regions
of the United Kingdom. Consequently, those acts of violence that
have been perpetrated by republicans have in the main been
directed against the agents and institutions of the British state.
The radical sedition that promotes the 'armed struggle' has invited
the preoccupation of the metropolis with the republican
movement. The military operations that have been undertaken
by the Provisional IRA in particular have threatened the actual
integrity of the United Kingdom. It is scarcely surprising,
therefore, that some figures within Westminster and Whitehall
should have come to associate 'terrorism' more or less exclusively
with republicanism.

The anxiety of the political establishment to demonise the
republican movement in particular is intimated in one of the earlier
advertisements produced by McCann Erickson. Viewers of *A
Future* are introduced to a disgruntled young father whose life has

been overshadowed by the troubles. The narrator insists that political violence has been the ruination of Northern Ireland. The actions of the paramilitaries are held to have denied the people of the province that security and prosperity that would have otherwise prevailed. The narrative formed within the advertisement draws towards a reasonably predictable finale. The young father that we encounter counsels that if future generations are to enjoy the lives that they deserve then people must begin to turn their backs on political violence. This realisation prompts the narrator to use the confidential telephone to pass on to the security forces information that he possesses concerning paramilitary organisations. Having performed his paternal duty, the informant returns to the warmth of the family living room where we leave him cradling his newborn child.

At least at first glance *A Future* appears to offer a universal denunciation of the political violence that has plagued Northern Ireland since the late 1960s. The disenchantment articulated by the central character seems to be directed at paramilitaries of each and every ideological hue. Closer examination, however, suggests that the advertisement encodes a distinct political prejudice. The viewer of *A Future* is provided with a series of clues as to the eth-noreligious affiliation of the narrator. At one stage the young father comments that he grew up among people with little regard for the security forces as he passes a wall displaying republican graffiti. At another the narrative alludes to 'the lads', a variation on 'the boys' which is frequently used to denote members of the Provisional IRA. The attentive viewer possessed of even the most rudimentary knowledge of the ethnographic cues that operate within Northern Ireland would be able to assemble these details in order to identify the narrator as a working class Catholic. Disclosure of the ethnoreligious persuasion of the central character reveals the very particular concerns that inform the advertisement. As soon as we realise that the narrator of *A Future* is in fact a working class nationalist we come to appreciate that the criticisms which he articulates are not targeted at all paramilitary associations but rather are targeted more specifically at the Provisional IRA. It becomes apparent, in other words, that the rationale that drives the advertisement is an ambition not to persuade all of the people of Northern Ireland to turn their backs on political violence but rather to drive a wedge between working class Catholics and those republicans who operate within their midst.

The storyline that unfolds within *A Future* illustrates the frequent preoccupation of official discourse with those forms of political violence that emanate from the republican movement. As the sequence of broadcasts compiled on *Advertising for Peace* progresses, however, this particular ideological asymmetry appears to dissolve. The more recent advertisements that appear on the compilation seek explicitly to condemn 'terrorism' in all its many guises. Those broadcast during the 1990s have often portrayed graphic scenes of political violence committed by individuals whose ideological credentials are almost impossible to discern. Indeed, the advertisements that the NIO have commissioned during the eventful period of what has come to be known as the 'peace process' have seemed to set out deliberately to confuse the viewer as to the ideological flavour of the carnage on the screen. This almost playful manipulation of the ethnographic knowledge and ideological prejudices of the audience is particularly apparent in the case of an advertisement which recounts two biographies marred by the troubles. *I Wanna Be Like You* tells the stories of a father and son both of whom are drawn to the path of terrorism. One scene depicts the father driving an accomplice to an inner city bar where the latter proceeds to rake the occupants with gunfire. Most viewers would probably intuitively read this particular indiscriminate act of barbarity as being more characteristic of the strategy adopted by loyalist paramilitaries. The presumption of the audience that the character of the father is a loyalist is disturbed, however, by a further scrap of ethnographic detail furnished during the closing moments of the advertisement. As the narrative of *I Wanna Be Like You* proceeds we discover that the character of the son has also been drawn into the conflict which will ultimately claim his life. At the funeral of the younger man a black beret and gloves are placed on the lid of the coffin. This particular rite would be instantly recognised by the viewer as one associated with the republican movement.

Hence, the storyline constructed within *I Wanna Be Like You* recounts the tragic tale of a family drawn into a version of political violence that might be loyalist, republican or indeed even both. The uncertainties which the advertisement engenders among the audience advances a distinctive moral argument. The symmetry realised within *I Wanna Be Like You* provides a strident denunciation of all forms of paramilitary violence. That the father might be a loyalist killer and his son a republican killer suggests that loyalism and republicanism should be read as (im)moral equivalents. The biographies of the main characters insist, in other words, that all versions of paramilitary violence are equally odious.

The various advertisements that have been financed by the NIO provide spirited and often compelling condemnation of politically motivated violence. The particular understanding of terrorism that informs these features is, however, distinctly ideologically loaded. The advertisements conceived by McCann Erickson proffer harrowing portrayals of the violence that has been committed in the name of loyalism and republicanism. These scenes provide the viewer with a version of recent Northern Irish history which should be acknowledged as strictly partial. Clearly loyalists and republicans have engaged in many acts of brutality over the last 30 years. The eruption and longevity of the troubles cannot, however, be attributed solely to the conduct of private citizens. Over the past three decades the agents of the state have inflicted multiple forms of violence upon many elements of Northern Irish society. The advertisements that have been sanctioned by the NIO decline, as one would expect, to acknowledge the frequently repressive conduct of the security forces. None of the atrocities that have been committed in the name of the state during the present conflict makes an appearance in the brief films aired on local television. These strategic omissions imply that state violence occurs either infrequently or not at all.

The absence of images of state repression from the advertisements created by McCann Erickson serves a further important ideological function. Throughout the current troubles the British political establishment has attempted to appropriate a position of moral authority. Accordingly, the representatives of metropolitan interests have sought to distinguish between those forms of violence that are carried out in the name of the state and those perpetrated by private citizens. These moral distinctions have given rise to some of the linguistic conventions that structure official discourse on the conflict. While influential figures within Westminster, Whitehall and Fleet Street have been keen to denounce loyalists and republicans as 'terrorists' they have offered stern resistance to the suggestion that such designations might prove equally appropriate when referring to members of the security forces.

The ambition of the state to secure the moral ascendancy shapes the substance of the brief films that feature on *Advertising for Peace*. The advertisements that have appeared on local television seem to advance a vehement and universal condemnation of the terrorism that has thrived within recent generations of Northern Irish society. Closer examination of the broadcasts, however, reveals that only those acts of political violence committed by private citizens are in fact identified and denounced as terrorist.

The omission of images of state repression articulates certain convenient ideological assumptions (Schlesinger 1978, p. 205; 1991, pp. 1–2, 18). That there are no such representations would seem to suggest that those acts of violence that are committed in the name of the state should not, and indeed cannot, be understood within the moral and conceptual category of terrorism. The advertisements commissioned by the NIO endeavour, therefore, to confer a certain moral legitimacy upon the local security forces. The meanings that jostle within these broadcasts insist that the violence of the state cannot be conceived as the moral equivalent of that of the citizen. While loyalist or republican paramilitaries may be roundly denounced as terrorists, the same accusation cannot be levelled against the soldier or the police officer.

The various political advertisements that have appeared on television screens throughout Northern Ireland over the last decade collude, therefore, to construct a distinctive interpretation of the troubles. Viewers are invited to share the understanding that the Northern Ireland problem is one simply of the existence of a small band of unrepresentative men with a proclivity to acts of terrorism. The reading of the troubles that we encounter within the frames of *Advertising for Peace* should be vigorously contested. The advertisements financed by the British state employ an understanding of political violence that transpires to be partisan and partial. The viewer is informed that the terrorism that has befallen the six counties since the late 1960s has been the exclusive preserve of the citizen. In reality, however, much of the violence that has defined the recent history of the province has been perpetrated by agents of the state. The distinctly repressive policies that successive Westminster administrations have introduced have served enormously to nurture and sustain the conflict.

Whether those incidents of violence that bear the imprint of the state should be considered terrorist is of course very much a matter of ideological preference. One plausible reading would define terrorism as a strategy designed to engender fear among communities with a view to the advancement of given political interests. Were we to adopt this particular definition then it would become possible to speak of 'state terrorism'. Perhaps the pre-eminent concern that has detained Westminster during the troubles has been to resist the attempts of republicans to dismantle the United Kingdom. In seeking to preserve its own integrity the British state has inevitably resorted to the classic methods of counter-insurgency. The military strategy that the metropolis has adopted has been designed largely to erode popular support for

the 'armed struggle'. Members of the security forces have
habitually employed the substantial powers at their disposal to
intimidate the residents of nationalist districts. The logic of
counter-insurgency counsels that these practices will visit sufficient
hardship upon nationalists to persuade them to reject the
republican militants that live among them. The intimidation of
nationalist communities by the security forces has typically taken
the prosaic form of routine surveillance and harassment. It has also
assumed the rather more dramatic and draconian guise of assassination. On 30 January 1972 British paratroopers shot dead 13
unarmed civilians who had been part of a civil rights demonstration organised to protest against the introduction of internment
without trial. The infamous events on 'Bloody Sunday' provide
arguably the most cogent illustration of the state terrorism that has
occurred during the present conflict.

The advertisements that have appeared on local television over
the last decade insist that those loyalists and republicans who
engage in acts of political violence enjoy little support within the
communities they claim to represent. The construction of paramilitary activists as 'strangers' simply fails, however, to stand up
to critical scrutiny. Paramilitary organisations have a rather greater
popular appeal than the agencies of the British state are willing to
allow (Butler 1995, p. 165). The Provisional IRA would appear
to have particularly strong roots within the community out of which
it operates. The campaign of insurgence sustained by republicans
over the past quarter of a century would have been simply
untenable without enormous practical and ideological support.
The legitimacy which many nationalists have conferred upon the
Provisional IRA has found partial reflection in the electoral
performance of Sinn Fein. Since the early 1980s a substantial
minority of the nationalist community has proved willing to vote
for the political wing of the republican movement. In recent
elections held in Northern Ireland two out of every four nationalists have cast their vote for Sinn Fein. The impressive electoral
performance of Sinn Fein flatly contradicts the official contention
that republicans are unrepresentative of the communities in which
they are based. It would appear that loyalist combatants enjoy considerably less popular appeal than the Provisional IRA. The
electoral performance of those parties which are associated with
loyalist paramilitary organisations has lagged well behind that of
Sinn Fein. While loyalist paramilitaries attract less communal
support than their republican counterparts, they are, however, far
from being 'outsiders'.

What are the Consequences of Terrorism?

The political advertisements that have been funded by the British state endeavour to convey the full horror of terrorism. Many of the broadcasts contain distinctly graphic scenes of violence. Consequently some have had to be shown after the 9pm watershed in an attempt to ensure they are not seen by younger viewers. Particularly harrowing are a couple of lengthy advertisements which were launched in the summer of 1993. The film entitled *Lady* provides a slow-motion portrayal of a lone gunman firing repeatedly from close distance at another man who had been fishing in an idyllic location. *I Wanna Be Like You* shows in painful detail a gruesome figure riddling the interior of a bar which resembles many in working class districts of Belfast and elsewhere. The brutality portrayed within these and other advertisements appeals strongly to the senses and the emotions of viewers. Scenes of carnage interrogate the morality of those campaigns of violence sustained by republicans and loyalists. In the process they establish a distance between paramilitary activists and those communities out of which they operate.

The endless miseries occasioned by terrorism are held to have impacted with particular force within the domestic realm. The suffering which political violence creates has been felt especially by families. The persistence of the troubles has deprived countless people of their loved ones. An advertisement first broadcast in November 1993 – in the immediate aftermath of the slaughter at Greysteel and on the Shankill Road – seeks to illustrate the desolation that the conflict has brought into homes throughout Northern Ireland. *Next* boldly poses the question of whose father, brother, mother, sister, son and so forth 'will be next to pay the terrorists' price'. The advertisement concludes by encouraging viewers to reject terrorism before it 'destroys your family'.

The injuries that the troubles have inflicted upon Northern Irish families are intimated further in a pair of advertisements alluded to already. The film *Lady* opens with a glowing depiction of one of the central rites of family life. A pair of couples – one Protestant, the other Catholic – are shown at the altar declaring their marriage vows. Both appear to have lifetimes of happiness ahead of them. The anticipated domestic bliss of the happy couples is destroyed, however, by a single act of political violence. In a particularly explicit scene one of the bridegrooms murders the other on the verge of a beautiful lake. The remainder of the advertisement chronicles the misery which the murder brings to the spouses of both perpetrator and victim. The wife of the man slain is of course utterly distraught. The bride of the murderer appears almost equally bereft. One scene reveals her unable to sleep, the space in the conjugal bed beside her vacated by her incarcerated husband. In order to underscore the misery suggested by the visual imagery the narrator concludes the advertisement with the observation: 'Two women, two traditions, two tragedies. One married to the victim of violence, the other married to the prisoner of violence. Both scarred, both suffering, both desperately wanting it to stop.'

The suffering that political violence brings into the home is illustrated further by *I Wanna Be Like You* which at two and a half minutes represents an extraordinarily long advertisement. The central narrative of the broadcast maps out the relationship between a father and his son. The film opens in the Belfast of 1972 introducing a man in his twenties who has evidently been drawn into the violence that consumed the life of the city at that time. Convicted of political offences on two separate occasions the central character spends most of the next two decades behind bars and consequently never sees his young son grow to be a man. By the time the father is eventually released from prison he and his son are effectively strangers. Moreover, the younger man has clearly inherited an appetite for violence. In a scene towards the end of the advertisement we witness him viciously shooting another man who happens to be accompanied by someone who is presumably his son. By the end of the advertisement the violence of the son has caught up with him. The film concludes with images of his apparently estranged parents grieving at his graveside.

The advertisements financed by the British state counsel, therefore, that the actions of republican and loyalist combatants ruin lives and families. The violence that corrupts Northern Irish society precludes even those most mundane certainties that seemingly govern everyday existence elsewhere. The actions of terrorists ensure that young women are widowed, that men miss the formative years of their children's lives, that sons grow up to engage in the same carnage as their fathers, that the simple comforting rhythms of Christmas are disturbed. Terrorism prevents the 'normal'. It is, therefore, 'abnormal', 'aberrant', 'wrong' (Taylor 1996, p. 329).

What are the Causes of 'Terrorism'?

The criticism that commentators have levelled at coverage of the troubles with perhaps greatest frequency has been that the media have failed typically to locate the Northern Irish conflict within an appropriate political context (Curtis 1984, p. 107; Miller 1993a, p. 73; 1994, pp. 248, 251; Schlesinger et al. 1983, pp. 3, 37; Taylor 1996, p. 69). Reporters have often chosen to overlook the full complexity of the historical backdrop against which the present crisis has been played out (Schlesinger 1984, p. 224). Moreover, commentators have frequently tended to ignore the nuances of the particular social and political conditions that have sustained three decades of violence within the province. The perennial reluctance of the media to place the turbulent recent history of Northern Ireland within a suitable context has frustrated an adequate popular understanding of the nature of the troubles (Elliott et al. 1996, p. 341). Journalists and broadcasters covering the troubles often provide little real sense of the intricacies of the past or of the complexities of the present. As a result, individuals confronted with the latest sequence of dramatic developments unfolding within Northern Ireland often lack the detail necessary to understand fully the events that they are witnessing. It is hardly surprising, therefore, that people living outside the six counties frequently encounter the troubles as infuriatingly incomprehensible.

The propensity within the media to 'decontextualise' the troubles conspires to promote a distinctive reading of the Northern Ireland problem (Schlesinger 1978, p. 243). Commentators have often proved content to ignore the ambitions, anxieties and memories that have fostered conflict within the province. Viewers, readers and listeners are rarely informed of the complex reasons that have prompted thousands of ordinary folk to take up arms over the last three decades. The reading advanced within the mainstream media suggests that the troubles represent not the articulation of certain resonant but incompatible political ambitions but rather a meaningless sequence of indistinguishable and senseless acts of violence (Butler 1991, p. 111; 1995, p. 86; Kirkaldy 1984, pp. 184–6; Schlesinger 1978, p. 243; Schlesinger et al. 1983, p. 37; Ziff 1991, p. 192). Having denied that the Northern Irish conflict might possess a political rationale, conventional commentators seek to ascribe other, rather less noble motivations to those citizens who have assumed the status of combatant. Within the media the actions of loyalist and republican paramilitaries are often routinely dismissed as the expression of criminal conspiracy or primordial bloodlust (Elliott et al. 1996, p. 341; Miller 1993a, p. 74; 1994, pp. 2, 7; Schlesinger et al. 1983, p. 4).

The propensity of the media to overlook the particular political context within which the troubles have taken place finds reflection in the advertisement campaign initiated by the NIO. The various features financed by the state offer no real explanation of the political circumstances and aspirations that have encouraged the violence of the last three decades. An overseas visitor to the province who happened upon the advertisements would be brought no closer to an understanding as to why 3,500 Northern Irish people should have lost their lives to political violence. That the advertisements conceived by McCann Erickson choose to overlook the political context of the troubles suggests that there is none. The stories and images provided within these brief films imply that the violence that has been perpetrated by loyalists and republicans possesses no proper political rationale. The actions of paramilitary bodies are portrayed as profoundly irrational. Viewers are consistently offered the view that loyalist and republican combatants are driven by psychopathic impulses. Members of paramilitary groupings murder other human beings not to advance certain political causes but rather because they derive a perverse pleasure from the carnage that they create. In *Silence* we are informed that those have taken lives during the conflict 'laugh' and 'sneer with cruel contempt'. Perhaps the most chilling image to appear during the advertisement campaign is that mentioned earlier which features in *I Wanna Be Like You*. A bloated, repulsive figure stalks into a bar and rakes the room with gunfire killing those staff who are present. The expression of gleeful mania on the face of the lone killer offers a resonant image that suggests that the actions of republican and loyalist combatants are irretrievably irrational.

The construction of the terrorist as a mindless psychopath that we encounter within the advertisements under consideration represents one of the guiding themes of official discourse on the Northern Irish conflict (Schlesinger et al. 1983, pp. 37–8). In the course of the troubles a substantial element of the nationalist community has issued a systematic challenge to the ideological and military hegemony of the state. Throughout the 1970s and 1980s the formal response of the metropolis to the republican movement was one of apparently implacable opposition. British politicians of various dispositions insisted that Westminster would never negotiate with those who had violated the codes of democratic practice through acts of political violence. Assorted establishment figures expressed the belief – in public at least – that the military defeat of the republican movement was possible. The resistance that the state offered to the campaign of insurgence mounted by republicans found numerous ideological expressions. One of the more important was the systematic attempt to demonise the republican movement. The vilification of republicans was in part intended to undermine their status and morale. The depiction of republican combatants as soulless monsters served further to legitimise some of the more unsavoury actions of the security forces. Soldiers and police officers serving in Northern Ireland have on numerous occasions acted outside the boundaries of the law. Representatives of the metropolis have often sought to defend the indiscretions of the security forces with the contention that these occasional violations of civil liberties are justified by the pursuit of the greater good, namely the defeat of a republican movement that exhibits utter disregard both for human life and the rudiments of democratic practice.

The political terrain within Northern Ireland has undergone a remarkable transformation during the 1990s. In recent years the tone of official discourse has become discernibly more equivocal and conciliatory. The metropolis would appear to have abandoned the resilient fiction that the security forces have the ability to defeat the Provisional IRA. Moreover, senior British politicians who had insisted that it would 'turn their stomachs' to talk to terrorists have come to emphasise the wisdom of dialogue with the republican movement. The changes that have occurred to the disposition of Westminster during the present decade have necessitated an important reformulation of official discourse on the Northern Ireland problem. The political establishment has of late been keen to encourage dialogue between certain elements of northern society and others that have been closely associated with political violence. The evolution of the peace process has demanded a radical recon-sideration of official constructions of the terrorist. Evidently it would be unreasonable for the state to expect 'constitutional' politicians to enter into negotiation with individuals closely connected to paramilitary groupings if the latter were still being portrayed as amoral maniacs immune to the counsel of reason. The promotion of political dialogue has, therefore, required the metropolis to advance a rather different representation of the terrorist.

The shifting composition of official discourse is clearly evident within the sequence of films collated on *Advertising for Peace*. The political advertisements that have been broadcast in the province have tendered graphic depictions of the multiple horrors occasioned by terrorism. Some of the later advertisements that have appeared, however, have tended to supplement chilling images of the terrorist with other, more flattering forms of repre-

sentation. The tension between these two rather different constructions of paramilitary activists is especially prominent in an
advertisement on which we have pondered at some length already.
I Wanna Be Like You contains some particularly harrowing illustrations of the horror that arises out of terrorism. Ironically, the
same advertisement also provides a distinctly complimentary
portrayal of the terrorist.

The latter strand of the narrative is actualised through the representative of the second generation of terrorism. The son who
features in *I Wanna Be Like You* emerges as decidedly glamorous.
He seems attractive, cleancut and resolute. The particular incident
of violence in which the younger man is involved appears almost
heroic. That he carries out the act of terror seemingly entirely alone
constructs the son as the fearless maverick so beloved of
mainstream cinema. The tone and pace of the scene that depicts
the gruesome murder affords the culprit an ironic glamour that
will be instantly recognisable to an audience largely familiar with
the codes and conventions of the action movie.

The advertisements that the state has financed during the 1990s
have, therefore, occasionally offered distinctly flattering images of
those who seek its demise. The meanings that arise out of these
apparently ironic representations of the terrorist have been expertly
deciphered by the cultural analyst Martin McLoone (1993). In a
brilliant article that appeared in the autumn of 1993 McLoone
suggested that although initially puzzling the appearance of
glamorous images of terrorists on local television would in time
prove a logical development within the strategy of the British state.
He contested that the strategic interests of the metropolis
ultimately demand that the various fractious elements within
Northern Irish society should collaborate to negotiate a lasting constitutional settlement. The promotion of political dialogue would,
however, require the rehabilitation of those who have for decades
been associated with countless acts of violence. The unanticipated
transmission of flattering images of the terrorist should, Martin
McLoone insisted, be regarded in this particular light. According
to McLoone, the portrayal of paramilitaries as almost heroic figures
within certain television advertisements represents a virtually
subliminal endeavour on the part of the state to prepare the people
of Northern Ireland for the day when those hitherto denounced
as terrorists would take their place at the talks' table. The interpretation that McLoone advanced was quickly offered credence.
Within a few weeks of the appearance of his article in the local
periodical *Fortnight* the British government finally summoned the

integrity to announce that for the past three years it had been engaged in dialogue with the republican movement.

Does the Conflict Reflect Insurmountable Divisions among the People of Northern Ireland?

A fundamental modern concern of the British political establishment – as we have seen – has been to resist the suggestion that the conduct of the executive might have contributed to the crises that have consumed the recent history of Northern Ireland (Taylor 1996, p. 68). Those interpretations that have emanated from the metropolis have tended to advance exclusively 'internal' explanations of the Northern Irish conflict. Official discourse has sought to attribute the troubles solely to the resilient ethnoreligious antagonisms that exist among the residents of the six counties. Representatives of the metropolitan interest have insisted that the role that the state has assumed within the conflict has been the reasonable and neutral one of referee (Rolston 1991a, p. 152). Westminster has been animated by the dual concerns of maintaining some semblance of order while attempting to resolve the manifold disputes that pollute relations between the two communities. The valiant efforts of the executive have, however, been undermined at every turn by ancient rivalries. The engrained recalcitrance of the Northern Irish has frustrated all of the bold initiatives that the British government has introduced in pursuit of a political settlement.

The construction of the modern conflict in Northern Ireland as merely the latest instalment of an ancient tribal squabble constitutes one of the enduring themes of official discourse (Thomas 1991, p. 125). The contention that the troubles represent an expression of obdurate sectarian enmities has proved persuasive for many people living in other regions of the United Kingdom. The 'internal' reading of the Northern Irish conflict has, however, proved altogether less popular among the residents of the six counties. The people of the province understandably tend to take offence at the insistence that they are mindless bigots ensnared by antediluvian passions. It should hardly come as a surprise, therefore, that those political advertisements aired on local television have elected not to depict the troubles as the outcome of the timeless animosity of two 'warring tribes'.

The advertisements transmitted over the last decade have in fact explicitly acknowledged that the peoples of Northern Ireland possess substantially different ethnoreligious personae. The narratives developed within the advertisements have sought, however, to advance a distinctly pluralist understanding of the nature and significance of the ethnic heterogeneity that characterises the province. The advertisements counsel that the ethnoreligious distinctions prevalent within Northern Ireland do not imperil or impoverish those who live there. On the contrary, the divergent cultural identities that coexist within the province represent an invaluable symbolic resource that promises to enrich the lives of everyone. This faith in the potential value of plural ways of being is declared by an advertisement entitled *Yours and Mine*. The images presented within the film intimate the manifold identities and attributes associated with Northern Ireland. At one stage a war memorial appears followed immediately by a stained glass window depicting Saint Patrick. The juxtaposition of images that are associated more or less exclusively with the unionist and nationalist traditions respectively is perhaps significant. The association of these emblems suggests that the cultural identities from which they are drawn are equally valuable and should therefore be cherished equally. The coincidence, moreover, serves to understate the differences between the ethnoreligious personae that the images signify. The figures of the unknown soldier and Saint Patrick appear to feed into a plurality of signifiers and identities from which all the people of the province are entitled to select.

The pluralist reading of ethnoreligious heterogeneity forms an enduring theme of that particular version of official discourse that exclusively addresses the people of Northern Ireland. Agents of the state have sought increasingly to emphasise the enormous opportunities that are afforded by the existence within the province of an array of ethnic personae. Successive Westminster administrations have encouraged the divided communities that coexist in the region to examine and appreciate both their own cultural identities and those of others. Millions of pounds of taxpayers' money has been channelled through various bodies established to promote the diverse 'cultural traditions' that collide within Northern Ireland.

The pluralist interpretation that drives the cultural traditions agenda rests upon a fundamental misconception of the nature of the ethnoreligious identities that hold sway in Northern Ireland. Those who frame public policy would seem to regard ethnic personae as ontological formations that find expression through culture rather than politics. The distinctive practices that arise out of ethnoreligious sentiment are conceived as purely aesthetic forms that possess no political significance. Banging a lambeg drum or speaking the Irish language become essentially the same as playing bridge or arranging flowers.

The shortcomings of this analysis become apparent as soon as we acknowledge that the ambitions and practices that attend ethnoreligious feeling are in fact overtly political (English 1994; Finlayson 1997a; McGarry & O'Leary 1995b). Ethnic sentiment invariably encourages and endorses an entire range of political aspirations and imperatives. The essential problem that troubles Northern Ireland is that the particular political ambitions that arise out of the divergent ethnoreligious traditions that rub shoulders within the six counties frequently prove mutually exclusive. Nationalists who loathe loyalist parades do so not because they regard the gait and attire of Orangemen as peculiar, but rather because they believe that the rites of the marching season encode a vision of society that condemns the nationalist community to the status of subordinates. By the same token, many unionists harbour an antipathy for Irish speakers not because of the inflection of their diction but rather because the language is considered a central element of a political enterprise that aspires to terminate the Union.

The ethnoreligious personae prevalent within Northern Ireland emerge, therefore, as profoundly political. An appreciation of the 'political' nature of identities that are supposedly simply 'cultural' reveals the contradictions that gnaw at the heart of both official discourse and public policy. During the last decade in particular the British state has sought to acknowledge and encourage the cultural diversity that exists within Northern Ireland. The people of the region have been strongly encouraged to explore the multiple identities that shelter within the six counties. The conduct of the executive has been guided by a concern to promote that climate of tolerance that may ultimately sustain a political settlement. The promotion of cultural pluralism within Northern Ireland may, however, have transpired to be rather less beneficial than anticipated. The 'cultural traditions' strategy has often required the metropolis to endorse sentiments and rituals that express and prolong communal division. The various relevant agencies that have been established by the state have effectively offered material and ideological encouragement to versions of ethnoreligious identity that promote conflict in the province (Butler 1995, pp. 107–9). The erroneous counsel of pluralism would appear, therefore, to have prompted Westminster to embrace a strategy that has been deeply dysfunctional. In seeking to advance mutual understanding within the six counties the state may have in fact elected to promote those feelings and practices that produce and reproduce intercommunal mistrust.

While the advertisements produced by McCann Erickson do refer explicitly to the ethnic differences and divisions that mark Northern Ireland these tend to be understated. Rather greater reference tends to be made to that which the peoples of the province are believed to have in common. As Martin McLoone (1993) has noted, the advertisements endorsed by the state have a pronounced humanist subtext. The understandings advanced within the features privilege the common humanity of the peoples of the province. The divisions among the inhabitants of the region are considered trivial compared to their shared status as humans. The people of Northern Ireland should, therefore, strive to overcome the comparatively insignificant differences that arise out of ethnic feeling in order to embrace the transcendent identity of humanity.

The humanist subtext that runs through the advertisements under examination features especially strongly in *Citizens* which received its first airing in the spring of 1995. Against the musical backdrop of the Van Morrison composition *Brown Eyed Girl* the advertisement opens with the narrator explaining the social experiment that is about to be carried out. As the camera pans a spacious sunlit room the voiceover states that a group of 'citizens' from various ethnoreligious backgrounds have been selected in order to illustrate the differences between the people of Northern Ireland. It transpires that these specimens of northern citizenry are in fact a group of young children who gradually appear as the film progresses. The remainder of the sequence portrays the toddlers frolicking joyously with the various playthings that have been provided. The infants are evidently only too keen to interact with one another.

The message encoded within the frames of *Citizens* should be immediately transparent. Although drawn from divergent ethnoreligious backgrounds, the toddlers who appear in the advertisement are perfectly content to interact with one another. The infants are evidently blissfully unaware of the animosities that define the society into which they have been born. Only later will they come to encounter and presumably share the antipathies that animate their elders. The rapturous conduct of the infants offered as 'citizens' mercilessly exposes ethnoreligious animosity as a form of prejudice that is socially learned. The unbridled enthusiasm of children to mix with others from different communal origins reveals the hostilities prevalent within the six counties as unnecessary and unnatural. The narrative advanced within the advertisement implies that progress will require the people of Northern Ireland to unlearn those forms of prejudice with which they have been inculcated. If the citizens of the six counties are to enjoy a peaceful future they must reclaim that ability that they possessed as children to see beyond the trivia of communal affiliation in order to embrace the human essence of the alleged 'other'.

The humanist sentiments expressed within *Citizens* appeal strongly to the emotions and common sense of the viewer. The distinctive reading of social prejudice embedded within the advertisement proves unable, however, to withstand rigorous examination. The storyline that unfolds within *Citizens* strives to unmask the communal divisions within Northern Ireland as senseless and aberrant. The ethnoreligious enmities that fester within the six counties are portrayed as pathologies that betray the human intellect and tarnish the human spirit. The entirely arbitrary nature of the intercommunal rivalries that characterise the province ironically offer reason for hope. As products of the human mind, the ethnopolitical distinctions between the peoples of Northern Ireland are open to transformation by the human mind.

The humanist reading advanced within *Citizens* simply fails to grasp the genuine nature of social prejudice. The ethnoreligious enmities that brood within Northern Ireland are of course reproduced in and through the myriad thoughts and deeds of social actors. The communal divisions that characterise the province do not, however, reside solely within the 'hearts and minds' of individuals. On the contrary, the contours of ethnopolitical distinction are indelibly inscribed upon the entire social formation that obtains within the six counties. The resilient structures of Northern Irish society place enormous constraints upon the conduct and outlook of even the most reflexive social actors. The children who appear in *Citizens* will of course grow up to shape society and perhaps even to make history. They will do so, however, under circumstances that are not of their own making. The infants who frolic throughout the advertisement will inherit a social formation within which ethnoreligious affiliation exercises an important bearing upon the allocation of material and figurative resources. Some will have considerably better prospects of securing employment than others; some will enjoy rather more amicable relations with the security forces than others; some will receive greater respect for their cultural identity than others. The structures that regulate the six counties afford divergent opportunities and experiences to the different elements within the local social formation. These distinctions ultimately find expression at the level of interpersonal and intercommunal relations. Consequently, were we to reassemble the cast of *Citizens* 20 years after their original appearance we would probably witness an altogether less harmonious mode of interaction. In the course of the intervening couple of decades many of those who appeared in the advertisement would have encountered injustice, discrimination, violence from numerous quarters, residential segregation, cultural attrition and so on. These experiences which are commonplace within Northern Ireland will have inevitably nurtured feelings of suspicion and animosity towards representatives of the other ethnoreligious tradition.

The souring of relations among the original cast of *Citizens* predicted here intimates the shortcomings of the interpretation of the Northern Ireland problem advanced within the advertisement. Although seductive, the notion that the ethnoreligious hatreds endemic within the six counties represent mere pathologies should be sternly contested. The communal tensions associated with Northern Ireland should not be regarded simply as further evidence of the inability of the human mind to resist the most odious and senseless brands of prejudice. While the ethnopolitical antagonisms evident within the six counties are undoubtedly abhorrent they are not particularly aberrant. On the contrary, the animosities that pollute group relations represent *inter alia* an acknowledgement – albeit a rather distorted one – of the distinctive patterns of privilege, injustice and anxiety that attend the particular social formation that exists within the province. The prejudices prevalent within Northern Ireland should be regarded, therefore, as the product not merely of 'human agency' but also of 'social structure'. It is precisely because *Citizens* chooses to privilege the former while obliterating the latter that the advertisement fails so glaringly to understand the nature of intercommunal hatred in the six counties.

An understanding of the structural foundations of communal division suggests that the ethnoreligious antagonisms common to Northern Ireland are likely to prove considerably more durable than the makers of *Citizens* would have us believe. The reading advanced within the advertisement depicts the prejudices prevalent within the six counties as mere phantoms conjured up by the darker recesses of the human mind. The pursuit of social progress will, therefore, require a transformation of the outlook of people living in Northern Ireland. If the violence that has tormented the province is to end then the residents of the six counties must begin to eschew the simple atavistic pleasures of mutual intolerance and come to acknowledge and appreciate one another as fellow humans. A resolution of the Northern Ireland problem will be the outcome exclusively of human agency. This familiar interpretation proves to be substantially wide of the mark. The ethnoreligious enmities that ferment within the six counties reside not only within the minds of individuals, but also within the distinctive social formation within the shadow of which they are forced to construct their lives. Given the structural foundations of communal tension, the resolution of the conflict in Northern Ireland will entail a rather more radical social enterprise than those who scripted *Citizens* would appear to allow. The formulation of a viable political settlement will of course demand that the Northern Irish come to embrace new ways of thinking and feeling. A lasting peace will also, however, demand a radical transformation of the social structures that order the lives and minds of people living in the six counties.

The political advertisements broadcast over the last decade or so exhibit enormous confidence that the Northern Irish people will prove able to overcome their divisions because they share the *universal* identity of humanity. The sequence of advertisements insists further that the residents of the six counties will in time cast off the fetters of ethnoreligious animosity due to their common possession of the rather more *particular* status of Northern Irishness. The features aired on local television offer a profoundly idealised vision of Northern Ireland. Many of the advertisements broadcast present the province as a rural arcadia. *Yours and Mine* guides the viewer around a host of idyllic settings located throughout the province. We witness mountains shrouded in mist, golden sunsets, arresting round towers, traditional turf cutters at work, sumptuous lakes and so on. The advertisement concludes with a striking image of a young girl walking her dog on a beautiful deserted beach. The splendour of the regional landscape is held to find reflection in the nature of the Northern Irish people. Many of the advertisements seek to ascribe a distinctive character to the people of the province. The Northern Irish are portrayed as possessing a particular spirit and sense of humour. One advertisement presents a procession of school children drawn presumably from a range of ethnoreligious backgrounds who tell a series of lame jokes with a local flavour. The calibre of the Northern Irish finds confirmation in the host of celebrities that the six counties has produced. While the population of the province may be small, Northern Ireland has managed to produce numerous individuals who have made enormous contributions to the wider communities of sport and the arts. The advertisement entitled *Stars* identifies some of those figures born in Northern Ireland who have secured fame far beyond the six counties.

A central subtext of the political advertisements aired within the province has, therefore, been the attempt to formulate a distinctive sense of Northern Irishness. Many of the advertisements set out to illustrate that which the people of Northern Ireland are believed to hold in common. The citizens of the province are portrayed as sharing a distinctive, admirable character, humour and landscape. The existence of a particular Northern Irish identity is assumed to bode well for the future of the six counties. That the people of the region share numerous attributes may in time enable them to transcend the comparatively trivial divisions between them. As the yoke of ethnoreligious enmity is shed the residents of the six counties will come to realise their genuine personality within the common fraternity of Northern Irishness.

What is to be Done?

The British state has consistently striven – as we have seen many times already – to disseminate a particular, ideologically loaded interpretation of the origins and nature of the Northern Irish conflict. The official version of events contends that the troubles are the outcome of a criminal conspiracy orchestrated by a small self-appointed band of terrorists (Miller 1993a, p. 82). Although the overwhelming majority of the population desperately desires peace, the people of the province are nonetheless compelled to live under conditions of turmoil due to the actions and ambitions of those heartless 'men of violence' who exhibit consummate disregard for the conventions of democratic practice. This distinctly convenient reading of the troubles prompts official sources to propose an entirely predictable solution to the conflict in Northern Ireland.

The sequence of political advertisements that have been broadcast over the last decade counsel that the troubles will only end when 'the people' make explicit their presumed opposition to the men of violence. The relevant broadcasts advocate that ordinary folk should begin actively to oppose the presence and actions of those terrorists who have, in the words of *A Future* aired for the first time in January 1988, 'lived off their backs' for many years. Viewers are informed that everyone has an invaluable role to play in the 'fight against terrorism'. The disclosure of even the most apparently innocuous information can make a telling contribution to the quest for peace. One simple though hugely effective broadcast entitled *Jigsaw* seeks to illustrate that the resolution of individuals who will never meet one another to act upon their desire to end violence will generate a momentum that will eventually liberate Northern Ireland from the threat of terrorism. The narrative of the advertisement invites viewers to pass on to the relevant authorities anything that they might happen to know about acts of terrorism. As each potential fragment of information is named a piece of a jigsaw puzzle materialises on screen. The volume of information anticipated as forthcoming from the audience soon becomes sufficient to insert the final piece of the jigsaw. This moment of closure may figure the successful completion of a criminal enquiry into a particular incident of political violence. The completion of the jigsaw puzzle may also of course have a rather broader resonance as a signifier of the resolution of the entire conflict within the six counties.

The advertisements sponsored by the NIO insist that the people of the province can contribute most effectively to the elimination of terrorism by offering unqualified support to the security forces. In particular viewers are encouraged to assist the investigations of the RUC. Police officers appear within the advertisements with rather greater frequency than members of the British army. The principal focus upon the RUC accords with the strategy of 'normalisation' that the British state has pursued since the mid 1970s. Images of police officers pursuing their investigations are considerably more redolent of a 'normal society' than the sight of heavily armed soldiers patrolling the streets of the province.

The advertisements produced by McCann Erickson construct a distinctly flattering vision of the RUC. Members of the force are portrayed as courteous and friendly. One scene casts a female RUC officer in an inevitably maternal role ensuring that a distressed girl who has become lost is returned to the arms of her family. Another from *Time to Build* broadcast in the wake of the ceasefires of the late summer and early autumn of 1994 portrays a jovial policeman instructing a young boy in the appropriate techniques of baseball. While RUC officers may be thoroughly personable they are also tirelessly dedicated to the campaign against terrorism. Running through many of the advertisements is the conviction that the RUC constitutes a thoroughly professional force capable of meeting and ultimately eliminating the threat posed by the men of violence. Viewers who might be tempted to contact the confidential telephone service are reassured that any information they might be able to supply would be employed by a body of skilled professionals in the fight against terrorism. While tireless and ruthless in their pursuit of terrorists, members of the RUC are evenhanded in their dealings with the wider community. The advertisements are at pains to establish that the RUC serves every citizen without favour. Given that they are a thoroughly professional force striving to protect everyone, the RUC deserves the support of everyone (Miller 1994, pp. 7–8). The community presumed to exist between the police and citizens is underscored by the slogan that closes *Bleak* which was broadcast during Christmas 1991: 'Help the Police to Help Us All'.

The portrayal of the RUC contained within *Advertising for Peace* emerges as profoundly ideologically skewed. The notion that the RUC represents a politically neutral force with the potential to appeal to persons drawn from all walks of life simply fails to square with the realities of contemporary Northern Irish society. The police are deeply distrusted and disliked by many nationalists (Brewer 1992, pp. 64–5; Hayes & Brewer 1997). The alienation that exists among the nationalist community has been encouraged by what is widely believed to be active strategies adopted by the RUC such as routine harassment, shoot to kill and collusion with loyalist paramilitaries. Relations between nationalists and the police have been undermined further by the manner in which the security forces have elected to handle certain controversial Orange parades in recent years. The disaffection endemic within nationalist districts has been exacerbated particularly by the dramatic events at Drumcree over recent summers which prompted allegations that the RUC had capitulated in the face of loyalist intimidation and had dealt with local Catholic residents in an excessively draconian fashion. The widespread violence that erupted in the wake of each decision that the Orange Order should be allowed to process along the Garvaghy Road may be read as the verdict of nationalists on the contention that the RUC represents an impartial force able to serve the interests of all.

Antipathy towards the police does not of course exist solely within the nationalist community. Over the course of the troubles many working class Protestants have become alienated from the RUC. The crucial period that followed the introduction of the Anglo-Irish Agreement in 1985 witnessed a pronounced deterioration in relations between loyalists and the police (Cochrane 1997, pp. 154–5). At various stages RUC officers were verbally and physically assaulted by loyalists who denounced them as the enforcers of a political initiative that would prove deeply injurious to the interests of the unionist community. The enmity that many loyalists expressed towards the police in the aftermath of the Hillsborough Accord has never entirely dissipated.

What Would be the Benefits of Peace?

The media analyst David Miller (1993a, pp. 77, 95; 1993b; 1994, pp. 88–9, 151) has astutely observed that official discourse on the troubles has been guided by two seemingly contradictory themes. On the one hand, those charged with disseminating the outlook of the state have sought to illustrate the devastation that terrorism has visited upon Northern Ireland. The people of the region are frequently portrayed as hapless victims held to ransom by a small band of evil men (Miller 1993a, pp. 78–9, 82). On the other hand, figures within the metropolis have often been keen to represent the residents of the six counties as a 'community on the move'. The Northern Irish are presented as an industrious and talented people who are turning their backs on the men of violence and who desire only to live in a normal society (Miller 1994, p. 88).

The impressive series of television advertisements financed by the British state accommodates the tension between these dual themes. Many of the advertisements offer harrowing images of the conflict that has defined and defiled the recent history of Northern Ireland. The numerous acts of violence that are represented are, needless to say, perpetrated exclusively by the personnel of paramilitary associations. The countless incidents of repression for which the security forces have been responsible are blithely overlooked. The advertisements created by McCann Erickson also attempt to illustrate the 'bright side' of life in Northern Ireland. Many of the broadcasts endeavour to convey the idyllic splendour of the local landscape and to celebrate the admirably doughty character of the people of the region. These glowing descriptions of Northern Ireland suggest a burgeoning optimism concerning the future. Once the contagion of terrorism is eradicated the genuine nature and potential of the people of the province will be realised. With the onset of peace the Northern Irish will be able to offer full expression to those talents and traits that will facilitate the revival of an economy previously encumbered by persistent political unrest. The optimism that informs official discourse on the conflict finds reflection in a series of advertisements designed to intimate the more positive aspects of life in Northern Ireland. Each concludes with the following epilogue which is delivered in a rather unconvincing northern accent: 'Wouldn't it be great if it was like this all the time?'

REGULATING THE MEDIA

Possession of substantial resources has enabled the political establishment of the United Kingdom to disseminate its own particular reading of the violent events of the past three decades to a wide audience. Each year millions of pounds of British taxpayers' money is spent to ensure that the official version of the troubles appears frequently in the columns of the press as well as on television and radio programmes. The interpretation of the conflict offered by Westminster and Whitehall is one with which most readers, viewers and listeners are readily familiar. While the media output that official agencies have generated has been considerable, the bulk of the coverage of the troubles has of course originated from sources that are formally independent of the state. In the main, those individuals who have sought to read and explain the conflict that has unfolded within the six counties have not been public employees.

The institutions of the state have inevitably sought to influence and regulate the output of the formally independent media. Official agencies have attempted to constrain journalists and broadcasters through recourse to the legal system. Since the outbreak of the conflict Westminster has introduced and amended legislation with a view to preventing the transmission of information deemed detrimental to metropolitan interests. Among the most important legal powers at the disposal of the British state are those provided under the terms of the Official Secrets Act 1911 (amended 1989), the Prevention of Terrorism Act 1974 and the Emergency Provisions (Northern Ireland) Act 1978. The discussion that follows provides a brief exposition of the Official Secrets Act in order to illustrate the constraints that are faced by journalists seeking to cover the conflict in Northern Ireland.

The essential purpose of the Official Secrets Act is to prevent the disclosure of information that may prove damaging to official agencies and in particular to the military (Miller 1994, pp. 30–2). The provisions of the Act are of enormous assistance to a British state keen to conceal some of the more clandestine activities of the security forces within the six counties. The amendments that were introduced to the Official Secrets Act in 1989 made it even more difficult than hitherto for journalists to scrutinise the conduct of military personnel stationed in Northern Ireland. The revised Act states that it is a criminal offence for current or former members of the military to disclose information pertaining to their period of service in Northern Ireland. Journalists who publish the testimony of security force personnel without official permission are liable to prosecution. The restrictions which the Official Secrets Act places upon journalists, and indeed upon other citizens, are shown most clearly perhaps by section five of the legislation. This particular provision declares that it is illegal for anyone to pass on information covered by the Act in the knowledge that the disclosure may injure the 'national interest'.

Official concern that the media may infringe the national interest prompted the creation of the Defence, Press and Broadcasting Committee (Schlesinger et al. 1983, pp. 117–18). This body includes representatives of the media and issues notices stating whether journalists are allowed to cover particularly sensitive issues. In the specific context of Northern Ireland these 'D notices' typically refer to coverage of the intelligence services, photographs of military installations and discussion of surveillance operations. In principle, the existence of the Defence, Press and Broadcasting Committee should assist those individuals working within the media. The deliberations of the body provide guidelines which may enable journalists to avoid reportage which inadvertently results in legal charges. In practice, however, the operation of the D notice committee offers little real protection to reporters seeking to cover the thorny issues that attend the conflict in Northern Ireland. Even if granted clearance for their investigations journalists may still ultimately face prosecution under the terms of the Official Secrets Act.

Consideration of the Official Secrets Act demonstrates the constraints that journalists and broadcasters encounter when setting out to cover the troubles. The terms of the Act produce enormous difficulties for those who seek to report the frequently clandestine conduct of the security forces. Consequently, the military and intelligence services have often been able to operate beyond the field of vision that delimits public scrutiny. The provisions of the Official Secrets Act are far reaching and often lack clarity. These particular traits of the legislation ensure that journalists assigned to the troubles are frequently unsure as to the boundaries of legal reportage. The understandable anxiety to avoid inviting criminal charges has inevitably meant that many reporters covering the political crisis that has descended upon Northern Ireland have tended to err on the side of caution (Rolston 1996, p. 240; Taylor 1996, pp. 71–2).

'KEEPING THEIR OWN HOUSE IN ORDER': SELF-CENSORSHIP AND THE 'REFERENCE UPWARDS' SYSTEM

The various legislative measures that have been introduced over the last quarter of a century have placed considerable external pressure upon those seeking to cover the Northern Irish conflict. Journalists concerned with the troubles have also encountered constraints that originate within those organisations which employ them. The numerous organs of the broadcast media have proved especially willing to monitor those programmes which they have devoted to the political upheaval that has overtaken the province. The willingness of broadcasters to 'keep their own house in order' acknowledges at least two pertinent considerations.

First, radio and television journalists covering the troubles are forced to negotiate a political and legal minefield. The enormous and enduring popular appeal of television has ensured that this particular medium has been afforded especial importance and attention by the agencies of the state. The prospect of escalating political pressure and, in extreme circumstances, legal retribution has convinced senior figures within television companies that it would be prudent not to offend the political establishment more than absolutely necessary. An institution like the BBC which receives funds from central government would appear to have a particular instrumental incentive to avoid ruffling feathers within the corridors of Westminster and Whitehall. The likely repercussions of alienating the government of the day have often persuaded broadcasters to exercise considerable discretion when dealing with the issues that arise out of the troubles. The television and radio networks have chosen to regulate their own affairs rather than invite the state to impose ever more draconian constraints upon their freedom (Schlesinger et al. 1983, pp. 121–5; Schlesinger 1984, pp. 225–6).

Second, the strategy of self-regulation that the broadcast media have adopted could be taken to suggest that they are rather less than politically impartial. The television and radio corporations licensed to operate within the United Kingdom should not be dismissed as mere organs of state propaganda. Broadcasters have frequently advanced interpretations of the political violence that afflicts Northern Ireland which have diverged sharply from those endorsed by the metropolis. In spite of its intimate associations with the state the BBC has produced numerous programmes that have challenged the official version of the troubles. While broadcasters should not be condemned as mere servants of the political elite, nor should they be regarded as entirely politically neutral (Miller 1994, pp. 63–6). The understated political allegiances of the broadcast media have been revealed through their response to the troubles.

The political crisis that has unfolded within the six counties over the past three decades arguably resembles no other in which the British state has become embroiled in recent times. The troubles do not represent an abstract, exotic skirmish in some distant colonial possession. On the contrary, the conflict in Northern Ireland should be understood as a profound challenge to the integrity of the British state. The evident gravity of the political crisis that has overtaken the province has forced representatives of the broadcast media to take sides. Given a choice between the state and those who seek the dissolution of the state it was always inevitable that broadcasters would align with the former. The broadcast media have in the main lent their considerable weight to those public agencies seeking to resist republican insurgence. More often than not broadcasters have elected to endorse the central elements of the official reading of the conflict in Northern Ireland (Taylor 1996, pp. 67–8). The typically subtle political allegiances of the broadcast media were declared with unusual frankness by a senior figure within the BBC during the early stages of the troubles. It is often claimed that the ethos of the BBC privileges the principle of impartiality (Fisk 1996). Nonetheless, during 1971 the Chairman of the Corporation was moved to inform the Home Secretary that 'between the British Army and the gunmen the BBC is not and cannot be impartial' (Miller 1994, p. 28).

In the course of 1971 the already volatile political climate within Northern Ireland deteriorated yet further. As tensions between republicans and British soldiers degenerated into open warfare, both of the television networks operating throughout the United Kingdom sought to establish internal guidelines that would govern coverage of the conflict escalating in the six counties (Curtis 1984, pp. 173–7; Miller 1994, pp. 58–9; Schlesinger 1978, pp. xvi, 210–15; Smith 1996, pp. 30–1). The regulations devised by the BBC were formalised in a document published in the following year. The 1972 edition of the Corporation's *News Guide* stated that every programme pertaining to the six counties should be referred for approval both to the Controller of BBC Northern Ireland and to other senior Belfast staff. The Independent Television (ITV) network introduced a similar 'reference upwards system'. The regulations that were formulated stipulated that programmes concerning Northern Ireland should be referred to senior personnel within the relevant region of the ITV system and that advice should be sought from the particular company licensed to broadcast within the province, namely Ulster Television (UTV). The body established to oversee the federal ITV network, the Independent Broadcasting Authority (IBA), would retain the power to veto the transmission of items on the six counties produced by any of the regional companies.

The upheavals of the early 1970s, therefore, prompted television companies to establish explicit mechanisms designed to monitor and regulate their own coverage of the political crisis that had erupted within Northern Ireland. Over the years the reference upwards systems adopted by both the BBC and ITV networks have become increasingly restrictive. During the 1970s and 1980s the BBC reviewed its own guidelines on programmes devoted to Northern Irish issues. The effect of each revision was to erode further the autonomy of broadcasters seeking to analyse the complex political affairs of the province. The internal regulations published by the BBC in December 1989 revealed how watertight the reference upwards system operating within the Corporation had become. The *Guidelines for Factual Programmes* stipulate that individuals who intend to make programmes on Northern Ireland must consult both senior personnel and other BBC journalists operating out of the regional station in Belfast. These consultations must take place at *every* stage of programme development – from conception to completion (Miller 1994, p. 61; Rolston & Miller 1996, pp. 145–50). The regulations governing coverage of the province within the ITV network have become comparably demanding with the passage of time.

The increased stringency of the reference upwards systems operating within the British television companies is reflected in the sheer volume of the regulations pertaining to programmes that deal with Northern Ireland. The guidelines for reporting Northern Irish affairs that the BBC issued in 1972 stretched to only three paragraphs. By 1989 the advice that the Corporation dispensed to journalists intending to cover the province had expanded to fill almost eight pages (Miller 1994, p. 62). The increasingly rigorous systems of internal referral adopted by the British television networks have ensured that programmes on Northern Ireland are subject to much greater critical examination prior to transmission than those pertaining to any other issue. As Liz Curtis (1984, p. 177) has commented, 'no item on Northern Ireland, however minor, escapes scrutiny'. Even *publicity* for BBC programmes which deal with the affairs of the province must be referred in advance to senior administrators for approval (Miller 1994, p. 60).

The formal regulations adopted both by the BBC and the ITV network have had an important bearing upon television coverage of the conflict in Northern Ireland. The operation of systems of referral within the television companies has enabled a small band of senior personnel to exercise considerable influence over coverage of the troubles. Down the years television executives have employed their authority to terminate numerous projects pertaining to Northern Ireland at various stages of their development. Moreover, those situated at the apex of the reference upwards system have frequently used their editorial powers to alter the content of programmes dealing with the six counties. The conduct of senior personnel within the British television companies reveals a distinct political bias. Those programmes that have been aborted have typically offered criticism of British policy in Northern Ireland or provided a forum for the expression of republican views. Somewhat predictably, no programme that has sought to advance a reading of the troubles similar to those that emanate from Westminster and Whitehall has ever been refused an airing on British television (Curtis 1984, p. 91).

The copious guidelines that govern coverage of Northern Irish matters have also influenced the conduct of those who occupy less elevated positions within the television networks. Reporters keen to analyse the conflict in Northern Ireland invariably soon discover that they have embarked upon a precarious mission. It is rather more difficult to make programmes about the troubles than about virtually any other issue one could mention. Broadcasters who seek to cover the affairs of the province will often encounter at various stages obstruction, intimidation and explicit censorship (Curtis 1984, pp. 186–9). The incessant pressures that are associated with investigating the troubles have tended to erode the resolve of less dogged journalists. As a result, many items contemplating the political life of the province that are planned simply never materialise.

The regulations that the broadcast media have voluntarily adopted have acted to weaken the resolve of many journalists who were originally committed to providing critical commentary upon the political crisis in Northern Ireland. The guidelines conceived by the senior personnel of the radio and television networks have further ensured that many broadcasters who might otherwise have filed valuable reports on the troubles have preferred to overlook the province. As David Miller (1994, p. 58) has noted, the wrangles that have attended numerous programmes devoted to Northern Irish affairs have produced 'a substantial chill factor throughout the whole media system in Britain'. Those reporters who set out to analyse the political violence that scars the province will inevitably and repeatedly come into conflict with their superiors. Choosing to cover the troubles could hardly, therefore, be considered an astute career move. The intimidating climate of regulation that exists within the radio and television networks has induced a debilitating conservatism. Journalists who possess the potential to shed light upon the political affairs of the province often choose to channel their energies into other, less controversial issues. The conservatism that pervades the broadcast media inevitably ensures that many potentially important examinations of the Northern Ireland problem simply never reach fruition. Indeed, one distinguished veteran of the media wars that have been occasioned by the troubles – the journalist Mary Holland – has estimated that for 'every programme [on Northern Ireland] that gets banned, there are about twenty that don't get made' (Curtis 1984, p. 188).

The systems of internal referral instituted within the broadcast media established not only general guidelines concerning coverage of Northern Irish affairs, but also more specific regulations governing interviews conducted with individuals associated with paramilitary organisations. In 1971 the BBC reviewed its entire approach to the conflict in Northern Ireland. One of the principles established by the review was that interviews with 'republican extremists' should only be transmitted after 'the most serious consideration' (Curtis 1984, p. 179). The manner in which journalists chose to interpret this particular guideline ensured that interviews with those associated with the republican campaign of political violence effectively came to be prohibited. In principle it remained permissable to air the views of republican paramilitaries – at least until the issue of a Home Office notice in the autumn of 1988 to which we shall return later. In practice, however, only a handful of interviews with republican insurgents were ever actually broadcast (Rolston 1996, p. 242).

The restrictions under which BBC journalists operate were refined further in the aftermath of an important controversy that broke in the winter of 1979. While making a documentary on the republican movement, the crew of a current affairs programme filmed a roadblock which members of the Provisional IRA had established temporarily in the County Tyrone village of Carrickmore (Curtis 1996, pp. 273–4; Miller 1994, pp. 34–5). The actions of the *Panorama* team inevitably drew vociferous criticism both from sections of the press and from politicians of various hues. Those who had filmed the republican roadblock were alleged to have provided terrorists with the invaluable 'oxygen of publicity'. The controversy sparked by the Carrickmore incident led swiftly to retribution. The editor of the proposed programme on the republican movement, Roger Bolton, was sacked. Sustained protests orchestrated by the media unions, however, subsequently ensured that Bolton was reinstated. While Roger Bolton managed to survive the Carrickmore controversy the same cannot be said of his programme. The particular edition of *Panorama* which proposed to explore the republican mind was never in fact completed.

The considerable embarrassment that resulted from the events at Carrickmore prompted the BBC to strengthen its restrictions on interviews with those connected to paramilitary groupings (Maloney 1991, p. 12). The new guidelines were set out in the 1980 edition of the *News and Current Affairs Index*. The document stipulates that BBC journalists must seek and secure permission both to interview paramilitaries and to transmit any such interviews that actually take place. The guidelines established in 1980 adopt a rather broader definition of terrorism than had been employed hitherto. The restrictions outlined in the *Index* apply not only to republicans but also to members of loyalist paramilitary bodies.

The measures introduced by the senior executives of the radio and television companies created guidelines for journalists seeking to interview not only the perpetrators of acts of political violence but also those who sympathise with them. The principal focus of these regulations has inevitably been the republican movement. Programmes which contain the expression of republican sentiments are expected to strike an 'internal balance' (Curtis 1984, pp. 181–3; Rolston 1995b). The arguments advanced by republicans are invariably countered with the views of other political interests which are frequently those of the security forces. Representatives of the republican movement who are offered the opportunity to appear on television or radio can expect to come in for rather sterner treatment than other participants. Among the conventions that operate within the broadcast media is the conviction that republicans should be subject to hostile interviews. In the 1989 *BBC Guideline for Factual Programmes* journalists interviewing those associated with, or sympathetic to, political violence are encouraged to provide 'challenging questions' (Rolston & Miller 1996, p. 149). This euphemistic recommendation adverts to the hostile stance which broadcasters have often adopted when dealing with republicans in particular.

MEDIA BATTLES: 'REAL LIVES' AND 'DEATH ON THE ROCK'

The eventful recent history of Northern Ireland has both exposed and compounded the essential conservatism of the broadcast media within the United Kingdom. Broadcasters have often tended to embrace passively the central components of official discourse on the troubles. Furthermore, senior figures within the radio and television companies have on occasion used their considerable authority to suppress the expression of views that threaten to invoke the wrath of the state. Clearly the broadcast media do not constitute the seedbeds of sedition sometimes claimed by disgruntled figures who move within the corridors of Westminster and Whitehall (Schlesinger et al. 1983, p. 166).

Nonetheless it would be inaccurate simply to dismiss television and radio as mere organs of state propaganda (Miller 1994, pp. 259–60). Broadcasters have occasionally provided important critiques of the approach which the British state has adopted towards Northern Ireland (Schlesinger 1984, p. 224). In addition, the various ranks within the television and radio networks have at times found common cause in resisting the attempts of government to influence their coverage of Northern Irish affairs. The troubles have invariably provided the context within which the often rather broader tensions between the state and media have been played out. Two of the more important controversies that have inflamed tensions between journalists and the political establishment arose out of the television documentaries *Real Lives: At the Edge of the Union* and *Death on the Rock* (Butler 1995, pp. 70–6, 124).

The relevant instalment of the *Real Lives* series set out to capture the everyday existence of two diametrically opposed political figures. Both hailed from Derry and had become embroiled in the political crisis heralded by the seismic events that occurred in the city during the summer of 1969. *At the Edge of the Union* invites the viewer to follow Gregory Campbell of the Democratic Unionist Party (DUP) and Martin McGuinness of Sinn Fein through a range of public and private settings. The documentary was originally scheduled to be aired on the evening of 7 August 1985. A strategic intervention by Rupert Murdoch's *News Corporation* media empire a couple of weeks prior to broadcast, however, placed the documentary at the eye of a political storm that would delay its transmission for a number of weeks (Leapman 1996; Miller 1994, pp. 35–8). At a speaking engagement in the United States, Prime Minister Margaret Thatcher was asked by a *Sunday Times* journalist for her reaction to the imminent broadcast of a programme which included an interview with someone, namely Martin McGuinness, who has been occasionally identified as the Chief of Staff of the Provisional IRA. The indignation which Mrs Thatcher predictably expressed at the alleged prospect of the BBC providing a forum for terrorists prompted the state into taking action. The day after *The Sunday Times* carried an article damning *At the Edge of the Union* the Home Secretary Leon Brittan issued a formal letter of complaint to the Corporation. Although he had not actually viewed the programme, Brittan felt able to condemn the edition of *Real Lives* on the grounds that it would 'materially assist the terrorist cause' (Miller 1994, p. 36).

The political storm that gathered around *At the Edge of the Union* drew a swift response from the hierarchy of the BBC. Alarmed by lurid reports that had surfaced in the press, those individuals who had been nominated by the government to sit on the Corporation's board of governors took the highly unusual step of demanding to view the documentary prior to transmission. The governors of the BBC clearly concurred with the judgement of the programme which other establishment figures had arrived at, and duly banned it. This dramatic measure inevitably generated a wave of protest within the media community. The National Union of Journalists organised a 24 hour strike to mark the day on which the documentary had originally been scheduled for transmission. There were no national news bulletins broadcast on 7 August 1985 and the BBC World Service was forced to play music for the entire day (Curtis 1996, p. 279).

The radical and united action taken by journalists forced those members of the establishment who were intent on banning *At the Edge of the Union* to compromise. In early September a statement was issued jointly by the governors and managers of the BBC stating that the documentary would appear on television screens the following month albeit with three relatively minor amendments. On 16 October 1995 the controversial profile of Gregory Campbell and Martin McGuinness was finally broadcast and drew an estimated audience of almost five million people (Leapman 1996, p. 117).

The tensions between the broadcast media and the state that had become readily apparent during the *Real Lives* controversy would dramatically resurface three years later. On the afternoon of Sunday 6 March 1988 three members of the Provisional IRA were shot dead in Gibraltar by members of the Special Air Service (SAS) operating under cover. Initial media reports provided broadly consistent versions of the incident (Miller 1991, p. 69; 1994, p. 42; 1997). Journalists claimed that an IRA active service unit had planted an enormous bomb on the British colony. When confronted by military personnel and requested to surrender, the three IRA members made movements which suggested that they were about to detonate the explosives by remote control. Fearing enormous casualties the SAS personnel present were forced to take drastic action and shot the republicans dead. This particular version of events consistently reiterated by the media on the day of the shootings was promptly contradicted by a statement which the Foreign Secretary Geoffrey Howe delivered to the House of Commons the following afternoon. Howe disclosed that no explosives had actually been unearthed on Gibraltar and that those republicans who had lost their lives had in fact been unarmed (Bolton 1996, p. 119).

The parliamentary statement issued by Geoffrey Howe cast a rather different light upon the bloodshed that had occurred in Gibraltar the previous day. The revelations in the House of Commons suggested that the deaths of Mairead Farrell, Sean Savage and Danny McCann had in fact been summary executions. The possibility that the Gibraltar killings may have constituted acts of state terrorism drew the attention of some of the more enquiring minds operating within the broadcast media. In particular, it caught the imagination of Roger Bolton. A veteran of the struggles occasioned by the Carrickmore incident, Bolton had by the mid 1980s become editor of *This Week*, a current affairs programme produced by Thames Television for the ITV network. Members of the *This Week* team were despatched to Gibraltar to investigate the increasingly confused and suspicious circumstances that surrounded the deaths of the three IRA volunteers. The programme's researchers were gradually able to trace a number of local residents who provided versions of the killings which diverged dramatically from those advanced by the British state. Various eye-witnesses claimed that the three IRA members had not in fact been challenged to surrender but were nonetheless attempting to do so when they were fatally wounded by military personnel. These testimonies would form an important element of the documentary *Death on the Rock* scheduled for broadcast on 27 April 1988.

The investigation of the Gibraltar killings initiated by Roger Bolton was as a matter of course subject to internal vetting.

Members of the body that regulates the independent television network, the Independent Broadcasting Authority (IBA), were given a preview of *Death on the Rock* on the eve of transmission. The IBA representatives present gave their consent for the programme to be broadcast, albeit with three amendments to the narrative (Bolton 1996, p. 129). The documentary had survived the internal system of referral relatively unscathed. The makers of *Death on the Rock* were, however, to come under enormous pressure from various sources outside the independent television network.

The documentary crafted by the *This Week* team cast considerable doubt on the veracity of the official version of the Gibraltar killings. It was thoroughly inevitable, therefore, that the transmission of *Death on the Rock* would meet with fierce resistance from the political elite. Two days before the programme was to be shown the Foreign Secretary Geoffrey Howe telephoned the Chairman of the IBA, Lord Thomson. Howe requested that the IBA postpone the documentary until after the official inquest into the deaths on Gibraltar had completed its deliberations. Lord Thomson offered a robust riposte to the Foreign Secretary's request. Noting that *Death on the Rock* assembled information similar to that already widely reported in the press, Thomson refused to accept that the evidence presented in the programme might prejudice the findings of the official inquest (Bolton 1996, pp. 130–1). The documentary was broadcast without delay.

The transmission of *Death on the Rock* immediately led to an enormous political row. The vilification which the documentary attracted was orchestrated primarily by certain sections of the press. The 'quality' broadsheet daily newspapers in the main supported the decision of the IBA to allow the programme to be shown. The tabloids, in contrast, were implacable in their condemnation of *Death on the Rock*. The daily newspaper which enjoys the largest circulation within the United Kingdom offered the most vociferous condemnation of Roger Bolton and his colleagues. The interpretation offered within the columns of the *Sun* was that the programme provided succour to terrorists and thereby endangered yet further the lives of innocent civilians. The flavour of the newspaper's analysis was captured in the vivid headline of its editorial on the day after the broadcast of *Death on the Rock* which declared: 'Blood on Screen – Thames' cheap telly scoop is just IRA propaganda' (Bolton 1996, p. 134).

The makers of *Death on the Rock* came under further pressure from figures within the Conservative government. Both the Home

Secretary and the Secretary of State for Northern Ireland denounced the programme as 'trial by television'. The Prime Minister Margaret Thatcher was characteristically strident in her denunciation of the documentary. Asked whether she was 'furious' about *Death on the Rock* Mrs Thatcher replied that her feelings ran 'deeper than that' (Miller 1994, p. 46). According to the Prime Minister, the investigation of the Gibraltar killings through the medium of television marked an erosion of those same freedoms upon which the media depend. Government ministers sustained their campaign of attrition against the programme throughout the summer until the official inquest convened in September. When one of the eyewitnesses who contributed to *Death on the Rock* appeared to retract his evidence during the inquest Thames Television considered that it would be prudent to hold an enquiry into the documentary. The subsequent report produced by two senior legal figures vindicated the decision to broadcast the investigation of the Gibraltar killings. Although minor criticisms were raised, the enquiry praised *Death on the Rock* as the work of individuals who were 'experienced, painstaking and persistent' (Miller 1994, pp. 46–7).

EXPLICIT CENSORSHIP: THE 1988 BROADCASTING BAN

The ambition to establish the hegemony of official discourse creates a perennial dilemma for the liberal democratic state. The political elite possesses considerable authority to regulate the flow of ideas that occurs through the media. It would scarcely be prudent, however, for the executive to deploy the full range of powers at its disposal. The adoption of a draconian stance towards the media would of course imperil the indispensable liberal credentials of the state (Schlesinger 1991, p. 21). The introduction of explicit measures of censorship in particular would be widely denounced as an insufferable violation of the cherished ideal of freedom of expression.

The anxiety of the liberal democratic state to be seen as the guardian of certain essential civil liberties has often persuaded Westminster to refrain from imposing crude forms of constraint upon the broadcast media. The political establishment has preferred instead the rather more subtle strategy of seeking to exercise influence over broadcasters through informal channels (Miller 1994, pp. 13–14; 1996, pp. 245–7). Private correspondence and conversations with senior media executives have frequently represented the principal methods employed by state functionaries in an attempt to alter the content of television and radio programmes.

The culture of 'gentlemen's agreements' that has traditionally defined relations between the state and media within the United Kingdom has to an extent persisted into the modern period. Those government ministers who were, for instance, outraged by the documentaries *At the Edge of the Union* and *Death on the Rock* chose to explore private avenues of influence rather than use the considerable legal powers available. In the course of the 1980s relations between the state and media deteriorated enormously. By the middle of the decade elements within the BBC and the Conservative administration were repeatedly at odds with one another (Schlesinger et al. 1983, pp. 110–21). For all its apparent shortcomings the BBC has managed to retain a commitment to the principle of public service. It was consequently viewed with considerable suspicion by a Conservative administration betrothed to the dogmas of the free market. The widespread tensions simmering between state and media came to a head over the specific issue of covering the conflict in Northern Ireland (Schlesinger 1978, p. xvii). The heated disputes that attended *Death on the Rock* had evidently convinced influential players within the Conservative administration of the need to exert greater control over broadcasters. Within months of the transmission of the documentary the British state had broken with tradition and introduced measures that amounted to explicit censorship (Maloney 1991, p. 27).

On 19 October 1988 the British Home Secretary Douglas Hurd issued a notice that henceforth it would be illegal to broadcast the words of representatives of eleven named organisations or comments made in support of those organisations specified (Curtis 1996, p. 285; Maloney 1991, p. 9). The principal targets of the ban were republicans. Both the political and military wings of the republican movement featured among the eleven organisations identified. The introduction of the ban served to erode yet further the already meagre profile of Sinn Fein within the media. The Glasgow University Media Group analysed news reports carried on British television during the year that preceded the Home Office notice and the year which followed it. The information collated by the Glasgow researchers reveals that after the implementation of the ban the number of television appearances made by members of Sinn Fein declined by 63 per cent (Henderson et al. 1990, p. 37). The draconian measure introduced by the

Westminster parliament in the autumn of 1988 would appear, therefore, to have performed its intended task of marginalising alternative readings of the troubles even further within the mainstream broadcast media.

The announcement that interviews with those associated with political violence could no longer be transmitted produced a wave of protest from various quarters. The notice issued by the Home Office proved especially offensive to television and radio journalists. Broadcasters roundly decried the ban as an intolerable erosion of the elementary right of freedom of expression. Journalists further opposed the introduction of censorship on the grounds that the move would ultimately prove counterproductive. The Conservative administration reasoned that the liberal ethos that prevails within the broadcast media had conspired to provide a valuable forum for the expression of extremist views. The rationale of the ban was to deprive terrorists and their fellow travellers of this priceless 'oxygen of publicity'. The inferences which appeared to inform the Home Office notice generated substantial resentment among broadcasters. Journalists working in television and radio were keen to point out that they had in fact never actually offered terrorists an hospitable environment. Over the years only a handful of interviews with republican and loyalist paramilitaries had actually been broadcast. Moreover, representatives of political parties associated with paramilitary bodies had been allowed to make only infrequent appearances on radio and television. Indeed, in the year that preceded the announcement of the Home Office notice, the ITV network devoted a total of only four minutes to members of Sinn Fein (Butler 1995, p. 79). Representatives of republican and loyalist parties who actually managed to appear on television or radio were of course subjected to rather robust examination. The hostile treatment that had been meted out to extremists prompted broadcasters to contend that the ban imposed on interviews with terrorists would inevitably defeat the very purpose for which it had been designed. In future, those sympathetic to the tactic of political violence could no longer be subjected to demanding questions. More specifically, representatives of Sinn Fein would no longer be obliged to grope around for justification for the latest atrocity perpetrated by the Provisional IRA. The effect of the ban would not, therefore, be to deprive republicans of valuable publicity but rather to shelter them from the critical scrutiny of professional journalists (Miller 1994, p. 63).

The advent of the Home Office notice also generated enormous resentment within republican circles. Sinn Fein denounced the ban as an undemocratic measure which illustrated the lengths to which the British state was prepared to go in order to marginalise and demonise the republican movement. In the years that followed the introduction of the ban, representatives of Sinn Fein would frequently cite censorship as a fundamental cause of the flagging electoral fortunes of the party. This rather convenient line of argument barely stands up, however, to close examination. The electoral performance of Sinn Fein had in fact levelled out *before* the implementation of the Home Office notice. Moreover, it is unlikely that the operation of the ban would have significantly undermined the profile of Sinn Fein within republican districts where there exist channels of communication which circumvent the mainstream media.

Like many of the other legal provisions pertaining to coverage of Northern Irish affairs, the terms of the Home Office notice were unclear and consequently engendered a great deal of confusion among those affected by them (Maloney 1991, p. 29). Over time broadcasters developed strategies which enabled them to avoid the restrictions associated with the ban while remaining within the law. The ability of journalists to adapt to the new climate of censorship meant that the endeavours of the state to exclude dissenting voices from the airwaves became increasingly ineffectual. One of the strategies that broadcasters adopted was to employ actors and actresses to provide synchronised deliveries of statements made by representatives of the various organisations that had been proscribed. This particular practice ensured that for a time television viewers living in Northern Ireland were subjected to the distinctly bizarre experience of watching, say, Gerry Adams being interviewed while listening to comments which, although precisely the same as those he had uttered, were in fact being spoken by an actor who sounded not entirely unlike him. Public discourse in the six counties had been reduced to the curious simulacrum of ventriloquism (Butler 1995, p. 79).

The strategies adopted by broadcasters ensured that the strategy of censorship pursued by Westminster increasingly served little purpose. The radical political developments that overtook Northern Ireland during 1994 heralded the demise of the evidently ludicrous broadcasting ban. On 31 August of that year the Provisional IRA declared a cessation of military actions. Two weeks later the British Prime Minister John Major announced that the Home Office notice outlawing interviews with eleven named organisations would be rescinded (Rolston & Miller 1996, p. 235).

198 CONTEMPORARY NORTHERN IRISH SOCIETY

CONCLUSION

The political violence that has engulfed Northern Ireland in the recent period has represented a fundamental crisis for the British state. The guerrilla warfare skilfully practised by republicans has threatened to redraw the existing boundaries of the United Kingdom. The gravity of the crisis figured by the troubles has been reflected in the vigour of the ideological response of the state. From the outset, the British political establishment has been determined to ensure that a convenient interpretation of the violence within the six counties would prevail. The official version of the Northern Irish conflict has been disseminated through various channels. Increasingly the state has sought to wage the 'battle for hearts and minds' through the influential medium of television. The considerable energies of the metropolis have also been devoted to the suppression of other, dissident voices. The events of the last 30 years or so have identified the limits that are placed upon freedom of expression under liberal democracy (Schlesinger 1978, p. xvi). Officials have engendered a climate of apprehension which has dissuaded many broadcasters and journalists from critically exploring the issues raised by the crisis in Northern Ireland. The metropolis has further sought to eliminate alternative readings of the troubles through recourse to the considerable statutory powers at its disposal. The formal regulation of the media assumed an especially draconian guise in the autumn of 1988 with the introduction of what the seasoned journalist Ed Maloney (1991, p. 27) has characterised as the 'most stringent piece of peace-time censorship'.

The recent period of civil unrest in Northern Ireland has served to illustrate the capacity of the political class to regulate the flow of ideas and images within a supposedly free society. The era of the troubles has at the same time, however, intimated the limits of the ideological authority of the state. Since the arrival of troops on the streets of the province, the British political establishment has invested enormous resources in order to promote its own distinctive stance on the Northern Ireland problem. The official version of the troubles has, however, proved rather less than persuasive for various elements within Northern Irish society. Many people living in the six counties simply refuse to accept that the violence of the last three decades can be attributed solely to the primordial urges of a small cadre of criminal conspirators. The refusal of a substantial swathe of the local population to embrace the metropolitan reading of the Northern Irish conflict has found various expressions. The willingness of tens of thousands of voters registered in the province to endorse political parties that have been consistently demonised within the media provides arguably the most important confirmation that the British state has emerged from the 'propaganda wars' that have accompanied the troubles somewhat less than victorious.

5 Alternative Representations of the Conflict in Northern Ireland: Republican and Loyalist Murals

The British state clearly occupies a privileged position within the ideological contest that has attended the conflict in Northern Ireland. Official agencies possess considerable political and legal authority. The substantial powers at their disposal have frequently enabled the institutions of state to influence the manner in which the formally independent media have covered the conflict in Northern Ireland. The various bodies that are charged with articulating the metropolitan perspective upon the troubles are generously financed. In recent years these financial resources have been employed to produce an expensive series of impressive advertisements aired on local television. The political authority and fiscal strength of the state have ensured that the official version of the Northern Irish war is that which is heard with greatest frequency.

Perhaps the most significant of the ideological contests that define the Northern Ireland problem is that between the British state and the republican movement. In the course of the troubles republicans have mounted a military campaign that has threatened the very unity of the United Kingdom. Consequently, the principal target of the ideological apparatus of the state has invariably been that offered by republicanism. The energies of official agencies have been channelled overwhelmingly into attempts to discredit and demonise the republican movement.

The ideological onslaught that the metropolis has unleashed during the recent conflict has inevitably prompted the republican movement to advance its own distinctive interpretation of the troubles. Republicans have entered the ideological fray, however, on distinctly disadvantaged terms. Those agencies concerned with the dissemination of the official version of the Northern Irish war frequently enjoy budgets that run into millions of pounds and often employ scores of full-time staff. The resources at the disposal of the republican movement, in contrast, are decidedly meagre.

At present Sinn Fein runs three press offices in Ireland which are located in Belfast, Derry and Dublin. Each office has three full-time workers. In addition, both of the republicans who secured seats at Westminster during the 1997 general election – Gerry Adams and Martin McGuinness – have personal press secretaries. The public relations activities of the republican movement, therefore, hinge upon the efforts of only eleven people. None of these individuals actually receives payment. Consequently the republican 'propaganda machine' manages to operate on a shoestring budget. Those within the republican movement who are in the best position to judge are either unwilling or unable to provide a guesstimate of the figure that Sinn Fein spends each year in an attempt to air its views within the mainstream media. But it is probably reasonable to assume that the annual public relations bill that republicans currently face – at least within Ireland – falls short of the yearly salary of any of the senior advertising executives who have submitted successful tenders to the Northern Ireland Office.

The principal audience towards which republican propaganda has been directed has of course been the people of Ireland. Over the course of the troubles, however, republicans have become increasingly mindful of the importance of winning hearts and minds beyond the island. As a result Sinn Fein has gradually stepped up its efforts to court international opinion. For a time during the 1990s the party operated a lobby in Brussels. At present there are plans to open another in London. The willingness of Sinn Fein to take its argument to the very heart of metropolitan power merely underlines the enormous intellectual self-confidence of contemporary republicanism. The principal focus of republican efforts to engage international sympathy has, however, been neither Great Britain nor continental Europe but rather the United States. In recent years senior republicans have gone to considerable lengths to win friends within the Clinton administration. The ambition to court the political and corporate elite of the United States has led to the opening in Washington of a Sinn Fein office which presently has two full-time staff.

The comparative poverty of the resources available to republicans demonstrates the obstacles confronted by those seeking to offer an interpretation of the conflict different from that which enjoys the endorsement of the metropolitan power. Irish republicans and Ulster loyalists simply cannot afford to commission slick television advertisement campaigns nor to finance excursions to the province by overseas journalists. Financial constraints have compelled some of the players in the Northern Irish conflict to improvise. Republicans and loyalists have endeavoured to create and explore alternative channels of communication. One important improvised medium adopted by the combatants in the propaganda war is that of the gable wall. Those who have visited working class districts situated in urban centres throughout the six counties will have noticed that walls marking the end of rows of terrace houses often play host to dramatic images and slogans. Wall murals represent an important device through which republicans and loyalists seek to advance their own particular reading of the conflict in Northern Ireland (Rolston 1991b, pp. 122–4; 1992, p. i).

THE HISTORY OF WALL MURALS IN NORTHERN IRELAND

The tradition of political murals that exists within the northeastern counties of Ireland dates back to the beginning of this century. The earliest documented wall mural appeared on the Beersbridge Road in Belfast in 1908 (Rolston 1991b, pp. 20–1). Until quite recently the practice was associated almost exclusively with the unionist community. The murals created during the early decades of the century were invariably inspired by the events of the Williamite wars (Rolston 1991b, pp. 20–1; 1992, p. i). The image of King William III astride a white stallion crossing the River Boyne in triumph featured on gable walls in many working class Protestant districts (Jarman 1998, pp. 83–4). While the practice predates partition, the drawing of political murals grew in importance after the formation of the vulnerable constitutional entity of Northern Ireland (Rolston 1991b, pp. 18–24; 1992, p. ii). In the main, unionists had resolutely opposed the establishment of a devolved legislature to govern the six counties. With the passage of time, however, their resistance dissipated and unionists gradually came to identify strongly with the institutions of state that existed for half a century within Northern Ireland. The creation of wall murals became an important element of the cycle of rituals through which the devotion of Ulster Protestants to the Stormont regime was actualised and reproduced. In the month of July – at the height of the Orange marching season – new or restored murals would be unveiled, usually by some dignitary drawn from the Unionist establishment (Rolston 1991b, p. 24).

The triumphalist murals which appeared each summer in working class Protestant districts convey the mood of confidence that existed within the unionist community during the Stormont era. The historic image of King William of Orange vanquishing the papist forces of King James evidently encoded a rather more contemporary conviction that the Unionist regime would survive and prosper. During the 1960s, however, it became increasingly apparent that the seeming political confidence of Ulster Protestants was misplaced. The decade witnessed the emergence of oppositional dynamics within northern society which heralded the demise of the partition settlement. Caught between the forces of nationalist resistance and unionist reaction the administration at Stormont became increasingly vulnerable and ineffectual. As the political life of Northern Ireland degenerated into chaos in the early 1970s the demise of the devolved legislature became all but inevitable. In March 1972 Westminster eventually decided to prorogue Stormont and exercise its constitutional prerogative to govern Northern Ireland directly.

The political upheavals which attended the onset of the present troubles were deeply disturbing for many within the unionist community. The introduction of direct rule in the spring of 1972 proved especially traumatic because it entailed the abolition of institutions that had long since become essential to Ulster Protestants' understanding of themselves. The gradual erosion of political confidence among the ranks of Northern Irish Unionists was chronicled on gable walls. As the province degenerated into chaos the unionist tradition of mural painting went into marked decline (Rolston 1991b, p. 31; 1992, p. ii). During the troublesome decades of the 1960s and 1970s few new murals appeared within loyalist districts. Moreover, existing murals were rarely restored. The neglected portraits of King Billy crossing the Boyne, sabre aloft in triumph, left to deteriorate in many loyalist areas provided crude metaphors for the dramatic decline in the political fortunes of the unionist community.

By the 1970s the loyalist mural tradition appeared to have all but died out. Ironically, the practice would be revived with considerable gusto by northern Irish republicans (Jarman 1998, pp. 84–6). In the period which preceded the troubles there were very few murals to be found in nationalist areas (Rolston 1991b, p. 71; 1992, p. iii). Until the emergence of the civil rights movement at least, northern nationalists were typically politically subdued. The lack of political confidence within the Catholic population was reflected in the absence of dramatic and assertive representations of history and community on the walls of nationalist districts. The era of the troubles has marked a dramatic shift in the disposition of the

nationalist community. During the current conflict northern
nationalists have come to articulate their grievances and ambitions
with ever greater vigour. The growing cultural and political self-
confidence of Northern Irish Catholics have found vivid
confirmation in the assertive and increasingly sophisticated
iconography that adorns the walls of many nationalist areas.

The specific catalyst which inspired republicans to take up the
brush was the campaign instigated by prisoners convicted of
scheduled offences in pursuit of political status (Rolston 1991b,
pp. 76–80; 1992, pp. iii–iv, 1995a, p. i). The ultimate tactic
employed by prisoners resentful of their designation as 'ordinary
criminals' was to refuse food. The hunger strikes clearly struck a
cord with a large section of nationalist opinion. Republicans
quickly realised that gable walls provided a valuable and convenient
medium through which to promote the prisoners' cause. In many
working class Catholic districts there appeared scores of slogans
and images promoting the demands of the hunger strikers. Many
of the early republican murals were somewhat crude and were often
quickly replaced. As the years have passed, however, the skills of
republican muralists have improved quite dramatically.
Consequently, some of the more recent murals in republican
districts have tended to be rather more sophisticated and durable
than their predecessors.

The highly charged period of the hunger strikes produced a wave
of republican wall murals. In the few months that followed the
death of Bobby Sands – the first prisoner to refuse food – one
hundred appeared in Belfast alone (Rolston 1991b, pp. 99–100).
The surge of republican street artistry which occurred during 1981
could not of course be sustained. In the aftermath of the hunger
strikes the number of new murals appearing within republican
districts declined substantially. According to Bill Rolston (1991b,
pp. 103–4) Belfast republicans painted only five new murals during
1986. The number of murals appearing in republican areas would
appear, however, to have grown again in recent years. In part the
resurgence of republican mural painting may be attributed to the
significant political developments that have occurred over the past
few years. Various republican street artists have sought to place
their own particular inflection upon the fragile peace process that
has evolved within the six counties.

The adoption of the wall mural as an ideological device by
republicans has inevitably produced a response from the loyalist
community. In recent years there has been a sustained attempt to
revive the unionist tradition of mural painting. The revival of

political art within working class Protestant neighbourhoods also owes its origins to a period of political upheaval (Rolston 1991b, p. 43; 1992, p. ii). The signing of the Anglo-Irish Agreement in November 1985 marked a thoroughly traumatic moment for Ulster unionists. Under the terms of the Hillsborough Accord the Irish government was afforded a consultative role in the affairs of Northern Ireland. The provisions revealed more graphically than hitherto that the constitutional status of the province was far from secure. Fearful that the Union was endangered, unionists became more willing to reflect upon and articulate their beliefs. In the aftermath of the Anglo-Irish Agreement, elements within the unionist community began to advance a range of arguments through a variety of media. An important medium adopted by one particular version of unionism was that of the gable wall. Many of the initial murals that appeared within working class Protestant districts were exceptionally crude. The standard of loyalist murals has, however, gradually improved with time.

The political mural represents an important, inexpensive ideological device at the disposal of various parties to the conflict in Northern Ireland that possess comparatively meagre financial resources. The dramatic images which adorn the gable walls of many working class districts throughout the six counties establish lines of communication both within and without the community. The declarations encoded within the wall murals seek to mobilise the local population over certain issues and in support of particular political enterprises. Street artists also endeavour to address a rather wider audience. Wall murals communicate distinctive inter-pretations of the Northern Irish conflict to individuals who may never actually visit the streets where they exist. The arresting iconography to be found on gable walls in many working class districts of the six counties has drawn considerable attention. Television journalists recounting the latest spate of political violence in Northern Ireland will frequently deliver their monologues in front of republican or loyalist murals. Lengthy articles in the Sunday supplements of the quality press will often feature engaging representations of the selfless sacrifice of the Easter Rebels or the triumphant majesty of King Billy navigating the Boyne. The attentions of the media have ensured that the creations of local street artists have enjoyed widespread exposure. Many of those who have never set foot in Northern Ireland will be nevertheless readily familiar with the political iconography that appears within urban centres throughout the six counties. The political mural represents, therefore, an effective medium for the dissemination of alternative versions of the conflict in Northern Ireland (Rolston 1991b, pp. 122–4; 1992, pp. vii–viii).

The discussion that follows analyses the distinctive readings of the troubles that are advanced within republican and loyalist murals respectively. At various stages we shall turn to examine the contents of specific political murals. Hopefully the descriptions offered will prove sufficient to convey the substance of the particular paintings under consideration. The more assiduous reader may, however, wish to see with his or her own eyes the political art discussed in the text. Most of the murals that are analysed in this chapter have been selected from two fascinating collections of photographs gathered by the sociologist Bill Rolston. The relevant volumes are entitled *Drawing Support: Murals in the North of Ireland* (1992) and *Drawing Support 2: Murals of War and Peace* (1995). Those murals that are mentioned in the chapter which have been drawn from either text are identified by means of a simple code. The prefix of the code alludes to the book in which a specific mural appears. The letter 'A' refers to *Drawing Support* while 'B' pertains to *Drawing Support 2*. The number featured in each reference corresponds with the plates which appear in the texts. Hence, for example, the code B63 identifies plate 63 collected in *Drawing Support 2* which you will find on page 33 of that particular volume.

IRISH REPUBLICANISM

Those Catholics who live in Northern Ireland are frequently characterised as the 'nationalist community'. There exists among the ranks of northern nationalists substantial common ground. Most nationalists living in the six counties share at least some level of commitment to the ideal of a united Ireland. While nationalists hold certain interests and ambitions in common they do not, however, form an homogeneous cultural or political bloc (McGarry & O'Leary 1995a, pp. 13–61; Ruane & Todd 1992b; 1996, pp. 87–103; Todd 1990). There are profound ideological differences among Northern Irish Catholics which are typically characterised through the distinction between 'nationalists' and 'republicans' (Ruane & Todd 1992a, pp. 189–94; 1996, pp. 71–4). The fissures existent within the nationalist community emerge partly out of divergent understandings of the origins of the Northern Ireland problem. Republicans invariably attribute the conflict in the province to the machinations of imperial Britain.

While nationalists concur that the neighbouring island has frequently exercised a malign influence over Irish affairs they also tend to acknowledge rather more fully the salience of the profound ethnoreligious distinctions that exist within the six counties. Divergent readings of the origins of the troubles lead the different elements within the nationalist fold to contrasting prescriptions for the ills of contemporary northern society. Republicans typically insist that armed force is required if Ireland is to be released from the snares of British imperialism. Nationalists, in contrast, tend to the view that political and cultural dialogue are necessary to promote that tolerance and understanding which may enable the divisions within the province to be resolved.

The discussion which follows sets out to examine that particular variant of Irish nationalist ideology which is usually designated as 'republican'. The ideological formation of Irish republicanism has prompted the campaigns of violence that have been sustained over recent decades by a range of paramilitary organisations, the most notable of which is of course the Provisional IRA. The concerns and ambitions of republicans find political expression principally through the agency of Sinn Fein. Recent electoral trends have underscored that there exists within the nationalist community a substantial minority of republicans. The spate of elections that have attended the Northern Irish peace process have witnessed a marked upsurge in support for the political wing of the republican movement. In June 1998 the province's voters were invited to employ the procedures of proportional representation (PR) to nominate delegates to a legislative assembly conceived within the Good Friday Agreement. Forty five per cent of nationalists who cast votes in the election offered Sinn Fein their first preference. The burgeoning electoral performance of Sinn Fein may be regarded as testimony to the capacity of republicans to articulate and represent the interests of a substantial swathe of nationalist opinion. In recent times the republican movement has sought to advance its own distinctive interpretation of the turbulent events that have consumed the six counties through a variety of means. One of the simplest and most effective media which republicans have employed in order to propagate their particular reading of the Northern Irish conflict is that of the wall mural.

Like the bearers of the other ideological traditions that exist on the island, Irish republicans often exhibit a heightened sense of history. Certain figures and moments drawn from the distant past exercise a palpable influence upon the manner in which republicans seek to understand and reconfigure the present (Ruane

& Todd 1991, p. 30). Intellectuals within the contemporary republican movement, moreover, routinely acknowledge the resonance of ideas that initially came into circulation in the latter stages of the eighteenth century. This apparent reverence for the past has served to promote the view that republicans essentially are slaves to history. Critics have at times asserted that republicanism represents an ideological programme that is incapable of renewal. According to Liam Clarke (1994, pp. 76–82), for instance, the violence that has consumed Northern Ireland since the late 1960s has had little meaningful impact upon the republican perspective. An unwillingness or inability to think beyond the presumed verities of inherited dogma has, Clarke insists, condemned recent generations of republicans to repeat the mistakes and relive the traumas of their predecessors.

The portrayal of republicanism as a moribund ideological formation offered by commentators like Liam Clarke fails to accommodate important developments that have unfolded over the past decade or more. A sense of history has of course played an important role in defining the contemporary republican movement. The distinctive philosophical orthodoxy bequeathed to the present generation of republicans has exerted considerable influence upon the manner in which they think and act. Moreover, the current leadership of Sinn Fein has remained perennially anxious to keep faith with the central tenets of the republican tradition – or at least to appear to do so. In many respects the ideological disposition of the contemporary republican movement marks a continuity with the past. The outlook of modern republicanism has also, however, undergone considerable change (Shirlow & McGovern 1998, pp. 171–2). Since the mid 1980s influential figures have sought to re-evaluate many of the interpretations, aspirations and methods that have been conventionally associated with the republican movement. This critical introspection has given rise to a series of ideological shifts that have been largely quite subtle. The ageless imperative of maintaining unity has ensured that the process of republican revisionism has unfolded at a fairly sedate pace. While gradual and understated, the changes that have occurred within republican thinking have been hugely significant nonetheless. In the absence of republican revisionism the current peace process that seemingly promises to transform the political life of the province would simply have been inconceivable.

Contemporary Irish republicanism represents an essentially vibrant and dynamic ideological construct. Reverence for the past has not prevented republicans from refining their readings and ambitions according to the more immediate demands of the present (Tonge 1998, pp. 135–7). The evolution of republican ideology over recent years has been chronicled on gable walls situated in working class nationalist districts. The seismic political developments that have unfolded during the 1990s have occasioned subtle though significant changes in the substance of republican murals. Street artists sympathetic to the republican cause have inevitably sought to place an ideologically convenient 'spin' upon the various events and processes that constitute the peace process. The murals that have appeared in poorer nationalist neighbourhoods over the past few years provide, however, a strictly partial account of the ideological development of contemporary Irish republicanism. The past decade has borne witness to a significant dilution of the moral certainty of the republican movement. The equivocation that has grown within republican discourse inevitably finds little expression in the murals that have appeared during the period of the peace process. The ambivalence that has come to define the disposition of republican intellectuals scarcely translates of course into the strident images and slogans that are the preferred style of the street artist. The ideological trajectory that the republican movement has followed over recent years would appear, therefore, to have signalled the limits of the mural as a discursive tool.

REPUBLICAN MURALS

The arresting images and slogans that have been devised by republican street artists assemble narratives of the turbulent recent history of the northeastern counties of Ireland. The iconography that appears on gable walls in many working class nationalist districts mirrors the concern of republicans to legitimise their own aspirations and actions and to invalidate those of other political interests. The narratives constructed within republican murals ask and answer a sequence of at least six questions.

Who Are We?

Among the fundamental preoccupations of all ethnic and national communities are definitions of selfhood. Ethnic and national identities are assembled out of that complex cluster of meanings that arise when the question is issued: 'who are we?' Intellectuals and others actively seek to establish the membership and character of the ethnie or nation. Moreover, ethnic and nationalist sentiment frequently prompts a concern to demarcate the boundaries between those who belong to the 'imagined community' and those who are designated as 'other'.

The ethnic nationalist preoccupation with selfhood has animated recent generations of Irish republicans. The political mural offers republican activists an important means through which to name the affective community to which they consider themselves to belong. The imagined community that engages the devotion of republicans is of course that delimited by the geographical boundaries of the island. The definition of selfhood to which republicans subscribe is that signified by the term 'Irishness'. Nationalists living in various settings seek to articulate their sense of being through the physical representation of the geopolitical entity to which they belong or aspire to belong. Irish republicans are no exception. The island of Ireland appears with predictable regularity in the work of republican street artists (B50). These 'map images' provide a simple though potent figurative expression to an ontological state that remains essentially ineffable.

The work of the American anthropologist Allen Feldman suggests that the representations of the island that appear in republican murals serve further important ideological and perhaps psychological functions. In his seminal text *Formations of Violence* Feldman (1991, pp. 21–45) contends that an adequate understanding of the nature of the conflict in Northern Ireland requires an appreciation of the processes through which social space is organised and disrupted. The violence that erupted in the late 1960s initiated a reconfiguration of the ethnopolitical geography of the six counties that has been especially pronounced in the context of Belfast. As patterns of residence throughout the city have become increasingly segregated, the local has come to be constructed as the site of refuge. The complex social and political processes that have redefined Belfast have served to ensure, however, that the integrity of communities has been incessantly disrupted. Agents of state violence, paramilitary assassins and urban planners have routinely violated the sanctuary that has been created out of communal space.

Feldman suggests that the upheavals that working class nationalist communities have experienced during the troubles provide the context within which we must interpret the substance of the republican imagination. The representations that are favoured by republican street artists inevitably overlook the ethnopolitical demarcations that exist within the island. The iconography that exists within working class nationalist districts depicts Ireland simply as a single geopolitical entity. These 'map images' offer an accessible 'metaphor of spatial integrity' to people who have endured persistent 'displacement and fragmentation' (ibid, p. 45). The work of republican muralists may be read, therefore, as an endeavour to reconstruct a sense of sanctuary within communities that have been routinely violated by multiple intruders.

The political murals that have appeared within republican districts advance visions of Ireland and Irishness that are inevitably deeply flattering. Ireland is held to be both ancient and mystical. Numerous republican murals delve into Celtic mythology. The belligerent figure of Cuchalainn appears with some regularity (B40, 53). An astonishing painting located in the Ardoyne district of North Belfast provides a heavily stylised portrait of the mythological queen Eire (B103). The spiritual majesty of Ireland is considered to be mirrored in the distinctive landscape of the island (B102). Republican street artists portray Ireland as a place of singular beauty. The particular idealised vision of the island that republicans construct suggests an apparent paradox. The republican murals that have been created over the past couple of decades have appeared typically within urban centres. Republican artists have tended, however, to overlook the immediate context of their work in order to construct the nation as a rural arcadia. Consequently, gable walls in republican neighbourhoods blighted with the multiple indices of urban deprivation have often provided a canvas for romantic images of sumptuous landscapes.

The elevation of the rural that we encounter within republican murals proves rather less anomalous than may appear at first glance. Those notions of beauty that have secured greatest currency within the prevailing social order frequently skew towards the rural. The senses of social actors are often cultivated to appreciate the topography of the land rather than that of the street. Like other nationalists, Irish republicans have sought to tap into popular sensibilities that pertain to the aesthetic. Dramatic landscapes are particularly likely to accord with existing definitions of the beautiful – even those in the possession of individuals more readily familiar with the contours of the urban.

The rural images that appear in republican murals serve further to suggest the ancient status of the Irish nation. The distinctive features of the landscape often seem timeless. It is hard to imagine that a particular mountain or river has not always been there. The bucolic scenes that have been created by republican artists intimate an ambition to confer upon the Irish nation the immutable status of the 'natural'. The romantic imagery that characterises many republican murals clearly implies that Ireland is, to employ a familiar colloquialism, as old as the hills.

The idealised images that inform the work of republican street artists are of course far from unique. Veneration of the landscape represents a trait common to many versions of nationalism. English nationalists have consistently imagined themselves as the blessed residents of a rural idyll (Loughlin 1995). The rural inflection of English nationalism was illustrated by the musings of the hapless former Conservative Prime Minister John Major in the early 1990s. In a speech that was greeted with widespread derision Major identified England as a place where one could relax and sip warm beer as the sun's last rays illuminate the closing overs of a cricket match on the village green. Rural images are also essential to that variant of nationalism that persists south of the Irish border. An increasingly substantial majority of the population of Ireland live in towns and cities. Irish nationalism has remained largely impervious, however, to the process of urbanisation. The denigration of the urban within the Irish nationalist imagination is revealed in the final sequence broadcast every evening by the national television station *Radio Telefís Eireann* (RTE). The substance of the closedown transmission offers a stirring declaration of the spirit of the nation. Predictably, the images that are presented throughout the sequence are overwhelmingly rural and organic. Those who seek the meaning of Irishness are invited to observe the spider weaving its web or the river following its course.

Irish republicans share with many other nationalists a propensity to construct the nation as a maternal figure (Rolston 1991b, p. 91). The imagery of 'Mother Ireland' is readily familiar to those weaned on the diverse traditions of Irish nationalism (O'Malley 1990, pp. 118–19). An ambition to feminise the nation has influenced the nature of republican iconography (Sawyer 1998). Numerous murals attest to the resonance that the notion of Mother Ireland has attained within the discourse of modern Irish republicanism. An arresting modernist image which adorns a gable wall in the Short Strand district of east Belfast casts Ireland in the heavily stylised guise of a woman (B101). The feminine imagery that pervades republican iconography represents in part an astute ideological device (A81, B103). The maternal metaphor that republicanism has adopted defines the relationship between nation and nationals as that between a mother and her children. The abstraction of Ireland is portrayed as a fount of maternal love. The unflagging devotion that Mother Ireland offers demands that the children of the nation respond in kind. The love of the Irish nation is merely an echo of the love which one has for one's own mother. The 'Irishness' felt by the people of Ireland constitutes, therefore, a sentiment that is inevitable, reasonable, above all 'natural'.

The essential splendour of the landscape of Ireland finds echoes in the nature and experience of its people. The Irish are held to comprise an ancient national community. Various murals seek to establish the connections between the present inhabitants of the island and previous generations. References are made both to fragments of Celtic mythology and to rather more literal incidents from Irish history. In part the murals seek to establish the authenticity of the nation. The Irish are portrayed as a people who have been defined by, and survived, the eventful passage of history. Irishness constitutes an identity that was formed neither yesterday nor the day before. These declarations of longevity seek to confer upon the Irish nation a certain moral authority. Feelings of Irishness have been sustained through many centuries and, therefore, possess a moral value greater than that of other ontological states of rather more recent vintage.

The ancient peoples of Ireland are depicted as having their own distinctive character and culture. Those chosen to represent the Irish nation are occasionally portrayed as possessing a marked physical beauty and strength. Some of the murals seek to intimate those cultural practices specific to the Irish. An impressive mural to be found in the Ardoyne district portrays an Uileann piper playing on the slopes of Belfast's Cave Hill (B102). Another represents various Gaelic sports which are proclaimed to be 'part of our heritage' (B104). The diverse images that appear within working class nationalist districts throughout the six counties underscore the growing cultural self-confidence of contemporary republicans (Ruane & Todd 1996, pp. 199, 319). The substance and form of the wall murals suggest that republicans possess a secure sense of who they are and where they come from.

What is the Problem?

The ideological formation of republicanism constructs Ireland as ancient, spiritual and beautiful. While the Irish nation may be majestic it has nonetheless been plagued with misfortune. The

(Porter & O'Hearn 1995, pp. 132–3; Ruane & Todd 1996, pp. 101–3). In recent years, however, an important refinement of republican orthodoxy has taken place. Since the late 1980s intellectuals within the republican fold have come to reflect anew upon the interests and intentions of the metropolis. These reflections have encouraged a belief in the *possibility* that it may no longer be in the interests of the British state to retain jurisdiction over a swathe of Irish national territory. Revisionist republicanism has increasingly come to the view that Britain *might* actually wish to leave Ireland voluntarily (Shirlow & McGovern 1998, pp. 176, 178, 184).

The refinements that have occurred within republican thinking of late have found some expression through the medium of political murals. In the main, muralists have kept faith with the familiar tenets of republican orthodoxy. Many of the murals that have appeared recently in working class nationalist communities denounce Britain as an imperialist tyrant. These traditional representations have been supplemented increasingly, however, with other, less harsh, images of the neighbouring island. The breathtaking political developments that culminated with the declaration of the first IRA ceasefire in the summer of 1994 provided republican street artists with considerable inspiration. Some of the republican murals that have been created during the peace process have sought to imagine the end of British jurisdiction over the six northeastern counties of Ireland. An especially memorable one provides a humorous depiction of a British soldier being escorted home across the Irish sea by a cooperative dove. Murals like these articulate sentiments that are of course rather old. The spectacle of a British military withdrawal clearly signifies the realisation of the traditional republican ideal of Irish unification. The newer murals also reveal, however, the revision that has occurred within contemporary Irish republicanism. Images of troops leaving Ireland intimate that there exists among some republicans a belief that the intentions of Britain may *perhaps* have begun to change in ways that will prove ultimately conducive to their political enterprise.

What Has Been the Response of Republicans?

Within the republican perspective the imperial designs of Great Britain are identified as the principal source of the problems that have plagued Ireland down the centuries. Republicans are often keen to point out that the 'natural' response of the Irish to the countless injustices of British imperialism has been to resist (Clarke 1994, p. 79; Rolston 1991b, pp. 96–7). Irish national resistance has at various stages of history assumed a military form (B52). A central concern of republican street artists is to establish the military credentials of the Irish people (A77, 107). The occasional appearance of the mythological character Cuchulainn declares that there has always been a 'warrior tradition' on the island (A 76, 108, B40). The frequent references that are made to the events of Easter 1916 illustrate the willingness of the Irish people to take up arms against British imperialism even in the face of superior military strength (A82, 83, 108, 112).

The tradition of armed resistance which Irish republicans believe exists on the island has of course been revived in recent times. Since the late 1960s republicans have striven to dismember the United Kingdom through force of arms. The absolute centrality of the 'armed struggle' within the strategy of the modern republican movement is underlined by a dramatic painting to be found in Strabane, County Tyrone (B39). Against the backdrop of the Irish tricolour an armalite rifle is formed out of the phrase 'tiocfaidh ar la' or 'our day will come' – the most famous and resonant rallying cry of modern republicanism. The sentiments of the mural issue a declaration that the objectives of the republican movement will be achieved through recourse to political violence. The particular form of the painting suggests, however, that the armed struggle represents rather more than a mere tactic. That the armalite rifle appears independently of any human being may perhaps be considered significant (Rolston 1995a, p. iv). The figurative autonomy of the weapon suggests that the military dimension of republican strategy possesses a value and logic of its own. It implies, in other words, that political violence represents not only a means but an end.

The sustained violence that has marred the recent history of Northern Ireland has come from many quarters. The republican movement, however, has been responsible for considerably more deaths during the troubles than any other single party to the conflict (McGarry & O'Leary 1995a, pp. 51–3). The creators of wall murals have been concerned to legitimise those acts of violence that republicans have committed over the last three decades. The actions and personnel of the Provisional IRA are predictably portrayed as heroic and glamorous. An ambition to glorify the armed struggle would appear to have animated those who drew an early republican mural in Rockville Street in west Belfast (A67). The relevant painting depicts the Provisional IRA in a manner reminiscent of those comic books devoted to war which have been read by generations of schoolboys. Fatigues strategically unbuttoned to reveal a manly torso, the lantern jawed republican combatant stares, noble and unblinking, into a distance which presumably heralds the dawn of the new Republic. The text which annotates this bold caricature of republican pugnacity rehearses the familiar mantra: 'They may kill the revolutionary but never the revolution'.

While muralists often romanticise the actions of republican militants, they also attempt to highlight the enormous costs that have arisen out of the armed struggle (Clarke 1994, p. 80). The paintings etched on gable walls throughout nationalist districts often serve as memorials to republicans and others who have lost their lives during the troubles. An especially skilful mural drawn during 1987 in Belfast's Springhill Avenue pays homage to the eight members of the Provisional IRA who died in that year at the hands of the Special Air Service (SAS) in Loughgall, County Armagh (A106). The distinctive style of the artist responsible portrays those who lost their lives as though figures from Irish mythology. The multiple meanings of the traditional celtic cross that dominates the visual memorial attests to the confluence of the secular and the sacred within republican iconography.

A motif that runs through the work of republican street artists is that of sacrifice (Rolston 1992, p. v). Fallen republican combatants are regularly portrayed as having selflessly offered their own lives in order to defend and enhance those of the wider community. The theme of sacrifice that embroiders republican murals is occasionally signified through explicitly religious imagery. Some of the early murals that were inspired by the hunger strikes had overtly religious overtones (Rolston 1991b, 79–81; 1992, p. iv; Ruane & Todd 1996, pp. 96, 110–13). The portraits of republican inmates fasting for the status of political prisoner occasionally bore a close resemblance to the popular western image of Jesus Christ. Some republican murals portrayed the hunger strikers clutching rosary beads and under the protective gaze of the Virgin Mary (A 57, 58).

Some critics have read a great deal into the religious sentiments that often seem to inform republican philosophy. The political scientist Padraig O'Malley (1990), for instance, has argued that the references to the sacred that exist within republicanism underline the intimacy of the relationship between religious feeling and ideological formation within Northern Ireland. The path-breaking work of Allen Feldman which we encountered earlier suggests a rather different interpretation. Feldman offers the view that republicans elected to employ occasional religious imagery in the period of the hunger strikes for reasons that were largely strategic. Catholicism offered a moral discourse and figurative code readily familiar to those beyond the prison gates whose support was vital if the demand for political status was to be realised. The adoption of religious images by republicans during the hunger strikes represented a largely pragmatic move to engage hearts and minds within the wider nationalist community and beyond. The references to the sacred that sometimes materialise within republican ideology should be read, therefore, as emblematic less of republicans' religious sensibility than of their appreciable discursive fluency.

The armed struggle has conventionally represented the central element of the wider republican strategy. Republicans have been keen to establish, however, that their objectives can also be advanced through means other than political violence. Numerous republican murals contest that British imperialism may be resisted through a variety of means. One that appeared in Derry in the mid 1980s presented several hands holding aloft assorted artifacts that promise to prise Ireland from the grip of the metropolitan power. The object held highest is inevitably that of the rifle. The other hands that are visible, however, clutch props associated with rather more peaceful modes of resistance – a brush, a spanner, some pencils, a book and a placard. The mural clearly seeks to suggest that the painter, the mechanic, the student, the intellectual and the street activist all have roles to play within the republican movement that are at least of comparable importance to that of the IRA volunteer.

These representations of the diverse forms through which resistance to British rule has been realised reveal a concern to locate the republican movement firmly within the wider nationalist community. Over the course of the troubles the British state has – as we witnessed in the previous chapter – consistently sought to denounce republicans as parasites who enjoy little popular support. The political mural has offered republicans an invaluable medium through which to resist this central strand of official discourse. Street artists have been keen to portray republicanism as a genuinely popular movement. The actions of the Provisional IRA are of course routinely identified as being of paramount importance. But republican murals insist that the armed struggle represents only one, albeit crucial, element of a broader republican strategy that demands the endorsement and participation of the entire community (Shirlow & McGovern 1998, p. 173, 179).

Republican murals frequently attempt to illustrate the various, often seemingly innocuous, contributions which ordinary working class nationalists have made to 'the cause' (A89). A gable wall situated in Derry's Rossville Street recounts the sequence of violence during August 1969 that has come to be known as the 'Battle of the Bogside' (B63). A local youngster sporting a gasmask appears preparing to hurl a petrol bomb at the lines of the loathed auxiliary police force, the 'B-Specials'. Other republican murals make reference to the opposite end of the age spectrum. An especially memorable one located on the Donegall Road in Belfast depicts the mundane scenario of a pair of old women barracking a bemused British soldier (B70). This prosaic act of resistance is considered to encapsulate 'the spirit of freedom'. The images that have been devised by mural artists seek to advance an inclusive vision of the republican movement. Republicanism is presented as a philosophy and strategy that is capable of accommodating everyone. Even the very young and the very old have a part to play in forging the new Republic. The work of republican muralists may be understood in part, therefore, as an endeavour to nurture and appropriate a sense of community among working class nationalists.

The rich iconography present within many poorer Catholic districts offers a highly idealised vision of the republican movement. Republican combatants are portrayed invariably as noble and fearless individuals who have risked their own lives to defend a grateful wider community. These romantic images conveniently overlook, however, some of the more unsavoury aspects of the armed struggle. Republicans have usually taken a rather dim view of political dissent. The efforts of the republican movement to maintain hegemony within their traditional strongholds has often led to considerable loss of life.

In the course of the troubles republican activists have become heavily involved in regulating the conduct of those they claim to represent. The particular political conditions that obtain within the six counties have served to ensure that conventional policing essentially does not exist within many working class nationalist districts. Fear of attack means that the RUC often cannot function adequately in those areas where republicans are influential. Furthermore, many working class nationalists who have been victims of crime simply refuse to seek the assistance of an official police force which is considered partisan and which has at times sought to recruit criminals as informers. The absence of 'normal' policing in many nationalist communities has created a vacuum which the republican movement has come to fill. Republicans have sought to eliminate criminal and deviant behaviour through methods that often border on sadism. In recent years 'punishment attacks' upon alleged miscreants have become an increasingly familiar aspect of life in areas where the republican movement holds sway. The horrific injuries which republican activists have routinely inflicted upon petty criminals and juvenile delinquents among others hardly square with the romantic images of noble soldiers beloved of mural artists.

Over the course of the present conflict the strategy of the republican movement has become increasingly sophisticated. The odious communal violence that heralded the onset of the troubles inevitably strengthened the hand of those traditionalists who asserted the primacy of the armed struggle. Although initially outnumbered the harrowing events of the early 1970s quickly ensured that the 'provisionals' became the dominant element within the republican fold. Throughout the rest of the decade the considerable energies of the republican movement were channelled overwhelmingly into military operations against the security forces. The narrow focus of republicans upon the armed struggle began to dissolve in the late 1970s, however, as the prison protests started to gather steam (Shirlow & McGovern 1998, pp. 174–6). The campaign to secure political status revealed more clearly than hitherto the appeal that republicanism has for many Northern Irish nationalists. The popular support mobilised around the hunger strikes laid the ground for the emergence of Sinn Fein as a mainstream political force. Throughout the early 1980s republicans registered remarkable electoral advances. Nonetheless, by the end of the decade the shortcomings of the dual strategy of the 'armalite and the ballot box' had become readily apparent. Although the Provisional IRA remained undefeated there appeared little prospect that political violence would prove sufficient to force a British withdrawal. Sinn Fein had, moreover, signally failed to make advances beyond the established centres of republican support.

The evident impasse of the late 1980s encouraged republicans to reflect upon issues of strategy. As the process of revision has progressed, elements within the republican movement have come to question the received wisdom of the armed struggle. Some republicans would seem to have arrived at the view that Britain will not, and indeed cannot, leave Ireland in the face of force. This

has been consistently prevalent within republican discourse? What are the liberties that will obtain within the new social order which republicans aspire to build? Would the citizens of the New Republic be entitled to freedom from the insidious exploitation of multinational capital, for instance? Hardly. The moral imperatives in which they trade cannot conceal that republicans possess only a limited sense of the course that national development would follow after partition. It would seem that republicans have persisted for three decades with a campaign of political violence designed to establish a social order of which they have only the vaguest of understandings.

Throughout the modern conflict in Northern Ireland the tone of republican discourse has been decidedly strident. Republicans have typically insisted that only the establishment of a united Ireland would be sufficient to persuade them to end their campaign of political violence. With the passage of time, however, the demands of the republican movement have become rather more circumspect. Over the last decade the view has grown among republicans that the unification of Ireland represents an unlikely prospect in the near future at least. This unpalatable realisation has nurtured the suspicion that the armed struggle serves little purpose other than mere performance.

The growing circumspection of the republican movement has offered invaluable encouragement to the Northern Irish peace process. During the present decade republicans have come to act upon their gnawing suspicion that political violence has become essentially futile. The ceasefires declared by the Provisionals have eased the assimilation of republicans into the political mainstream. In spite of enormous odds, republicans and other delegates to political negotiations convened in Belfast managed in the spring of 1998 to arrive at a series of proposals which may provide the foundation for a durable constitutional settlement. The endorsement which Sinn Fein eventually offered the Good Friday Agreement reveals just how far republicans have travelled over recent years. For all its nuance and ambivalence, the deal brokered under the guidance of George Mitchell clearly envisages that Northern Ireland will remain within the United Kingdom for quite some time to come. The current generation of republicans would seem, therefore, to have settled for substantially less than the cherished ideal of a united Ireland.

The pragmatism that has advanced within contemporary republicanism has had little apparent bearing upon the work of political artists. Recent republican murals have continued to issue undiluted demands for the unification of Ireland. The essential orthodoxy of republican street artists has led some to advance rather tendentious interpretations of those events and processes that have charted the peace process. The initial ceasefire which the IRA declared late in the summer of 1994 inspired a wave of political murals. In some of these the decision of republicans to lay down their arms was portrayed as heralding the imminent creation of a united Irish state (O'Reilly 1998, pp. 57–8). British troops occasionally appeared trudging home beneath banners wishing them a safe journey (B 67, 68, 69).

The somewhat disingenuous readings of the peace process advanced within certain political murals suggest that there exists substantial distance between the rhetoric and the practice of contemporary republicanism. Republican politicians would seem to have grasped that the six counties will probably remain under the jurisdiction of Westminster for some time to come. Republican muralists, on the other hand, would appear to have retained the conviction that the creation of a united Irish state in the near future remains within the realm of the possible. The seeming inability of political art to capture the drift towards pragmatism within the modern republican movement may be explained in at least three ways.

First, the political mural offers a text for the projection not only of the realistic but also of the fantastic. The images that appear on gable walls primarily articulate what republicans want rather than what republicans are willing to accept. The substance of contemporary murals serves to underline, therefore, that many working class nationalists remain attached to the ideal of a united Ireland even if some have come to the realisation that the institutions of partition are likely to remain in place for the foreseeable future.

Second, the particular interpretations of the peace process that have been developed within recent republican murals should be acknowledged as forms of political intervention (Shirlow & McGovern 1998, p. 182). Republican revisionists have of course embarked along an extremely perilous path. The current leadership of Sinn Fein has assumed a direction that has infringed some of the central tenets of republican orthodoxy. Inevitably, the revisionist turn within republicanism has generated substantial resistance and dissent. The narratives that have been constructed by political artists seek to defend the republican leadership in the face of considerable internal criticism. Recent republican murals have portrayed the peace process as a sequence that promises to lead ultimately to the unification of Ireland. The leaders of Sinn

Fein are considered, therefore, to have guided republicans in a direction that remains altogether consistent with traditional ideals. Although wildly implausible, the readings of the peace process that have been offered by republican street artists represent a vital strategic attempt to hold together a political movement that has in the past been given to bloody schism.

Third, the disjuncture that seems to exist between the rhetoric and practice of contemporary republicanism may be attributed to the limitations of the wall mural as a political text. For much of the present troubles the republican movement kept faith with a fairly straightforward political strategy. The orthodox republican demand that Britain should withdraw from Ireland readily translates into those bold emblems and texts that provide the substance of the political mural. In recent times, however, the outlook of the republican movement has become rather more subtle and sophisticated. The strategy which republicans have embraced during the 1990s has been marked by a growing ambivalence and willingness to take the longer view. Some of the changes that have occurred within republican thinking of late have hardly been conducive to the substantial, though ultimately limited, talents of the street artist. Ambivalence draws upon sentiments that cannot find adequate expression through the stirring but often crude iconography of the political mural. The traditional republican slogan of 'Brits Out' seems appropriate etched on a gable wall. The more recent equivocation that 'Britain should join the ranks of the persuaders in order to encourage the unionists that their future lies outside the United Kingdom and in the interim should establish consociational institutions which possess an inherent dynamic that promises ultimately to produce a unitary Irish state' would clearly seem out of place.

What about the Protestants?

The present generation of Irish republicans consider themselves heirs to an ideological tradition which is both secular and inclusive. A central article of faith within republicanism asserts that all of those who live on the island of Ireland are members of the same national community. Republicans insist that their actions are motivated by concerns which transcend sectional interests. The campaign of resistance to British rule which they have sustained is held by republicans to advance the interests of all of the diverse peoples of Ireland. With the establishment of the Republic, a new social order will emerge that will cherish equally the rights and identities of all of the children of the nation – whether Catholic, Protestant or Dissenter.

The secular idealism that informs republican philosophy contrasts starkly with many of the frequently unpleasant realities of contemporary life in the six counties. The contention of the republican movement that the boundaries of the island coincide with those of the nation has encountered stout resistance from the unionist tradition. Ulster Protestants have simply refused to accept that they are members of the Irish nation. These ontological disputes arise out of ethnic distinctions which have over the past three decades produced sustained political violence. In the course of the troubles more than 3,000 people have died at the hands of individuals whom republicans would insist are in fact fellow Irish men and women.

The republican tradition attributes the deadly divisions that fester among the children of the nation to the malign influence of British imperialism. Republicans argue that the political establishment in London has sought to retain authority through fostering distinctions among the Irish people (Rolston 1995a, p. v). The metropolitan power has conferred comparative material and cultural advantage upon those Protestants who congregate in the northeastern counties of Ireland. Ulster unionists have been encouraged to believe that they are both different from, and better than, the other residents of the island. The cultural supremacism considered to contaminate the unionist mind finds especially insidious expression for republicans in the ritualised practices of the Orange Order.

As the peace process has progressed, the attentions of the republican movement have turned away from military operations and towards other more popular forms of political agitation. The shifts that have occurred recently within republican strategy have fuelled further the controversies that surround the loyalist 'marching season'. In the last few years the residents of certain nationalist districts have heightened their efforts to ensure that the Orange Order does not process through their midst. Although a matter of some conjecture, the role that republicans have played in mobilising communal opposition to Orange parades would seem to have been substantial. The residents' groups that have been formed within many nationalist communities in recent years have sought to air their grievances through a variety of means. The political mural has inevitably provided an important medium through which the case against contentious Orange processions has been articulated (Jarman 1998, p. 87). In recent summers the international media have been drawn to Northern Ireland by the parades issue. Viewers and readers living abroad have become familiar with some of the murals that have been created by opponents of particular Orange processions. The images of Orangemen trampling over the bodies and rights of local residents that adorn gable walls in districts like the Lower Ormeau Road in Belfast or the Garvaghy Road in Portadown have skilfully translated the grievances of nationalists and republicans into forms that are readily intelligible to an international audience.

The republican tradition counsels that the metropolitan ambition to foster division within the Irish nation finds further pertinent expression in the guise of military strategy. Republicans regard the British state as an expansionist force which has throughout history sought the military conquest of Ireland. In the republican mind the desire of the metropolitan authority to retain influence within Ireland has made inevitable the lamentable violence that has marked the last three decades. During the early stages of the troubles Westminster had sought to resist the rising tide of republican insurgence through the deployment of the British army. The ideological costs associated with the deaths of British soldiers soon became sufficient, however, to alter the course of official military strategy. In the mid 1970s British troops gradually began to be replaced with other members of the security forces who had been recruited within the six counties. This significant revision of security policy served merely to sharpen further the enmities that exist between the principal ethnopolitical traditions in Northern Ireland.

The strategy of Ulsterisation has inevitably substantially altered the composition of the fatalities that have arisen out of republican violence. Since the mid 1970s those who have lost their lives at the hands of the republican movement typically have not been British soldiers. Rather, they have been in the main Northern Irish Protestants who have joined the ranks of the Royal Ulster Constabulary (RUC), the Ulster Defence Regiment (UDR) and the Royal Irish Regiment (RIR). Over the last couple of decades, therefore, the ambition to liberate the Irish nation has frequently prompted republicans to take the lives of people whom they profess to regard as Irish men and women (McGarry & O'Leary 1995a, p. 53).

The republican movement has sought to interpret this particular deadly paradox as an unfortunate necessity of war. The orthodox republican reading of the troubles suggests that the political violence that has defined the recent history of the six counties represents the inevitable outcome of the British presence in Ireland. In the republican imagination Britain constitutes an imperial monster which has sought down the centuries to retain authority over Ireland through expressly draconian means. Resistance to British imperialism has, therefore, necessitated recourse to violence. In seeking to terminate the sovereignty which Westminster continues to exercise over a large tract of the country, the republican movement has been compelled to use force against those Irish people who have chosen to collude with the 'British war machine'. The murder of RUC officers and UDR soldiers, therefore, represents for republicans simply another necessary, if unpleasant, facet of war. The killing of fellow Irish men and women is considered merely one further indignity which British imperialism has forced upon the present generation of republican activists.

The anxiety of republicans to rationalise the violence which they have directed against those Ulster Protestants who happen to work for the security forces becomes evident when we consider the substance of certain political murals. Many of the murals that have appeared in republican districts have advanced damning indictments of the various repressive apparatus of the British state. Political artists have endeavoured to capture the multiple miseries which they consider the British army, RUC, UDR and RIR to have visited upon members of the nationalist community. Those Northern Irish people who have joined the 'Crown forces' and who happen to have been overwhelmingly Protestants are represented in predictably unflattering terms (B76–80). The depiction of those unionists who have secured employment within the security forces implies a concern on the part of the political artist to establish the secular and inclusive credentials of the republican movement. The juxtaposition of images of the RUC officer with those of the British soldier offers a denial to the accusation that republican combatants have committed acts of violence that have been sectarian. The messages that are embedded within the murals assert that republicans who have killed Northern Irish Protestants working for the security forces have done so not because of their ethno-religious orientation, but rather because they are considered to perform functions essential to British rule in Ireland. The work of sympathetic political artists seeks to suggest, therefore, that the republican movement has claimed the lives of some Irish men and women in the recent past so as to ensure that at some stage in the future all of the peoples of Ireland will be able to live free from the oppression of British imperialism.

The process of Ulsterisation has ensured that since the mid 1970s at least Northern Irish Protestants have represented the principal agents of official security policy. Republicans would contend further that over the period of the modern conflict the British state has employed elements within the unionist community as conduits through which to direct unofficial violence against northern nationalists. The work of republican street artists frequently claims that figures within the security forces have systematically colluded with loyalist paramilitaries (B46–48). Numerous republican murals assert that British military intelligence has both financed and orchestrated those loyalist organisations which have terrorised nationalist communities over the course of the troubles.

While allegations that the state has conspired with loyalist paramilitaries are substantially true they also advert to an important shortcoming within the republican disposition. The belief that Britain has exercised an entirely baleful influence over the development of Ireland has often ensured that republicans have simply refused to take unionism seriously. In the republican mind Ulster Protestants represent unfortunate pawns of British imperialism (Clarke 1994, pp. 92–3; Finlayson 1997b, p. 75; McGarry & O'Leary 1995a, pp. 48–51). Unionists are considered to have been fooled into regarding themselves as 'British' by the silver tongues of metropolitan authority. Moreover, the violence of loyalist paramilitaries is conceived as simply an appendage of official security policy. The orthodox republican reading, therefore, tends to construct unionism and loyalism as mere epiphenomena of British imperialism. Once the ties with the imperial overlord are severed, republicans insist, these retarded ideological formations will inevitably proceed to dissolve. With the creation of the Republic, unionists will quickly come to their senses and realise their 'true' identity as Irish men and women (Bruce 1994a, pp. 129–31).

The distinctly patronising understandings of unionism that inform the republican imagination have proved remarkably resilient. Over the past decade, however, some republicans would appear to have begun to take rather more seriously the other principal ethnopolitical tradition that exists on the island. Influential figures within the republican movement would seem in recent years to have revised substantially the conventional conception of unionism as simply the bastard child of British imperialism. Elements within Sinn Fein have become increasingly amenable to the view that the unionist tradition has a value – and perhaps ultimately a dynamic – of its own. The growing realisation that unionists may not simply be the pathetic dupes of a machiavellian metropolitan power has altered the inflection of modern republican strategy (Hazelkorn & Patterson 1994, p. 60; Shirlow & McGovern 1998, p. 175). If Ulster unionism actually represents a largely autonomous ideological formation then it might be reasonably expected to survive (in some form) any decision taken by a Westminster administration to terminate the Union. The emergence of a genuinely united Ireland would not, therefore, be assured simply by the declaration of a British withdrawal. Rather, it would also require that unionists abandon their former beliefs and take the historic decision to assimilate fully into the Irish nation.

The burgeoning understanding that the consent of unionists is essential to the realisation of the entire republican enterprise has had important implications. In recent years Sinn Fein representatives have adopted a rather more conciliatory approach towards the unionist tradition (McGarry & O'Leary 1995a, p. 367; Ryan 1994, pp. 12–17; Shirlow & McGovern 1998, p. 176). Unionists have been consistently assured that their optimal future remains as equal citizens of a united Irish state. The shifts that have occurred recently within republican discourse have become evident in speeches and newspaper articles. The increasingly pluralist tone of contemporary republicanism has had little bearing, however, upon the substance of political art. This is hardly surprising of course. The political mural provides an ideal forum for the strident polemic and cultural supremacism that often characterise the discourse of war. The cruder forms of political art provide a rather less conducive medium for the conciliatory and pluralist sentiments that frequently typify the language of peace.

Who is Like Us?

Akin with other nationalists, Irish republicans are eager to establish as unique that place which they happen to call home (Smyth 1995, p. 213). The adherents to the republican faith typically portray Ireland as a place with a distinctive history and people. While acknowledging the particularities of that community to which they imagine themselves to belong, republicans are also keen to draw parallels between the Irish experience and that of peoples elsewhere. The creations of republican mural artists often feature bold international(ist) statements (Rolston 1992, p. v; 1995a, p. v). Murals situated in working class nationalist districts often invite the viewer to make associations between the republican cause and that of black South Africans, native Americans and the beleaguered peoples of Central America (A109, 110, 111).

These international references perform certain essential political and psychological tasks. Critics have frequently alleged that the violence of the modern republican movement has marked a descent into atavism. Republicans have sought to refute these allegations in part by locating the Northern Irish conflict within a rather broader context. Analogies with other situations of conflict suggest that the conduct of the republican movement during the present troubles has been neither irrational nor aberrant. International references imply, in other words, that the actions of Irish republicans over the past three decades have been essentially no different from those of plain folk elsewhere who have also been forced to live through oppression and political change.

The analogies which republican mural artists make between the troubles and other political conflicts may be read further as claims upon moral authority. In republican murals the experiences of Northern Irish nationalists are variously compared to those of the residents of South African townships, the inhabitants of North American reservations and the occupants of Central American shanty towns. These highly questionable comparisons are clearly intended to confer moral legitimacy upon a republican movement that bears more responsibility than any other single agency for the horrendous death toll of the modern conflict in Northern Ireland.

The international references that appear in some political murals indicate the willingness of the republican movement to look beyond the confines of the island. The political stalemate that has prevailed within Northern Ireland for much of the last three decades has persuaded republicans and others of the need to court opinion outside the six counties. The universal ideals and rhetorical power that define republican discourse have ensured that Sinn Fein has often received a sympathetic audience abroad in recent years (Ruane & Todd 1996, p. 288; Shirlow & McGovern 1998, p. 177). The anxiety to win influential friends outside Ireland has inevitably softened the tone of contemporary republicanism. The gradual and partial rehabilitation of Sinn Fein that has occurred during the 1990s has owed much to the energies of various influential American politicians and businessmen. Reliance upon the political and corporate elite of North America has clearly diluted the radicalism that once defined republican rhetoric. Few contemporary republican murals advance the cause of international revolution. Potential American investors being escorted around west Belfast would scarcely be impressed were they to happen upon an enormous political mural bearing the likeness of Che Guevara.

ULSTER LOYALISM

The Protestant community clustered within the northeastern counties of Ireland has over the last century often exhibited a remarkable capacity for political cohesion. Ulster unionists have frequently agreed to overlook their many differences in order to secure the connection with Great Britain. In recent decades, however, the ideological formation of unionism has become increasingly prone to schism. Over the course of the troubles the divisions that have always existed within the unionist fold have become ever more apparent. The scale of the fragmentation that has occurred within modern unionism was mercilessly exposed in the early summer of 1998. In elections convened to nominate delegates to the new Northern Ireland assembly half a dozen parties and countless maverick individuals vied for the affections of a clearly bewildered unionist electorate.

Many commentators have sought to capture the tensions that characterise the unionist tradition. Perhaps the most persuasive attempt to map out the ideological fissures within Ulster unionism to date can be found in the writings of the political scientist Jennifer Todd. In a seminal essay which appeared in the 1987 volume of *Irish Political Studies* Todd sets out to delineate the multiple strands of unionist thought. Two of these ideological currents are teased out for systematic examination and are designated 'Ulster Loyalist' and 'Ulster British' respectively.

The 'Ulster Loyalist' tradition is possibly the one with which readers will be more readily familiar (Todd 1987, pp. 3–11). The primary community to which Ulster Loyalists feel themselves to belong is that formed by the six northeastern counties of Ireland. Loyalists often denote the constitutional entity of Northern Ireland with the historically inaccurate term 'Ulster'. The ideological disposition of Ulster Loyalism often tends towards the exclusive and sectarian. The particularism that defines the outlook of the Ulster Loyalist is evinced most dramatically in the ritual triumphalism of the Orange marching season.

The contrast with the ideological tradition of 'Ulster Britishness' could hardly be more profound (Todd 1987, pp. 11–20). The principal 'imagined community' of the Ulster British is that demarcated by the boundaries of the United Kingdom. The ideological formation of Ulster Britishness endorses those liberal, secular and pluralist values assumed to be enshrined within the institutions of the modern British state. The Ulster British tend towards modes of cultural and political expression which are rather more sober and bourgeois than those adopted by Ulster Loyalists. The characteristic beliefs and identities which cluster around Ulster Britishness are channelled through distinctly dignified modes of intellectual and political engagement. The sectarian rites of the Orange marching season are frowned upon as boorish and parochial.

The discussion which follows seeks to delineate that strand of unionist ideology which Jennifer Todd has persuasively characterised as 'Ulster Loyalist'. An essential means through which loyalists have sought to voice their ambitions and anxieties has been that of the political mural. It should be remembered, however, that not all of the sentiments that are encoded within loyalist murals would be acceptable to all of those who would readily identify themselves as loyalists. One of the most important bones of contention within the loyalist fold pertains to the issue of political violence. The paintings that often adorn gable walls in less affluent Protestant neighbourhoods are typically the work of individuals sympathetic to organisations like the Ulster Defence Association (UDA), the Ulster Freedom Fighters (UFF), and the Ulster Volunteer Force (UVF). These paramilitary bodies have, however, managed to secure only limited support within the loyalist community. Many of those who regard themselves as loyalists have proved loth to condone the countless acts of violence that have been carried out in their name.

The aversion, or at least ambivalence, towards political violence that exists within the loyalist community has been borne out in recent electoral trends. The two political parties which have organic associations with loyalist paramilitary factions have played an important role in the peace process that has gathered pace over recent years. Neither the Progressive Unionist Party (PUP) nor the Ulster Democratic Party (UDP) have managed, however, to garner substantial electoral support. In the elections to the Northern Ireland assembly held in June 1998 less than four per cent of the electorate offered their first preferences to either party. The electoral performance of the PUP and UDP particularly fails to impress when compared to that of the other political party which articulates an outlook which could be considered 'loyalist' (McAuley 1994, pp. 58–81; 1997, pp. 172–4).

In the 1998 Northern Ireland Assembly elections the Democratic Unionist Party (DUP) attracted the support of 18 per cent of the local electorate. Critics have frequently claimed that figures within the DUP have provided moral encouragement to the loyalist campaign of political violence. The formal stance of the party remains nonetheless one of explicit opposition to loyalist paramilitarism. The evidence offered by recent electoral trends would seem to suggest, therefore, that loyalists have in the main chosen to withhold their support from those who have killed and maimed in their name. The results of recent polls would indicate that the loyalist community has been rather more willing to endorse a party which – for all its apparent equivocation – remains formally opposed to political violence than to support those parties which are intimately associated with loyalist paramilitary groupings.

LOYALIST MURALS

In light of the foregoing discussion we should exercise caution when attempting to interpret loyalist murals. While the dramatic slogans and images on view within many working class Protestant communities capture the disposition of many loyalists, they by no means represent the views of all. The work of loyalist street artists nonetheless provides an important alternative reading of the Northern Irish conflict. The narratives that are constructed within loyalist murals centre upon a sequence of six questions. Each shall be considered in turn.

Who are We?

The function of the loyalist mural is in part to acknowledge and affirm a distinctive sense of ethnic – and perhaps national – being. Through political art loyalists seek to delineate the community of descent to which they consider themselves to belong. The 'imagined community' of Ulster loyalism is occasionally constructed in exclusively religious terms. In some political murals the formal status of loyalists as members of the Protestant faith is affirmed (B24). The image of an open bible appears from time to time (B31, 32). The references to the sacred that appear in the work of loyalist street artists are, however, remarkably rare. Those murals that voice the perspective of loyalism are typically located in districts where religious observance has declined dramatically over recent generations. The individual who feels moved to paint an image of the bible on a convenient stretch of wall may not in fact have darkened the door of a church in a very long time. The advance of secularisation within working class Protestant communities has had an important bearing upon the content of loyalist iconography. The community of descent imagined within the loyalist mural invariably owes considerably less to the religious sentiments that arise out of confessional status than to the secular impulses that drive ethnic and national feeling.

Ulster loyalists tend to define themselves as being essentially 'British' both in origin and culture. The declaration that 'Ulster is British' is a slogan readily familiar to the residents of working class Protestant districts (A15). While loyalist murals often boldly assert the Britishness of Northern Ireland, remarkably few actually attempt to represent the connection between the province and the 'mainland'. One form through which loyalism could seek to imagine the Union would be the 'map image' of the United Kingdom. In practice, however, loyalists have proved strangely reluctant to provide visual representation of the neighbouring island. The map image of Great Britain does not constitute an important element of political art designed to advance the loyalist cause. The fact that representations of the mainland are absent from murals located in working class Protestant areas suggests that Ulster loyalists may in fact have relatively little sense of kinship with their fellow citizens who happen to reside in other regions of the United Kingdom. The substance of contemporary loyalist iconography implies, that is to say, that the identity of Britishness may be rather less important to loyalists than they frequently profess.

The map image that actually does appear with some regularity in the work of loyalist street artists is inevitably that of Northern Ireland. In numerous loyalist murals the six counties are portrayed as though they exist as a discrete geopolitical entity (Rolston 1991b, p. 40). The recurrent representation of Northern Ireland casts light upon the ontological disposition of contemporary loyalism. The images of the province that pervade loyalist murals indicate that the community to which many working class Protestants feel themselves to belong is not that of the United Kingdom but rather that bounded by the six counties. The figurative system of contemporary loyalism suggests, therefore, that the sense of being to which the loyalist subscribes is not that designated by the term 'Britishness' but rather that denoted by the phrase 'Northern Irishness'. It implies, in other words, that Ulster loyalists are simply and precisely that – loyal to 'Ulster' (Finlayson 1997b, pp. 82–3).

The representations of Northern Ireland that appear regularly in loyalist murals are often wildly inaccurate (A29, 30, B5, 28). The apparent inability of many loyalist muralists to capture the physical likeness of the six counties may simply reveal a dearth of artistic prowess. It may, alternatively, reflect an altogether more important trait of contemporary loyalism. The map image represents a crude though valuable device which allows social actors to offer spatial expression to feelings of belonging that may otherwise remain intangible. The often unconvincing representations of Northern Ireland on view within working class Protestant communities, therefore, expose Ulster loyalism as a distinctly underdeveloped ideological programme. The apparent inability of loyalists to imagine the six counties accurately suggests that they possess only a limited sense both of self and place (Graham 1997, pp. 36–7). The relative poverty of contemporary loyalist iconography implies, that is, that many working class Protestants are somewhat confused as to who they are, where they come from and, most importantly of all, where they are going.

The suspicion that ontological confusion reigns within Ulster loyalism is heightened further by the absence of detail in the work of loyalist street artists. In loyalist murals Northern Ireland typically appears in silhouette. Usually little effort is made to flesh out the resemblance of the six counties. The images of a spiritual, ancient, rural arcadia which we found earlier in republican political art are all but absent from loyalist murals. That loyalists have proved unwilling or unable to embellish their representations of the six counties with flattering detail implies that their sense of who they are and indeed where they are remains somewhat retarded. It suggests that loyalists have not as yet fully imagined that place which they claim to call home.

What Is the Problem?

The ideological formation of Ulster loyalism advances a reading of history that centres upon the fractious relations between the two dominant ethnoreligious traditions that coexist uneasily in Northern Ireland. Loyalists consider that Irish Catholics have consistently adopted an implacably hostile stance towards those Protestants who have settled in the historic province of Ulster (Porter 1996, pp. 87–8). The loyalist interpretation of history affords particular significance to the events of the Williamite wars. The siege of Derry has left an indelible impression upon the popular imagination of loyalism. The image of the papist forces of King James massed at the gates of the walled city is frequently employed to signify the beleaguered position which Ulster Protestants occupy as a minority on the island (A26).

Ulster loyalists often hold to the view that the threat which Catholic nationalism has posed to the Protestant community throughout history remains as strong as ever today (McGovern & Shirlow 1997, pp. 178–9). The ideological enterprise of loyalism insists that the ageless hostility of Irish Catholics to those outside the confessional group has in recent times found expression in the guise of a ruthless campaign of political violence. Loyalists interpret the actions of the Provisional IRA as an attempt not to resist British imperialism but rather to drive Protestants from the island. The objectives of the republican armed struggle are not, therefore, national liberation but rather 'ethnic cleansing'.

The loyalist perspective contends that the innumerable perils that confront Northern Irish Protestants sometimes originate outside the six counties. Ulster loyalists have traditionally regarded the Irish Republic as irretrievably hostile. The southern Irish state is considered to harbour improper designs upon the cherished territory of Northern Ireland. Dublin politicians are believed to want to reclaim the six counties and to force the Protestant people against their will into a united Ireland. Hence, loyalists are threatened both from within by a 'fifth column' of republican insurgents and from without by the irredentism of the Irish Republic (B16, 21).

The particular grievances that fester within the imagination of Ulster loyalism have inevitably ensured that gable walls in working class Protestant neighbourhoods have often provided a forum for the expression of hostility towards the Irish Republic. The creations of loyalist mural artists frequently proclaim an indomitable will to resist the alleged irredentism of the southern Irish state. One mural located in the loyalist heartland of the Shankill Road eschews 'any Eire involvement in our country' (B16). Another Belfast mural located in the east of the city announces the refusal of loyalists 'to submit to the rule of the Irish' (B21).

What has Been the Response of Loyalists?

The loyalist reading of history asserts that the unprovoked aggression of Irish Catholics has inevitably and consistently compelled the Protestants of Ulster to resist. Loyalists note that through the ages the Protestant people have been forced to defend both themselves and their interests through force of arms. Many of the murals that exist within loyalist communities strive to delineate a military tradition. In recent years the mythological figure of Cuchulainn has been occasionally claimed as a loyalist icon (B32). Given that he has been associated traditionally with Irish republicanism the appropriation of Cuchulainn by loyalists would seem a bold ideological venture (Rolston 1995a, pp. iii–iv). It should be acknowledged, however, that the role which Cuchulainn plays within Irish mythology is that of the defender of Ulster against attacks launched from the south. Regarded in this particular light, the 'hound of Ulster' would seem a plausible emblem of the determination of loyalists to resist the perceived hostile forces of Catholic nationalist irredentism (McAuley 1991, pp. 55–7).

The warrior tradition to which loyalists lay claim finds expression in various historical settings (Rolston 1992, p. iii). The iconography of contemporary loyalism draws heavily of course from the period of the 'glorious revolution'. The triumph at the Boyne represents a hardy perennial of the loyalist wall mural (A1–8, B 1–3, 99). Images of a victorious King Billy constitute perhaps the most potent expression of confidence among loyalists that they will survive and perhaps even prosper in a land where they remain heavily outnumbered. The willingness of Ulster Protestants to take arms is further signified through reference to the events of World War I. Numerous loyalist murals introduce the viewer to glorious images of the carnage at the Somme. The horrific casualties incurred during the summer of 1916 are offered as emblematic of the indomitable spirit of the Ulster Protestant.

Present day loyalists have, like those they regard as their predecessors, taken up arms (Clayton 1996, pp. 148–56). The murals that are a feature of many poorer Protestant neighbourhoods heap praise upon those who have employed violence to resist the hostile forces considered to be ranged against the loyalist community. Loyalist political art frequently attempts to draw connections between the present troubles and previous periods of military engagement. In particular the members of the modern UVF are often portrayed as direct descendants of those who joined the ranks of the organisation of the same name which played a central role in unionist opposition to Home Rule in the early years of this century (A19–21). Few historians would accept the comparison. The frequently spurious analogies that are drawn in loyalist murals reveal a concern to legitimise the violence that has emanated from the Protestant community over recent decades (Bruce 1994b, pp. 115–17). References to previous historical periods suggest that the present troubles do not constitute an aberrant expression of specific modern conditions. On the contrary, the actions of contemporary loyalist paramilitary factions represent merely the latest instalment of the historic quest of the Ulster Protestant community for survival. Historical analogies, therefore, seek to afford to the actions of loyalist paramilitaries that moral authority which only the passage of time can confer.

The work of loyalist street artists invariably provides glorious portrayals of the particular paramilitary organisations to which they are sympathetic (Rolston 1991b, p. 41). One particularly arresting political mural located in the Woodstock Link areas of east Belfast pays homage to the UVF. The dramatic sunburst and rich colours that are featured in the painting describe the conduct of the UVF in a distinctly noble light (B92). Those murals that have appeared in working class districts that are predominantly Protestant tend to be particularly menacing (Rolston 1992, p. ii; 1995a, pp. ii–iii). Members of loyalist paramilitary factions are frequently depicted entering the fray wearing balaclavas and brandishing rifles (A31–35, B13–22, 92, 96–98). These dramatic images clearly declare that loyalists are competent and dedicated combatants who will provide steadfast defence for the communities to which they belong. The monotonous militarism that defines the loyalist mural adverts to the machismo which infests Northern Irish society.

The images that characterise contemporary loyalist iconography are almost entirely masculine. The principal subject of the loyalist mural is the hooded male paramilitary. Women virtually never appear in the work of loyalist street artists. On the rare occasions that women actually do feature in loyalist murals they are typically presented as passive and vulnerable. A painting that appeared in a working class Protestant district of Lurgan in the early 1980s, for instance, cast a male loyalist in the role of defender of a cowering woman (Rolston 1991b, p. 44). Examination of contemporary political art reveals, therefore, that loyalist muralists are loth to imagine women in those active, public roles which they are frequently afforded by republican street artists. Even within the profoundly reactionary political context of Northern Ireland, loyalism would seem to represent a particularly patriarchal ideological formation.

Most loyalist murals are designed to narrate the supposed glories of warfare. Some endeavour, however, to acknowledge the enormous human costs that have attended the actions of loyalist paramilitaries (Porter 1996, pp. 87–8). In the course of the modern conflict scores of loyalist activists have lost their lives to political violence. Loyalist murals often serve as memorials to particular casualties of the troubles (B25–27, 95). These valedictions typically suggest that those who have died have given their lives to defend the interests of the wider loyalist community (Rolston 1991b, p. ii). The noble sacrifices which loyalist paramilitaries are assumed to have made during the modern troubles are underscored through comparison with those of previous generations of Ulster Protestants. The most frequent point of reference for these analogies is the valour of the 36th (Ulster) Division of the British Army at the Somme (A22,23,24).

Those who are sympathetic invariably claim that the actions of loyalist militants are motivated solely by a selfless concern for the interests of the communities from which they come. Loyalist murals frequently suggest that the conduct of groupings like the UVF, UDA, UFF and so forth attracts the endorsement of the Ulster Protestant people. Loyalist paramilitaries are represented as the vanguard of a genuinely popular social movement that seeks to advance the interests of the entire community. The contention that loyalist paramilitarism enjoys widespread support provides the substance of a striking political mural that appeared on the Shankill Road in the latter months of 1994. The mural in question issued the familiar demand that loyalist prisoners convicted for scheduled offences should be released (B94). Beneath a pair of red hands breaking the chains of incarceration are two slogans which mirror one another in order to construct a community between loyalist paramilitaries and the wider Protestant populace. One proclaims that 'ALL GAVE SOME' while the other opines that 'SOME GAVE ALL'.

The work of sympathetic muralists offers a deeply flattering portrayal of loyalist paramilitary organisations. The notion that loyalist paramilitaries are selfless defenders of the people scarcely stands up to examination, however. Presumably there are loyalists who have taken up arms out of a sense of obligation to a community considered to be under threat. There are clearly others though who have been attracted to the cause for reasons other than pure altruism. The loyalist paramilitary factions that emerged at the outset of the troubles soon descended into multiple forms of gangsterism. The numerous rackets that have been organised over the last quarter of a century have generated considerable personal benefit for some loyalist activists. The ostentatious affluence of certain loyalist figures has been cast into even starker relief by the crippling poverty often endured by those they claim to represent.

The bold assertion of numerous political murals that loyalist paramilitary organisations have offered steadfast defence to Protestant communities that otherwise would have been deeply vulnerable frankly fails to convince. The role that loyalist paramilitaries have played in the Northern Irish conflict has, as we shall return to see later, invariably been to launch indiscriminate attacks upon defenceless Catholics. The actions of loyalist militants have inevitably drawn a violent response from the republican movement. The casualties of republican retaliation have at times been Protestants who have no connection with loyalist paramilitarism. Hence, the actions of groups like the UVF, UDA and UFF which have been intended ostensibly to offer defence to beleaguered loyalist communities have ironically often invited violence upon working class Protestants.

Loyalist paramilitary factions have also provided a rather more direct route for violence within those districts where they are influential. Since the beginning of the troubles loyalist paramilitaries have become an increasingly important source of local authority. Loyalists have proved no more tolerant than their republican counterparts of political dissent and social deviance. Those individuals who have challenged the hegemony of particular paramilitary bodies or persisted with criminal activity have often become victims of an horrifically crude form of summary justice. Over recent years in particular, punishment attacks have become an increasingly familiar element of life within those districts where loyalist paramilitary factions enjoy or pursue dominance. The methods of violence and intimidation which these groupings have habitually employed to police certain communities scarcely square with the images of doughty defenders of the people that are a central motif of the work of loyalist street artists.

Numerous political murals contest, as we have seen, that loyalist paramilitarism attracts widespread communal support. These claims are, however, questionable at best. It is certainly the case that loyalist paramilitaries have enjoyed considerable legitimacy among the Protestant working classes. The various loyalist factions simply could not have sustained campaigns of political violence for the last three decades without substantial active and passive communal support. Nonetheless it remains true that loyalists have proved unable to attain a popular appeal comparable to that of their republican counterparts. The limits to the tolerance of paramilitarism that exists among working class Protestants are suggested by recent electoral trends. Both of the political parties that have organic connections with loyalist paramilitary groupings have attained public prominence and even upon occasion critical acclaim as the peace process has evolved throughout the present decade. Neither has managed as yet, however, to make substantial electoral gains. The performance of the political party understood to reflect the outlook of the largest loyalist paramilitary faction has been particularly poor. In the elections held in June 1998 to nominate delegates to the new Northern Ireland assembly the UDP failed to secure even a single seat. The notable absence of the political representatives of the UDA from the legislative body designed to map out the future of the province may be read as a withering comment by working class Protestants upon the claims of loyalist paramilitaries to represent their interests.

The political analysis and strategy that have been advanced by those diverse elements of the 'unionist family' that are typically designated as loyalist have often proved exceptionally crude. The loyalist imagination has conventionally identified a range of hostile forces considered to be intent upon forcing the 'Ulster Protestant people' into a united Ireland against their will. The conviction that the Union is in peril has frequently persuaded loyalists that force is required if the countless 'enemies of Ulster' are to be vanquished. Many loyalists have issued repeated demands that the state employ draconian measures to resist republican insurgence. Others have come to the view that the interests of the Protestant community will be best safeguarded through unofficial forms of violence.

The disposition of Ulster loyalism often appears to have altered little with the passage of time. The outlook of that political party which has consistently claimed the support of most loyalists would seem particularly impervious to change. The DUP has largely persisted with a mode of discourse which orbits around the paranoid sectarian cant of party leader Ian Paisley. While the occupants of the loyalist mainstream have consistently proved incapable of ideological renewal, those on the margins have exhibited rather greater capacity for critical reflection. Over the last decade the outlook of those small parties which have close associations with loyalist paramilitary organisations has undergone remarkable change (Finlayson 1997b, pp. 87–91; McAuley 1996). Opinion formers within the UDP and PUP have come increasingly to the view that the interests of the loyalist community would be best served through methods other than force. The growing realisation of the futility of political violence bore fruit in the autumn of 1994 when the main loyalist factions declared an immediate end to military operations. While the various paramilitary groups which for a time clustered beneath the umbrella of the Combined Loyalist Military Command (CLMC) have infringed their ceasefire on many occasions, the prospect has grown nonetheless that loyalists may in the future permanently and unequivocally renounce the use of force.

As faith in the value of political violence has declined, loyalists have come to place rather greater store in political dialogue. In recent times loyalists have adopted an altogether less hostile approach towards the other principal ethnopolitical tradition that exists within the six counties. The increasingly conciliatory tone of contemporary loyalism found pertinent expression in the ceasefire statement issued by the CLMC which extended abject apologies to the victims of loyalist paramilitarism. While the sentiments expressed in the text are unlikely to have provided much comfort to those injured or bereaved by the likes of the UVF, UFF and Red Hand Commando, they nevertheless mark an important departure within loyalist discourse.

The apparent drift towards moderation within contemporary loyalism has enabled the present leaders of the UDP and the PUP to envisage political developments and compromises that would have been inconceivable to their predecessors. The political analysis that loyalists advance suggests that political progress within Northern Ireland requires an appreciation of the rights and misgivings of everyone. Loyalists have often proved rather more willing than mainstream unionists to acknowledge the grievances of nationalists. Figures within the UDP and PUP have argued for some time that political stability will only be secured if members of the nationalist community come to regard themselves as truly belonging to Northern Ireland. Consequently, loyalists have contended that nationalists must be afforded a substantial role in the future governance of the six counties. While members of the DUP have clung tenaciously to the ultraunionist fantasy of a return to majority rule, elements within the UDP have for at least the last decade argued the case for consociational forms of government.

The increasingly conciliatory tone of contemporary loyalism has also become evident in the approach which parties like the UDP and PUP have adopted recently towards the other state on the island. The Irish Republic has traditionally been the central figure within loyalist demonology. Loyalists have conventionally assumed Dublin politicians to have improper designs upon the beloved territory of Ulster. In recent years, however, loyalist leaders have adopted a rather more amicable stance towards the Irish Republic. As Dublin has come to exert ever greater influence over the affairs of Northern Ireland, elements within the UDP and PUP have become concerned to bring the loyalist case to a southern Irish audience. As a result, former loyalist prisoners like David Ervine and Billy Hutchinson have become increasingly familiar and intelligible personalities to readers, viewers and listeners who live in the Irish Republic. The leader of the UDP, Gary McMichael, even pens a regular column for a southern Irish Sunday newspaper.

The current decade has overseen remarkable changes in the thinking of those associated with loyalist paramilitarism. The comparatively moderate stance that senior players within the 'fringe' loyalist parties have adopted has encouraged the seemingly progressive political developments that have occurred over recent years. Indeed figures like David Ervine and Gary McMichael have attracted widespread praise for the role that they have played in the present peace process. The recent apparent refinement of loyalist thought has failed to find expression, however, at the level of political art. The seismic political events that have unfolded during the present decade have altered little the work of loyalist street artists. The dominant emblem of the loyalist mural remains the sinister hooded figure brandishing a firearm. The persistent belligerence of loyalist muralists is reflected in the distinctly tendentious reading of the peace process which they often seek to advance. In the late summer of 1994 the Provisional IRA called a halt to its military operations. Some loyalists sought to promulgate the distinctly dubious interpretation that the ceasefire represented an admission on the part of republicans that they had in fact lost the war. A mural that appeared soon after on the Shankill Road declared that the UVF was prepared 'on behalf of the loyalist people' to 'accept the unconditional surrender of the IRA' (B90).

Examination of the content of recent political art suggests the existence of important distinctions within contemporary loyalism. Over the last decade the outlook of loyalist leaders has come increasingly to centre upon peace and accommodation. The disposition of many grassroots loyalists has continued, however, to emphasise conflict and triumph. The persistence of military images within the iconography of contemporary loyalism suggests that we should exercise caution when seeking to transpose the views of men like David Ervine or Gary McMichael onto the wider loyalist community.

The substance of recent loyalist murals may be interpreted further perhaps as a strategic ideological intervention. The political developments that have defined the 1990s have proved as troubling for loyalists as for many others. Elements within the loyalist fold have expressed concern that the likely benefits of the peace process will accrue overwhelmingly to the republican movement. Many loyalists have found it inconceivable that the IRA would have declared either of its ceasefires without the promise of substantial concessions from Westminster. The work of loyalist muralists represents in part an attempt to engender confidence within working class Protestant communities unnerved by recent political change. Some loyalist street artists have, as we have seen, chosen to interpret the IRA ceasefires as abject admissions of defeat. The bold assertion that republicans have 'surrendered' accommodates an insistence that the constitutional future of Northern Ireland within the United Kingdom is secure. The military symbols that still dominate loyalist iconography are perhaps intended to offer the reassurance that the political developments currently afoot within Northern Ireland will not leave loyalists physically vulnerable. The images of armed men in balaclavas that continue to appear on gable walls suggest that should the province ever return to war loyalists will once again offer steadfast and selfless defence to threatened working class Protestant communities. In sum, therefore, the form of contemporary loyalist iconography seeks to persuade loyalists that the political process to which their leaders have lent their support promises ultimately to guarantee the safety both of themselves and the Union. The images of war that appear in certain neighbourhoods, in other words, may ironically represent an attempt to win working class Protestants over to the cause of peace.

The substance of contemporary murals not only fails to capture recent developments in loyalist thinking but also captures the failure of these developments. In recent times the leaders of loyalism have sought to devise a political strategy rather broader than hitherto. As the value of force has come increasingly into question loyalists have turned towards other forms of political engagement considered to have greater popular appeal. The political wing of the UVF has placed particular emphasis upon the potential of community development projects. Members of the PUP have attempted to encourage particular working class

Protestant communities to articulate with greater clarity and vigour their identities and interests. The efforts of the party to promote a version of 'class politics' contrast starkly with the profound social conservatism of the unionist mainstream (McAuley 1997, p. 165).

The attempts of elements within loyalism to construct a broader political strategy have proved somewhat less than successful. The networks of representation that have emerged within working class Protestant communities have remained relatively underdeveloped. Moreover, the process of cultural introspection that loyalists have sought to encourage has invariably proved unable to produce definitions of self more progressive and endearing than those actualised in the crude rituals of the 'marching season'. The inability of loyalists to stimulate and harness the energies of the communities in which they are based contrasts strongly with the experience of the modern republican movement. In the course of the troubles republicans have been transformed from a relatively small political sect into a genuinely popular social movement. The images of Irish dancers and Gaelic athletes on view in many working class nationalist districts offer rich testimony to the cultural self-confidence of contemporary republicanism. Examination of recent loyalist murals reveals rather less ontological security. The preoccupations of political artists suggest that loyalists have proved unable to construct a notion of self other than that realised through acts of political violence. The military monotone of the loyalist mural fuels further the suspicion that working class Protestants possess only a limited sense of who they are and what they want.

What do Loyalists want?

Ulster loyalists have inevitably been keen to suggest that their ambitions and motivations are entirely noble. The principal rationale which loyalists employ in order to legitimise their own conduct echoes that advanced by the republican movement. Those who are sympathetic often insist that the actions of loyalist para-militaries are an unfortunate necessity prompted by an insatiable desire to be free. The discourse of contemporary loyalism abounds with references to freedom. The term and its various cognates feature prominently in the work of loyalist muralists. Indeed a stretch of the Newtownards Road in east Belfast which plays host to a series of loyalist murals has been given the rather curious unofficial title 'freedom corner'.

The concept of liberty that exists within Ulster loyalism centres upon the right to live unmolested by the allegedly hostile and intolerant forces of Irish nationalism. The definition of freedom to which loyalists adhere is almost entirely negative. While loyalists are invariably unequivocal concerning what they do *not* want they tend to be rather less clear about what they do want. Those murals that articulate the loyalist case contain no models of the good society. There are no intimations of the halcyon days that will follow once the spectre of Irish nationalism is banished. The essentially negative inflection of Ulster loyalism occasionally gives way to bona fide pessimism. Those emblems that are employed by political artists sympathetic to loyalism typically signify decline rather than rebirth. The images that appear within loyalist murals are often those of sunset rather than sunrise (B30).

The insistence that the 'Ulster Protestant people' are entitled to live free from the allegedly pernicious influence of the Irish Republic has been an enduring feature of loyalist discourse. The last few years have, however, witnessed a significant dilution of the traditional loyalist demand for freedom. In the course of the 1990s the leaders of Ulster loyalism have come to adopt a rather less pugnacious approach towards Dublin. At various stages during the present decade senior loyalist figures have engaged in both clandestine and overt negotiations with southern Irish politicians. Moreover, opinion formers within the small loyalist 'fringe' parties would seem to have arrived at an understanding that the formulation of a durable political settlement for Northern Ireland will necessarily involve an 'Irish dimension'. The growing pragmatism of contemporary loyalism has ensured that the UDP and PUP have been among the most committed supporters of the Good Friday Agreement. The increasingly conciliatory tone of prominent loyalist politicians has thus far failed to find expression in the guise of political art. Gable walls within working class Protestant districts still proclaim implacable opposition to 'Dublin rule'. Loyalist street artists who have for decades declared that as long as 100 Protestants remain in Ulster there will be resistance to the irredentism of southern Ireland have inevitably proved unwilling and unable to acknowledge that a solution to the Northern Ireland problem will require an Irish dimension.

What about the Catholics?

The community of descent to which loyalists consider themselves to belong emerges as distinctly narrow and exclusive. Loyalists invariably imagine Ulster to be solely British and Protestant (Clayton 1996, pp. 101–12; Porter 1996, p. 72). Those who exist outside the laager are frequently viewed with suspicion and hostility. Some loyalist murals vent antipathy towards the entire Catholic population that resides within the six counties (A43). These blanket expressions of ethnopolitical enmity are, however, surprisingly rare. Sympathetic artists are clearly keen to resist the accusation that loyalist paramilitaries are driven simply by blind prejudice. In loyalist murals the actions of factions like the UVF, UDA and UFF are represented as clinical and discriminate. Loyalist militants are portrayed as having directed their ire not towards Northern Irish Catholics as a whole but rather towards those republican activists who exist within their midst.

The representation of loyalist paramilitarism advanced within ideologically conducive murals simply fails to convince. In practice the definition of republican activism that loyalist paramilitaries have chosen to employ has tended to be conveniently broad. Loyalists have often proved content to assume that all Northern Irish Catholics are in fact republicans. As a consequence, the multiple acts of violence which they have perpetrated have been invariably indiscriminate (McAuley 1997 p. 163; McGovern & Shirlow 1997, p. 177). Remarkably few of the Catholics who have died at the hands of loyalists during the troubles could be described accurately as republican activists (Fay et al. 1999, pp. 168–71). Indeed reliable data would indicate that only one in twelve of the nationalists murdered by loyalist paramilitary bodies over the last three decades have actually been directly involved in the republican movement (McGarry & O'Leary 1995a, pp. 160–1).

The other principal military target identified within loyalist murals is that of the southern Irish state. Loyalist street artists frequently insist that the Irish Republic has imperial designs upon Northern Ireland. The unwarranted irredentism of the southern state is considered to invite and indeed merit a military response from the imperilled Ulster Protestant people (McGarry & O'Leary 1995a, pp. 95–6). A brief survey of the murals located within working class Protestant neighbourhoods suggests that loyalists actually harbour greater enmity and distrust for the southern Irish state than for northern Irish republicans. That the Irish Republic should be demonised with particular vigour seems puzzling given the strategy that loyalists have adopted during the troubles. Loyalist paramilitaries have made relatively few incursions south of the border. Admittedly, the supposedly loyalist bombings of Dublin and Monaghan in May 1974 produced the highest death toll for a single day of the conflict. It remains true, nevertheless, that loyalist military activity in southern Ireland has remained mercifully rare.

We would seem, therefore, to be faced with a paradox. While the actions of loyalist paramilitaries suggest that northern Irish nationalists represent the greatest risk to the constitutional status of the province, the work of loyalist artists implies that the southern Irish state poses the principal threat to the Union. The disjuncture that exists between the practice and the iconography of contemporary loyalism arises largely out of a concern for legitimacy. The discursive strategies which loyalists have adopted during the troubles have centred upon the concept of 'war'. Loyalist combatants have been keen to portray themselves simply as soldiers fighting for their country. Hence the various analogies drawn with previous periods of war stretching back over the last three centuries. The substance of loyalist murals may be read as an acknowledgement of the conventions associated with the description of conflict. While the violence which citizens of the same state visit upon one another is invariably vilified, that which states inflict upon one another is often venerated. Consequently, civil wars are typically regarded as squalid and interstate wars are frequently considered to be noble.

These discursive conventions would seem to have had some influence upon the work of loyalist street artists. Those acts of violence which social actors direct towards fellow citizens are typically regarded as odious. Individuals who engage in such conduct are invariably denounced as barbarians, criminals or terrorists. Consequently perhaps, loyalists have often preferred to understate the considerable enmity which they seem to harbour towards members of the other principal ethnopolitical tradition. The ferocious hostility that informs contemporary loyalist iconography is targeted less frequently at northern Irish national- ists than at the southern Irish state. The vilification of the Irish Republic within loyalist murals represents an endeavour to construct an ideologically convenient reading of the horrific events that have marked the recent history of Northern Ireland. The frequent references to the supposed irredentism of the southern Irish state imply that the troubles actually represent a mode of conflict more properly designated as a war. Regarded against this particular backdrop, the actions of loyalists begin to appear as though driven by an honourable concern to defend their own nation against the hostility of another. The distorted narrative advanced within loyalist murals seeks to suggest, in other words, that those loyalists who have murdered hundreds of nationalist civilians over the last three decades are not criminals or terrorists, but rather soldiers whose only crime has been to remain loyal to their country.

Who is Like Us?

Ulster loyalists would appear rather less willing or able than Irish republicans to make connections between their own plight and concerns and those of other peoples living in other parts of the world (Rolston 1991b, pp. 37–9). The focus of loyalist political art rarely strays outside Northern Ireland. The sole reference beyond the six counties that occurs with any regularity is that to Scotland (A9, B13). Ulster Protestants have traditionally considered themselves to share a history, temperament and dialect with the Scots. The few other references which loyalists make to communities beyond the six counties typically pertain to white settler societies which usually fall within the British Commonwealth (Clayton 1996, pp. 39–42). One mural painted in Derry during the early 1980s, for instance, featured the national flags of Australia and Canada (A14). The reluctance of loyalists to draw connections between their own struggle and that of other peoples elsewhere may perhaps be regarded as significant. The absence of international references within the iconography of contemporary loyalism adverts to the failure of Ulster Protestants to generate meaningful political support abroad (Ruane & Todd 1996, p. 143).

CONCLUSION

Since the early 1980s gable walls in working class districts throughout the six counties have provided increasingly important spaces for the dissemination of alternative readings of the conflict in Northern Ireland. The sustained popularity of the political mural acknowledges its distinct value as an ideological medium. Murals generate political discourse in forms that are accessible – if not necessarily palatable – to all. Political artists take the most complex historical and contemporary processes and translate them into simple images that engage both the mind and the senses. The contents of the political mural bombard the intellect and the emotions with a vigour that few other modes of political discourse can match. Images of the defeated Easter rebels or the fallen at the Somme exercise a resonance which even the most skilful political tracts and speeches can rarely attain.

Although considerable, the discursive value of the political mural remains strictly limited nonetheless. Political artists are clearly adept at capturing the dogmatic certainties of specific ideological programmes. Gable walls invariably provide a fitting context for the familiar declarations of 'No Surrender' or 'Brits Out'. The talents of the muralist are somewhat less amenable, however, to the nuance and ambivalence that often define political discourse. As a result, loyalist and republican street artists have often proved unable to capture the subtle but important ideological developments that have taken place during the present decade. The political mural has in the recent past provided an important, if often inaccurate, chronicle of a place at war. There are reasons to doubt, however, that political artists will in the future prove to be as compelling biographers of a region that will have hopefully found peace.

Conclusion

It is often difficult to resist the temptation to regard Northern Ireland as a place where little ever changes. The issues and identities that animate the people of the province as we approach the end of the twentieth century are remarkably similar to those that held sway during the closing moments of the nineteenth. The concepts and terms that frame public discourse within the six counties, moreover, are hardly of recent vintage. The loyalties and enmities that endure in Northern Ireland mean that social actors are frequently reluctant to countenance compromise or change. Hence the fateful political stalemate that has characterised the recent history of the region. The apparent intractability of the conflict in Northern Ireland has inevitably encouraged despondency in various quarters. Ordinary folk living in the six counties have frequently said that they are unable to see an end to the troubles. British politicians have at times been unable to conceal their despair at the intransigence of their Northern Irish counterparts. Academics have with some regularity chosen to characterise the Northern Ireland problem as one that has no obvious solution.

The gloom that has shrouded most commentaries on the political life of the province has of course been entirely under-standable. Since the outbreak of the troubles it has been enormously difficult to imagine how precisely the political logjam might be broken. The events that have unfolded in Northern Ireland during the present decade suggest, however, that there now exist grounds for greater optimism. The advance of the peace process implies that the residents of the six counties are beginning to think and talk their way out the mess in which they find themselves. The unexpected direction that Northern Irish politics has taken in the last few years makes the task of commenting on the public life of the province even more problematic. In a climate of distinct political flux it is difficult to arrive at authoritative judgements as to the likely future course that Northern Ireland

CONTEMPORARY NORTHERN IRISH SOCIETY

will take. Indeed the pace of recent political change in the six counties makes it hard at times even to know which tense to write in. Are we to speak of the troubles as a period that the citizens of Northern Ireland have left behind or as one through which they continue to live?

The remarkable political developments that have occurred during the 1990s have engendered widespread hope among people in Northern Ireland that an end to the troubles might finally be in sight. The blueprint of a prospective political settlement for the province emerged out of tortuous negotiations convened in Belfast under the watchful eye of former US Senator George Mitchell. On 10 April 1998 the final draft of a document was published which met with the approval of the British and Irish governments and most of the local political parties (O'Leary 1999). The focus of the Good Friday Agreement takes in the 'totality of relationships' between all of the peoples of Britain and Ireland. The principal concern of the document though is to alter the manner in which unionists and nationalists living in Northern Ireland relate to one another. The principles that inform the political agreement thrashed out in Belfast are those of consociationalism and pluralism. It is proposed that in future the people of Northern Ireland should govern themselves and that unionists and nationalists should share power with one another. Furthermore, the text of the agreement insists that all of the diverse cultures that exist in the province are innately valuable and are, therefore, equally worthy of respect.

The political arrangements conceived under the terms of the Good Friday Agreement are of course far from original. Indeed some pundits have observed wryly that the political deal struck at Stormont in the spring of 1998 represents 'Sunningdale for slow learners'. What *is* new though is the political climate in which the Belfast Agreement has been devised and advanced. The political package that emerged out of the multiparty negotiations enjoys unprecedented widespread support. The overwhelming majority of people living on both sides of the Irish border have endorsed the agreement in simultaneous referenda. Outside fundamentalist unionism, support for the deal would appear close to universal. The Belfast Agreement also has the backing of most political parties based in Northern Ireland. More importantly perhaps, the document has been endorsed by most of the local parties that have organic connections to paramilitary organisations.

That Sinn Fein, the Progressive Unionist Party (PUP) and the Ulster Democratic Party (UDP) should have given their blessing to the Good Friday Agreement is evidently of crucial significance. For the first time perhaps a proposed political settlement for Northern Ireland has the support of a critical mass of those agencies that possess the military capacity to undermine the fledgling institutions involved. With most republicans and loyalists on board there is a very real prospect that the Belfast Agreement might act as a catalyst for genuine political progress in the six counties. The full implementation of the arrangements agreed at the multiparty talks would probably mean that the brutal campaigns of violence that paramilitary bodies have sustained over the last three decades would effectively come to a halt. Young working class men would stop killing and maiming other young working class men in the name of competing, though equally worthless, nationalisms. Such a turn of events would, needless to say, be one genuinely worth celebrating.

The orchestrated euphoria that has surrounded the Good Friday Agreement should not, however, be allowed to cloud our critical judgement. The arrangements imagined during the negotiations at Stormont amount not to a political solution but rather to a political settlement. The origins of the Northern Ireland problem are to be found in the demands that emanate from alternative eth-nonational enterprises. While most unionists are content to continue to live in the United Kingdom many nationalists would prefer citizenship of an Irish Republic. The authors of the Good Friday Agreement seek to forge an historic compromise that can accommodate these divergent ambitions. The institutions that are envisaged within the text are intended to chime with a sense both of Britishness and Irishness.

The essential, and perhaps unavoidable, flaw of the Good Friday Agreement is that it pursues and presumes the reconciliation of ideological enterprises that simply cannot be reconciled. Fundamentally, Ulster unionism and Irish nationalism represent mutually exclusive political schemes. The proper realisation of one necessarily presupposes the annihilation of the other. It is hardly surprising, therefore, that unionists and nationalists should often find it difficult to get along with one another. The advent of the Belfast Agreement would seem to herald that the troubles are finally coming to an end. In reality though it means merely that the particular form of the conflict in Northern Ireland is currently in the process of change. The terms of the agreement seek to encourage a rejection of violence as a medium for advancing political interests. Politics will become the pursuit of war through other means. In addition the document envisages that 'culture' will provide a channel through which communities in Northern Ireland will articulate their identities and grievances. It is understood that the public life of the province will come to centre increasingly upon issues such as marching and language rights.

The foreseen shift towards politics and culture in Northern Ireland would seem to mark a progressive development. It would of course be great if unionists and nationalists were to choose to argue with one another rather than kill one another. The optimism that has attended recent developments in the province remains, however, questionable at best. While the Good Friday Agreement may for a time at least succeed in removing the symptoms of conflict in Northern Ireland it will inevitably prove unable to eradicate its cause. People living in the six counties will continue to aspire to citizenship of different states. As time passes and the demographic balance becomes increasingly precarious the communal ambitions and grievances that exist in Northern Ireland will strengthen rather than diminish. That the interests and misgivings of unionists and nationalists will be expressed increasingly through the media of what are conventionally understood to be 'politics' and 'culture' will not preclude the possibility of further violence. On the contrary in fact. Walter Benjamin (1973, p. 234) has reminded us that those schemes that seek to render aesthetic that which should be conceived as political lead inevitably towards one destination – that of war. With this in mind it might be suggested that the cultural turn that the Belfast Agreement proposes for Northern Ireland is likely to signal not an end to the conflict but rather a period of interregnum.

The inability of the Good Friday Agreement to eliminate the fundamental causes of division within Northern Ireland scarcely comes as a surprise. Resolving the differences between Ulster unionists and Irish nationalists is probably beyond the capability of any conceivable set of political arrangements. After all, as Marx (1977) once observed, societies tend only to set themselves those tasks that they can reasonably expect to fulfil. The Belfast Agreement exhibits at least one further shortcoming, however, that might be considered rather less inevitable. In certain respects the document seeks to encourage and legitimise identities and dispositions that were essential in producing the conflict in the first place. The tone of the Good Friday Agreement orbits around a currently fashionable liberal reading of pluralism. In reality, however, the text rests upon an understanding of the nature of contemporary Northern Irish society that transpires to be oppressively narrow.

The document that provides the blueprint for the political future of Northern Ireland constructs the people of the province purely as representatives of one or other of the principal ethnonational traditions within the six counties. Under the terms of the Good

Friday Agreement the citizens of Northern Ireland are entitled solely to be either unionists or nationalists. Admittedly the text does allow delegates to the new assembly at Stormont to designate themselves as 'other'. It is telling, however, that the votes of those politicians who refuse to identify themselves as unionist or nationalist are simply ignored during calculations to ascertain whether particular legislative decisions accord with the consociational ideals agreed during the multiparty talks and hence will be allowed to go on statute. The substance of the Good Friday Agreement advances a depressingly stunted and prescriptive understanding of how Northern Irish people see themselves and the world around them. The prospect that social actors in the province might actually prefer to construct themselves in terms of gender, sexuality, age or more individuated inclinations is blithely overlooked. The most important distinctions that exist in Northern Ireland as in all bourgeois societies – namely those that pertain to class – are inevitably simply written out of existence.

The architects of the Good Friday Agreement clearly presume that ethnonational feeling represents the only really important source of social and political identity in Northern Ireland. This presumption will almost inevitably come to assume the status of a self-fulfilling prophecy. The impulses that drive the Belfast Agreement seek not to bury unionism and nationalism but rather to praise them. The deal brokered at Stormont signals that enormous material and figurative resources are to be employed in order to confer legitimacy upon the unionist and nationalist projects. The most prevalent voices within contemporary public discourse insist that unionism and nationalism are inherently worthy ideals that deserve 'parity of esteem'.

It is precisely here that we encounter the reactionary soul of the Good Friday Agreement. The substance and spirit of the document insist that we should acknowledge Ulster unionism and Irish nationalism as innately valuable philosophical programmes. This insistence is really very difficult to swallow. Unionism and nationalism are not in fact ways of being in the world that have enhanced the lives of all of the residents of Ireland. On the contrary, they are political programmes that have nothing to offer the peoples of this island other than yet more death, division and disadvantage. Which of the ideologies happens to be the more venal is a question of distinctly negligible significance. Rather than choosing to venerate or simply accept unionism and nationalism we should be attempting to deconstruct and transcend them. Perhaps the time has come for a little more parity of *dis*esteem.

References

Aughey, A. (1989), *Under Siege: Ulster Unionism and the Anglo-Irish Agreement*. Belfast: Blackstaff.

Aughey, A. (1995), 'The Idea of the Union', pp. 8–19 in J.W. Foster (ed.) *The Idea of the Union: Statements and Critiques in Favour of the Union of Great Britain and Northern Ireland*. Vancouver: Belcouver.

Aughey, A. (1997), 'The Character of Ulster Unionism', pp. 16–33 in P. Shirlow and M. McGovern (eds) *Who are 'the People'? Unionism, Protestantism and Loyalism in Northern Ireland*. London: Pluto Press.

Aunger, E.A. (1975), 'Religion and Occupational Class in Northern Ireland', *Economic and Social Review* 7 (1).

Bairner, A. (1997), '"Up to their Knees?" Football, Sectarianism, Masculinity and Working Class Protestant Identity', pp. 95–113 in P. Shirlow and M. McGovern (eds) *Who are 'the People'? Unionism, Protestantism and Loyalism in Northern Ireland*. London: Pluto Press.

Bairner, A. and P. Shirlow, (1998), 'Loyalism, Linfield and the Territorial Politics of Soccer Fandom in Northern Ireland', pp. 163–77 *Space & Polity* 2 (2).

Beck, U. (1992), *Risk Society: Towards a New Modernity*. London: Sage.

Beck, U. (1994), 'The Reinvention of Politics: Towards a Theory of Reflexive Modernisation', pp. 1–55 in U. Beck, A. Giddens and S. Lash (eds) *Reflexive Modernisation: Politics, Tradition and Aesthetics in the Modern Social Order*. Cambridge: Polity.

Benjamin, W. (1973), *Illuminations*. London: Fontana.

Bew, P., P. Gibbon, and H. Patterson, (1979), *The State in Northern Ireland 1921–72: Political Forces and Social Classes*. Manchester: Manchester University Press.

Bew, P. and H. Patterson, (1985), *The British State & the Ulster Crisis: From Wilson to Thatcher*. London: Verso.

Bew, P. and G. Gillespie, (1993), *Northern Ireland: A Chronology of the Troubles 1968–1993*. Dublin: Gill & Macmillan.

Boal, F. (1971) 'Territoriality and Class: A Study of Two Residential Areas in Belfast' *Irish Geography* 6:3.

Boal, F., J. Campbell, and D. Livingstone, (1991), 'The Protestant Mosaic: A Majority of Minorities', in P. Roche and B. Barton (eds) *The Northern Ireland Question: Myth and Reality*. Aldershot: Avebury.

Bolton, R. (1996), 'Death on the Rock', pp. 118–41 in B. Rolston and D. Miller (eds) *War and Words: The Northern Ireland Media Reader*. Belfast: Beyond the Pale.

Borooah, V. (1993), 'Northern Ireland: Typology of a Regional Economy', in P. Teague (ed.) *The Economy of Northern Ireland*. London: Lawrence & Wishart.

Bourdieu, P. (1986), *Distinction: A Social Critique of Judgements of Taste*. London: Routledge & Kegan Paul.

Boyce, D.G. (1991), 'Northern Ireland: A Place Apart?', pp. 13–25 in E. Hughes (ed.) *Culture and Politics in Northern Ireland 1960–1990*. Milton Keynes: Open University.

Breen, R. and P. Devine, (1999), 'Segmentation and Social Structure', pp. 53–65 in P. Mitchell and R. Wilford (eds) *Politics in Northern Ireland*. Boulder: Westview.

Breen, S. (1994), 'Middle Classes Find a Silver Lining', pp. 26–7 *Red Pepper*, 5 October.

Breen, S. (1999), 'Mandarin Mayhem', p. 7 *Fortnight* 377, March.

Brennock, M. (1991), 'Guess Who's Coming to Belfast 9?', *Irish Times*, 23 March.

Brewer, J. (1992), 'The Public and the Police', pp. 52–66 in P. Stringer and G. Robinson (eds) *Social Attitudes in Northern Ireland: 1991–92*. Belfast: Blackstaff.

Brewer, J. and K. Magee, (1991), *Inside the RUC*. Oxford: Clarendon.

British & Irish Communist Organisation (B&ICO), (1977), *Against Ulster Nationalism*, 2nd Edition. Belfast: B&ICO.

Bruce, S. (1986), *God Save Ulster! The Religion and Politics of Paisleyism*. Oxford: Oxford University Press.

Bruce, S. (1994a), *The Edge of the Union: The Ulster Loyalist Political Vision*. Oxford: Oxford University Press.

Bruce, S. (1994b), 'The Politics of the Loyalist Paramilitaries', pp. 103–20 in B. Barton and P. Roche (eds) *The Northern Ireland Question: Perspectives and Policies*. Aldershot: Avebury.

Butler, D. (1991), 'Ulster Unionism and British Broadcasting Journalism, 1924–89', pp. 99–121 in B. Rolston (ed.) *The Media and Northern Ireland: Covering the Troubles*. London: Macmillan.

Butler, D. (1995), *The Trouble With Reporting Northern Ireland: The British State, the Broadcast Media and Nonfictional Representation of the Conflict*. Aldershot: Avebury,

Campbell, D. (1996), 'Still Dark in Paranoia Gulch', pp. 191–6 in B. Rolston and D. Miller (eds) *War and Words: The Northern Ireland Media Reader*. Belfast: Beyond the Pale.

Carey, M. (1997), 'Women in Non-Traditional Employment in Northern Ireland: A Marginalised Form of Femininity', pp. 97–110 in A. Byrne and M. Leonard (eds) *Women and Irish Society: A Sociological Reader*. Belfast: Beyond the Pale.

Cathcart, R. (1996), '2BE Consolidates: The Early Years of the BBC in Northern Ireland', pp. 5–21 in B. Rolston and D. Miller (eds) *War and Words: The Northern Ireland Media Reader*. Belfast: Beyond the Pale.

Cebulla, A. and J. Smyth, (1995), 'Industrial Collapse and Post-Fordist Overdetermination of Belfast', in P. Shirlow (ed.) *Development Ireland*. London: Pluto Press.

Clarke, L. (1994), 'Contemporary Republican Politics', pp. 76–101 in B. Barton and P. Roche (eds) *The Northern Ireland Question: Perspectives and Policies*. Aldershot: Avebury.

Clar na mBan, (1994a), *A Women's Agenda for Peace*. Belfast: Clar na mBan.

Clar na mBan, (1994b), *Submission to the Forum for Peace and Reconciliation*. Belfast: Clar na mBan.

Clayton, P. (1996), *Enemies and Passing Friends: Settler Ideologies in Twentieth Century Ulster*. London: Pluto Press.

Cochrane, F. (1997), *Unionist Politics and the Politics of Unionism Since the Anglo-Irish Agreement*. Cork: Cork University Press.

Collins, P. (1994), 'Irish Labour and Politics in the Late Nineteenth and Early Twentieth Centuries', pp. 123–54 in P. Collins (ed.) *Nationalism & Unionism: Conflict in Ireland, 1885–1921*. Belfast: Institute of Irish Studies.

Cormack, R. and R. Osborne, (1995), 'Education in Northern Ireland: The Struggle For Equality', in P. Clancy et al. (eds) *Irish Society: Sociological Perspectives*. Dublin: Institute of Public Administration.

Coulter, C. (1996), 'Direct Rule and the Unionist Middle Classes', pp. 169–91 in R. English and G. Walker (eds) *Unionism in Modern Ireland*. Dublin: Gill & Macmillan.

Coulter, C. (1997), 'The Culture of Contentment: The Political Beliefs and Practice of the Unionist Middle Classes', pp. 114–39 in P. Shirlow and M. McGovern (eds) *Who are 'the People'?*

Unionism, Protestantism and Loyalism in Northern Ireland. London: Pluto Press.

Courtney, D. (1995), 'Demographic Structure and Change in the Republic Of Ireland and Northern Ireland', pp. 39–89 in P. Clancy et al. (eds) *Irish Society: Sociological Perspectives.* Dublin: IPA.

Cunningham, M. (1991), *British Government Policy in Northern Ireland 1969-89: Its Nature and Execution.* Manchester: Manchester University Press.

Curtis, L. (1984), *Ireland: The Propaganda War.* London: Pluto Press.

Curtis, L. (1996), 'A Catalogue of Censorship 1959–93', pp. 265–304 in B. Rolston and D. Miller (eds) *War and Words: The Northern Ireland Media Reader.* Belfast: Beyond the Pale.

Davanna, T. (1999), 'Carmelites and Ballot Boxes', pp. 10–11 *Fortnight* 337, March.

Department of Education for Northern Ireland (DENI), (1997), *Annual School Census.* Bangor: DENI.

Department of Finance & Personnel, (1994), *Equal Opportunities in the Northern Ireland Civil Service.* Fifth Report of the Equal Opportunities Monitoring Unit, Belfast.

Douds, S. (1996), 'All Croppies Together', *Fortnight* 353.

Douglas, N. (1998), 'The Politics of Accommodation, Social Change and Conflict Resolution in Northern Ireland', pp. 209–29 *Political Geography* 17 (2).

Elliott, P., G.Murdock, and P. Schlesinger, (1996), 'The State and "Terrorism" on British Television', pp. 340–76 in B. Rolston and D. Miller (eds) *War and Words: The Northern Ireland Media Reader.* Belfast: Beyond the Pale.

English, R. (1994), 'Cultural Traditions and Political Ambiguity', pp. 97–106 *The Irish Review* No 15 (Spring).

Equal Opportunities Commission for Northern Ireland (EOCNI), (1997), *Equality Now and Then: Statistics Report.* Belfast: EOCNI.

Evans, G. and M. Duffy, (1997), 'Beyond the Sectarian Divide: The Social Bases and Political Consequences of Nationalist and Unionist Party Competition in Northern Ireland', pp. 47–81 *British Journal of Political Science* 27.

Fagan, H. and R. Munck, (1997), 'Gender, Citizenship and National Identity in Northern Ireland', pp. 101–12 in A. O'Day (ed.) *Political Violence in Northern Ireland: Conflict and Conflict Resolution.* London: Praeger.

Farrell, M. (1976), *Northern Ireland: The Orange State*. London: Pluto Press.

Fawcett, L. (1996), 'Confined to Stereotypes' in Democratic Dialogue, Report No 4: *Power, Politics, Positionings*. Belfast.

Fay, M., M. Morrissey, and M. Smyth, (1999), *Northern Ireland's Troubles: The Human Costs*. London: Pluto Press.

Fearon, K. (1996a,b,c), 'Introduction', 'Painting the Picture', 'Conclusion' in Democratic Dialogue, Report No. 4: *Power, Politics, Positionings*. Belfast.

Feldman, A. (1991), *Formations of Violence: The Narrative of the Body and Political Terror in Northern Ireland*. London: University of Chicago Press.

Finlayson, A. (1997a), 'The Problem of "Culture" in Northern Ireland: A Critique of the Cultural Traditions Group', pp. 76–88 The Irish Review No 20, Winter/Spring.

Finlayson, A. (1997b), 'Discourse and Contemporary Loyalist Identity', pp. 72–94 in P. Shirlow and M. McGovern (eds) *Who are 'the People'? Unionism, Protestantism and Loyalism in Northern Ireland*. London: Pluto Press.

Fisk, R. (1996), 'The BBC and the 1974 Ulster Workers' Council Strike', pp. 38–55 in B. Rolston and D. Miller (eds) *War and Words: The Northern Ireland Media Reader*. Belfast: Beyond the Pale.

Flackes, W. and S. Elliott, (1989), *Northern Ireland: A Political Directory 1968–88*. Belfast: Blackstaff.

Foot, P. (1996), 'Colin Wallace and the Propaganda War', pp. 158–90 in B. Rolston and D. Miller (eds) *War and Words: The Northern Ireland Media Reader*. Belfast: Beyond the Pale.

Fukuyama, F. (1989), 'The End of History', pp. 13–18 *The National Interest*, Summer.

Fukuyama, F. (1992), *The End of History and the Last Man*. London: Hamish Hamilton.

Gaffikin, F. and M. Morrissey, (1995), 'Taxation: The Cost of Inclusion', pp. 53–5 in Democratic Dialogue, Report No. 2: *Social Exclusion, Social Inclusion*. Belfast.

Gallagher, A., R. Osborne, and R. Cormack, (1994), *Fair Shares? Employment, Unemployment and Economic Status*. Belfast: Fair Employment Commission.

Gallagher, T. (1995), 'New Schools For New Times', pp. 62–4 in Democratic Dialogue, Report No. 2: *Social Exclusion, Social Inclusion*. Belfast.

Galligan, Y. and R. Wilford, (1999), 'Women's Political Representation in Ireland', pp. 130–48 in Y. Galligan, E. Ward, and R. Wilford (eds) *Contesting Politics: Women in Ireland, North and South*. Oxford: Westview Press.

Giddens, A. (1994), 'Living in a Post-Traditional Society', pp. 56–107 in U. Beck, A. Giddens, and S. Lash (eds) *Reflexive Modernisation: Politics, Tradition and Aesthetics in the Modern Social Order*. Cambridge: Polity.

Giddens, A. (1998), *The Third Way: The Renewal of Social Democracy*. Cambridge: Polity.

Gorecki, P. and C. Keating, (1995), 'Welfare: Piloting Change', pp. 49–52 in Democratic Dialogue, Report No 2: *Social Exclusion, Social Inclusion*. Belfast.

Graham, B. (1997), 'Ulster: A Representation of Place Yet To Be Imagined', pp. 34–55 in P. Shirlow and M. McGovern (eds) *Who are 'the People'? Unionism, Protestantism and Loyalism in Northern Ireland*. London: Pluto Press.

Gray, A. and D. Heenan, (1996), 'In a Wider World...' in Democratic Dialogue, Repat No 4: *Power, Politics, Positionings*. Belfast.

Hall, M. (1995), *Beyond the Fife and Drum*. Newtownabbey: Island Publications.

Hall, M. (1996), *Reinforcing Powerlessness: The Hidden Dimension to the Northern Ireland 'Troubles'*. Newtownabbey: Island Publications.

Harvie, S. (1996), '17 November 1993 – A Night to Remember?', pp. 192–219 in R. English and G. Walker (eds) *Unionism in Modern Ireland: New Perspectives on Politics and Culture*. Dublin: Gill and Macmillan.

Hayes, B. and J. Brewer, (1997), 'Ethnic Minority Status and Attitudes Towards Police Powers: A Comparative Study of Great Britain, Northern Ireland and the Republic of Ireland', pp. 781–96 *Ethnic and Racial Studies* Vol. 20 No. 4, October.

Hayes, B. and I. McAllister, (1995), 'Social Class, Class Awareness and Political Beliefs in Northern Ireland and the Republic of Ireland', *Economic and Social Review*, 26:4.

Hayes, B. and I. McAllister, (1997), 'Economic Beliefs and Politics in Northern Ireland', pp. 153–74 in R. Breen, P. Devine, and L. Dowds (eds) *Social Attitudes in Northern Ireland: The Sixth Report*. Belfast: Blackstaff.

Hazelkorn, E. and H. Patterson, (1994), 'The New Politics of the Irish Republic', pp. 49–71 *New Left Review* 207.

Heenan, D. and A.M. Gray, (1999), 'Women and Nominated Boards in Ireland', pp. 185–200 in Y. Galligan, E. Ward, and

R. Wilford (eds) *Contesting Politics: Women in Ireland, North and South*. Oxford: Westview Press.

Henderson, L., D. Miller and J. Reilly, (1990), *The British Broadcasting Ban, the Media and the Conflict in Ireland*. Glasgow: Glasgow University Media Group.

Hickey, J. (1984), *Religion and the Northern Ireland Problem*. Dublin: Gill & Macmillan.

Hinds, B. (1999), 'Women Working for Peace in Northern Ireland', pp. 109–29 in Y. Galligan, E. Ward and R. Wilford (eds) *Contesting Politics: Women in Ireland, North and South*. Oxford: Westview Press.

Hoggart, S. (1996), 'The Army PR Men of Northern Ireland', pp. 153–7 in B. Rolston and D. Miller (eds) *War and Words: The Northern Ireland Media Reader*. Belfast: Beyond the Pale.

Irvin, C. and E. Moxon-Browne, (1989), 'Not Too Many Floating Voters Here', *Fortnight* 273.

Jarman, N. (1998), 'Painting Landscapes: The Place of Murals in the Symbolic Construction of Urban Space', pp. 81–98 in A.D. Buckley (ed.) *Symbols in Northern Ireland*. Belfast: Institute of Irish Studies.

Jenkins, R. (1983), *Lads, Citizens and Ordinary Kids: Working Class Youth Lifestyles in Belfast*. London: Routledge & Kegan Paul.

Jenkins, R. (1986), 'Northern Ireland: In What Sense 'Religions' in Conflict?', Royal Anthropological Institute of Great Britain and Ireland, Occasional Paper No. 41. London.

Kellas, J.G. (1991), *The Politics of Nationalism and Ethnicity*. London: Macmillan.

Kenney, M. (1998), 'The Phoenix and the Lark: Revolutionary Mythology and Iconographic Creativity in Belfast's Republican Districts', pp. 153–70 in A.D. Buckley (ed.), *Symbols in Northern Ireland*. Belfast: Institute of Irish Studies.

Kilbane, P. (1995), 'Partners in Health?', pp. 65–7 in Democratic Dialogue, Report No 2: *Social Exclusion, Social Inclusion*. Belfast.

Kirkaldy, J. (1984), 'Northern Ireland and Fleet Street: Misreporting a Continuing Tragedy', pp. 171–200 in Y. Alexander and A.O' Day (eds) *Terrorism in Ireland*. Beckenham: Croom Helm.

Kitson, F. (1971), *Low Intensity Operations: Subversion, Insurgency and Peace-Keeping*. London: Faber & Faber.

Kremer, J. and P. Montgomery (eds), (1993), *Women's Working Lives*. Belfast: HMSO.

Leapman, M. (1996), 'The "Real Lives" Controversy', pp. 96–117 in B. Rolston and D. Miller (eds) *War and Words: The Northern Ireland Media Reader*. Belfast: Beyond the Pale.

Leonard, M. (1994), *Informal Economic Activity in Belfast*. Aldershot: Avebury.

Leonard, M. (1995), 'Women and Informal Economic Activity in Belfast', pp. 235–49 in P. Clancy et al. (eds) *Irish Society: Sociological Perspectives*. Dublin: IPA.

Leonard, M. (1997), 'Women Caring and Sharing in Belfast', pp. 111–26 in A. Byrne and M. Leonard (eds) *Women and Irish Society: A Sociological Reader*. Belfast: Beyond the Pale.

Loughlin, J. (1995), *Ulster Unionism and British National Identity Since 1885*. London: Pinter.

Macauley, C. (1994), 'Catholics Scarce on Movers and Shakers List', *Irish News*, 16 March.

MacDonald, M. (1986) *Children of Wrath: Political Violence in Northern Ireland*. Cambridge: Polity.

MacKinnon, I. (1993), 'Ulster Few Enjoy a Golden Age', *Independent on Sunday*, 8 August.

Maloney, E. (1991), 'Closing Down the Airwaves: The Story of the Broadcasting Ban', pp. 8–50 in B. Rolston (ed.) *The Media and Northern Ireland: Covering the Troubles*. London: Macmillan.

Marx, K. (1977), 'Preface to *A Critique of Political Economy*', pp. 388–92 in D. McLellan (ed.) *Karl Marx: Selected Writings*. Oxfordl: Oxford University Press.

McAll, C. (1990), *Class, Ethnicity and Social Inequality*. London: McGill – Queen's University Press.

McAuley, J.W. (1991), 'Cuchulainn and an RPG-7: The Ideology and Politics of the UDA', pp. 45–68 in E. Hughes (ed.) *Culture and Politics in Northern Ireland 1960–1990*. Milton Keynes: Open University.

McAuley, J.W. (1994), *The Politics of Identity: A Loyalist Community in Belfast*. Aldershot: Avebury.

McAuley, J.W. (1996), '(Re)Constructing Ulster Loyalism: Political Responses to the "Peace Process"', pp. 127–53 *Irish Journal of Sociology* 6.

McAuley, J.W. (1997), 'Flying the One-Winged Bird: Ulster Unionism and the Peace Process', pp. 158–75 in P. Shirlow and M. McGovern (eds) *Who are 'the People'? Unionism, Protestantism and Loyalism in Northern Ireland*. London: Pluto Press.

McDonough, R. (1996), 'Integration or Independence?' in Democratic Dialogue, Report No 4: *Power, Politics, Positionings*. Belfast.

McGarry, J. and B. O'Leary, (1995a), *Explaining Northern Ireland: Broken Images*. London: Blackwell.

McGarry, J. and B. O'Leary, (1995b), 'Five Fallacies: Northern Ireland and the Liabilities of Liberalism', pp. 837–61 *Ethnic and Racial Studies*, Vol. 18 No. 4.

McGill, P. (1995), 'Far More Catholic Children in North Live in Poverty', *The Irish Times*, 28 December.

McGovern, M. and P. Shirlow, (1997), 'Counter-Insurgency, Deindustrialisation and the Political Economy of Ulster Loyalism', pp. 176–98 in P. Shirlow and M. McGovern (eds) *Who are 'the People'? Unionism, Protestantism and Loyalism in Northern Ireland*. London: Pluto Press.

McGregor, P. and P. McKee, (1995), 'A Widening Gap?', pp. 39–44 in Democratic Dialogue, Report No 2: *Social Exclusion, Social Inclusion*. Belfast.

McKeown, K. (1989), *Two Seven Six Three*. Lucan: Murlough.

McKiernan, J. and M. McWilliams, (1997), 'Women, Religion and Violence in the Family', pp. 327–41 in A. Byrne and M. Leonard (eds) *Women and Irish Society: A Sociological Reader*. Belfast: Beyond the Pale.

McKittrick, D. (1994), *Endgame: The Search for Peace in Northern Ireland*. Belfast: Blackstaff.

McLoone, M. (1993), 'The Commitments', *Fortnight* 321.

McWilliams, M. (1994), 'The Woman "Other"', *Fortnight* 328.

McWilliams, M. (1995), 'Struggling for Peace and Justice: Reflections on Women's Activism in Northern Ireland', *Journal of Women's History* 6 (4) and 7 (1).

McWilliams, M. (1996), 'Dinosaurs Not Extinct', *Fortnight* 354.

McWilliams, M. and J. McKiernan, (1993), *Bringing it all out in the Open*. Belfast: HMSO.

Meade, R. (1997), 'Domestic Violence: An Analysis and Response From Community Activists', pp. 342–56 in A. Byrne and M. Leonard (eds) *Women and Irish Society: A Sociological Reader*. Belfast: Beyond the Pale.

Milburn, A. (1994), 'Class Act', *Fortnight* 328.

Miller, D. (1991), 'The Media on the Rock: The Media and the Gibraltar Killings', pp. 69–98 in B. Rolston (ed.) *The Media and Northern Ireland: Covering the Troubles*. London: Macmillan.

Miller, D. (1993a), 'The Northern Ireland Information Service and the Media', pp. 73–103 in J. Eldridge (ed.) *Getting the Message: News, Truth and Power*. London: Routledge.

Miller, D. (1993b), 'Selling Northern Ireland: The Strategy of the Northern Ireland Information Service', *Irish Reporter*.

Miller, D. (1994), *Don't Mention the War: Northern Ireland, Propaganda and the Media*. London: Pluto Press.

Miller, D. (1996), 'The History Behind a Mistake', pp. 244–52 in B. Rolston and D. Miller (eds) *War and Words: The Northern Ireland Media Reader*. Belfast: Beyond the Pale.

Miller, D. (1997), 'Dominant Ideologies and Media Power: The Case of Northern Ireland', pp. 126–45 in M. Kelly and B. O'Connor (eds) *Media Audiences in Ireland: Power and Cultural Identity*. Dublin: University College Dublin Press.

Miller, R.L., R. Wilford and F. Donoghue, (1996), *Women and Political Participation in Northern Ireland*. Aldershot: Avebury.

Mitchell, E. (1991), *Class and Ethnicity in the Perpetuation of Conflict in Northern Ireland*, unpublished PhD dissertation. Rutgers: New Jersey.

Montgomery, P. (1993), 'Paid and Unpaid Work', pp. 15–42 in J. Kremer and P. Montgomery (eds) *Women's Working Lives*. Belfast: HMSO.

Montgomery P. and C. Davies, (1991), 'A Woman's Place in Northern Ireland', pp. 74–95 in P. Stringer and G. Robinson (eds) *Social Attitudes in Northern Ireland: 1990–91 Edition*. Belfast: Blackstaff.

Morgan, V. (1992), 'Bridging the Divide: Women and Political and Community Issues', pp. 135–48 in P. Stringer and G. Robinson (eds) *Social Attitudes in Northern Ireland: The Second Report 1991–92*. Belfast: Blackstaff.

Morgan V. and K. Lynch (1995), 'Gender and Education: North and South', pp. 529–62 in P. Clancy et al. (eds) *Irish Society: Sociological Perspectives*. Dublin: IPA.

Morrissey, H. (1991), 'Economic Change and the Position of Women in Northern Ireland', pp. 101–18 in E. Hughes (ed.) *Culture and Politics in Northern Ireland*. Buckingham: Open University Press.

Moxon-Browne, E. (1991), 'National Identity in Northern Ireland', in P. Stringer and G. Robinson (eds) *Social Attitudes in Northern Ireland: 1990–91*. Belfast: Blackstaff.

Murray, D. (1985), *Worlds Apart: Segregated Schools in Northern Ireland*. Belfast: Blackstaff.

Nairn, T. (1977), *The Break-Up of Britain*. London: New Left Books.

Nelson, S. (1984), *Ulster's Uncertain Defenders: Protestant Political, Paramilitary and Community Groups in the Northern Ireland Conflict*. Belfast: Appletree.

268 CONTEMPORARY NORTHERN IRISH SOCIETY

Northern Ireland Abortion Law Reform Association (NIALRA), (1992), 'Abortion: The Case For Legal Reform in Northern Ireland', pp. 40–6 in A. Smyth (ed.) *The Abortion Papers: Ireland*. Dublin: Attic.

Northern Ireland Department of Finance & Personnel (NIDFP), (1998), *Northern Ireland Expenditure Plans & Priorities: The Government's Expenditure Plan 1998–99*. Belfast: NIDFP.

Northern Ireland Women's Coalition (NIWC), (1997), 'Manifesto Election Communication', pp. 1–3 *Irish Journal of Feminist Studies* 1(2).

Northern Ireland Women's Coalition (NIWC), (1998), *Common Cause: The Story of the Northern Ireland Women's Coalition*. Belfast: NIWC.

Northern Ireland Women's Rights Movement and Downtown Women's Centre, (1996), *Who's Making the News? Women in the Media Industry in Northern Ireland*. Belfast.

O'Connor, F. (1993), *In Search of a State: Catholics in Northern Ireland*. Belfast: Blackstaff.

O'Connor, M. (1995), 'The Prognosis is Political', *Fortnight* 339.

O'Dochartaigh, N. (1997), *From Civil Rights to Armalites: Derry and the Birth of the Troubles*. Cork: Cork University Press.

O'Dowd, L. (1990), 'New Introduction', pp. 29–66 in A. Memmi *The Coloniser and the Colonised*. London: Earthscan.

O'Dowd, L. (1991), 'Social Class' in P. Stringer and G. Robinson (eds) *Social Attitudes in Northern Ireland: 1990–91*. Belfast: Blackstaff.

O'Dowd, L. (1995), 'Development or Dependency? State, Economy and Society in Northern Ireland' in P. Clancy et al. (eds) *Irish Society: Sociological Perspectives*. Dublin: Institute of Public Administration.

O'Dowd, L. (1998), '"New Unionism", British Nationalism and the Prospects for a Negotiated Settlement in Northern Ireland', pp. 55–69 in D. Miller (ed.) *Rethinking Northern Ireland: Culture, Ideology and Colonialism*. London: Longman.

O'Dowd, L., Rolston, B. and Tomlinson, M., (1980), *Northern Ireland: From Civil Rights to Civil War*. London: CSE.

O'Faolain, N. (1997), 'Attempts to Smear Show Mowlam Has Rocked a Few Boats', *The Irish Times*, 10 November.

O'Hearn, D. (1998), *Inside the Celtic Tiger: The Irish Economy and the Asian Model*. London: Pluto Press.

O'Leary, B. (1999), 'The Nature of the British-Irish Agreement', pp. 66–96 *New Left Review* 233.

O'Malley, P. (1990), *Biting at the Grave: The Irish Hunger Strikes and the Politics of Despair*. Belfast: Blackstaff.

O'Malley, P. (1995), 'The Question of Religion', *Fortnight* 336.

O'Reilly, C. (1998), 'The Irish Language As Symbol: Visual Representations of Irish in Northern Ireland', pp. 43–62 in A.D. Buckley (ed.) *Symbols in Northern Ireland*. Belfast: Institute of Irish Studies.

O'Toole, F. (1993), 'On the Other Foot', *The Irish Times*, 30 November.

Oakley, A. (1976), *Housewife*. Harmondsworth: Penguin.

Porter, N. (1996), *Rethinking Unionism: An Alternative Vision for Northern Ireland*. Belfast: Blackstaff.

Porter S. and D. O'Hearn, (1995), 'New Left Podsnappery: The British Left and Ireland', pp. 131–47 *New Left Review* 212.

Regional Trends, Various Years. London: Office for National Statistics.

Rolston, B. (ed.), (1991a), *The Media and Northern Ireland: Covering the Troubles*. London: Macmillan.

Rolston, B. (1991b), *Politics and Painting: Murals and Conflict in Northern Ireland*. London: Associated Universities Press.

Rolston, B. (1992), *Drawing Support: Murals in the North of Ireland*. Belfast: Beyond the Pale.

Rolston, B. (1993), 'The Contented Classes', pp. 7–9 *Irish Reporter* 9.

Rolston, B. (1995a), *Drawing Support 2: Murals of War and Peace*. Belfast: Beyond the Pale.

Rolston, B. (1995b), 'Gagging For It', *Fortnight* 340.

Rolston, B. (1996), 'Political Censorship', pp. 237–43 in B. Rolston and D. Miller (eds) *War and Words: The Northern Ireland Media Reader*. Belfast: Beyond the Pale.

Rolston, B. and D. Miller (eds), (1996), *War and Words: The Northern Ireland Media Reader*. Belfast: Beyond the Pale.

Rooney, E. (1995a), 'Women in Political Conflict', *Race & Class* 37:1.

Rooney, E. (1995b), 'Political Division, Practical Alliance: Problems for Women in Conflict', *Journal of Women's History* 6(4)/7(1), Winter/Spring.

Rooney, E. (1997), 'Women in Party Politics and Local Groups: Findings From Belfast', pp. 535–51 in A. Byrne and M. Leonard (eds) *Women and Irish Society: A Sociological Reader*. Belfast: Beyond the Pale.

Rose, R. (1971), *Governing Without Consensus: An Irish Perspective*. London: Faber & Faber.

Rose, R. (1982), 'Is the UK a State? Northern Ireland as a Test Case', pp. 100–36 in P. Madgwick and R. Rose (eds) *The Territorial Dimension in UK Politics*. London: Macmillan.

Ruane, J. (1996), 'The Core of Reason in Irish Revisions', pp. 1–2 *Anthropology Today* 12(6).

Ruane, J. and J. Todd, (1991), '"Why Can't You Get Along With Each Other? Culture, Structure and the Northern Ireland Conflict', pp. 27–43 in E. Hughes (ed.) *Culture and Politics in Northern Ireland 1960–1990*. Milton Keynes: Open University.

Ruane, J. and J. Todd, (1992a), 'The Social Origins of Nationalism in a Contested Region: The Case of Northern Ireland', pp. 187–211 in J. Coakley (ed.) *The Social Origins of Nationalist Movements: The Contemporary West European Experience*. London: Sage.

Ruane, J. and J. Todd, (1992b), 'Division, Diversity and the Middle Ground in Northern Ireland', pp. 73–98 *Irish Political Studies* 7.

Ruane, J. and J.Todd, (1996), *The Dynamics of Conflict in Northern Ireland: Power, Conflict and Emancipation*. Cambridge: Cambridge University Press.

Rutter, M. et al., (1979), *Fifteen Thousand Hours*. London: Open Books.

Ryan, M. (1994), *War and Peace in Ireland: Britain and the IRA in the New World Order*. London: Pluto Press.

Sales, R. (1997a), *Women Divided: Gender, Religion and Politics in Northern Ireland*. London: Routledge.

Sales, R. (1997b), 'Gender and Protestantism in Northern Ireland', pp. 140–57 in P. Shirlow and M. McGovern (eds) *Who are 'the People'? Unionism, Protestantism and Loyalism in Northern Ireland*. London: Pluto Press.

Sawyer, R. (1998), 'The Symbolism of Womanhood', pp. 171–88 in A.D. Buckley (ed.) *Symbols in Northern Ireland*. Belfast: Institute of Irish Studies.

Schlesinger, P. (1978), *Putting 'Reality' Together: BBC News*. London: Methuen.

Schlesinger, P. (1984), '"Terrorism", the Media and the Liberal Democratic State: A Critique of the Orthodoxy', pp. 213–32 in Y. Alexander and A. O'Day (eds) *Terrorism in Ireland*. Beckenham: Croom Helm.

Schlesinger, P. (1991), *Media, State and Nation: Political Violence and Collective Identities*. London: Sage.

Schlesinger, P., G. Murdock, and P. Elliott, (1983), *Televising 'Terrorism': Political Violence in Popular Culture*. London: Comedia.

See, K. O'Sullivan, (1986), *First World Nationalisms: Class and Ethnic Politics in Northern Ireland and Quebec*. Chicago: University of Chicago Press.

Sennett, R. and J. Cobb, (1972), *The Hidden Injuries of Class*. Cambridge: Cambridge University Press.

Shannon, C. (1989), 'Catholic Women and the Northern Irish Troubles', pp. 234–48 in Y. Alexander and A. O'Day (eds) *Ireland's Terrorist Trauma: Interdisciplinary Perspectives*. London: Harvester Wheatsheaf.

Shara, L. (1994), 'Thugs and Hooligans?', *Fortnight* 325.

Sharrock, D. (1995), 'Wealth of Evidence Points to a Quiet Revolution in the Suburbs', *Guardian*, 25 May.

Sheehan, M. and M. Tomlinson, (1995), 'Unemployment: A Long-Term Problem', pp. 56–61 in Democratic Dialogue, Report No 2: *Social Exclusion, Social Inclusion*. Belfast.

Shirlow, P., and M. McGovern, (1998), 'Language, Discourse and Dialogue: Sinn Fein and the Irish Peace Process', pp. 171–86 *Political Geography* 17 (2).

Silver, H. (1995), 'Fighting Social Exclusion', pp. 8–31 in Democratic Dialogue, Report No 2: *Social Exclusion, Social Inclusion*. Belfast.

Smith, A. (1996), 'Television Coverage of Northern Ireland', pp. 22–37 in B. Rolston and D. Miller (eds) *War and Words: The Northern Ireland Media Reader*. Belfast: Beyond the Pale.

Smyth, A. (1995), 'Paying Our Disrespects to the Bloody States We're In: Women, Violence, Culture and the State', pp. 190–215 *Journal of Women's History*, Winter/Spring.

Smyth, J. (1980), 'Northern Ireland: Conflicts Without Class?', pp. 33–52 in A. Morgan and B. Purdie (eds) *Ireland: Divided Nation, Divided Class*. London: Ink Links.

Smyth, J. (1991), 'Weasels in a Hole: Ideologies of the Northern Ireland Conflict', in Y. Alexander and A. O'Day (eds) *The Irish Terrorism Experience*. Aldershot: Dartmouth.

Social Trends, Various Years. London: Office for National Statistics.

Springfield Inter-Community Development Project, (1994), *Ulster's Protestant Working Class: A Community Exploration*. Newtownabbey: Island Publications.

Steedman, C. (1986), *Landscape for a Good Woman: A Story of Two Lives*. London: Virago.

Sugden, J. and A. Bairner, (1991), 'The Political Culture of Sport in Northern Ireland', pp. 133–41 *Studies* 80.

Sugden, J. and A. Bairner, (1993a), *Sport, Sectarianism and Society in a Divided Ireland*. Leicester: Leicester University Press.

Sugden, J. and A. Bairner, (1993b), 'National Identity, Community Relations and the Sporting Life in Northern Ireland', pp. 171–206 in L. Allison (ed.) *The Changing Politics of Sport*. Manchester: Manchester University Press.

Sugden, J. and A. Bairner, (1994), 'Ireland and the World Cup: "Two Teams in Ireland, There's Only Two Teams in Ireland..."', pp. 119–39 in J. Sugden and A. Tomlinson (eds) *Hosts and Champions: Soccer Cultures, National Identities and the World Cup*. Aldershot: Arena.

Taylor, P. (1996), 'Reporting Northern Ireland', pp. 67–79 in B. Rolston and D. Miller (eds) *War and Words: The Northern Ireland Media Reader*. Belfast: Beyond the Pale.

Teague, P. (1993), 'Not a Firm Basis', *Fortnight* 317.

Thomas, J. (1991), 'Toeing the Line: Why the American Press Fails', pp. 122–35 in B. Rolston (ed.) *The Media and Northern Ireland: Covering the Troubles*. London: Macmillan.

Todd, J. (1987), 'Two Traditions in Unionist Political Culture', pp. 1–26 *Irish Political Studies* 2.

Todd, J. (1988), 'The Limits of Britishness', pp. 11–16 *The Irish Review* 5.

Todd, J. (1990), 'Northern Irish Nationalist Political Culture', pp. 31–44 *Irish Political Studies* 5.

Tomlinson, M. (1995), 'Can Britain Leave Ireland? The Political Economy of War and Peace', *Race & Class* 37:1.

Tonge, J. (1998), *Northern Ireland: Conflict and Change*. Hemel Hempstead: Prentice Hall.

Walker, L. (1997), *Godmothers and Mentors: Women, Politics and Education in Northern Ireland*. Belfast: December Publications.

Ward, M. (1995), 'Finding a Place: Women and the Irish Peace Process', *Race & Class* 37:1.

Ward, M. and M. McGivern, (1982), 'Images of Women in Northern Ireland', pp. 66–72 *Crane Bag* 4 (1).

Whyte, J. (1986) 'How is the Boundary Maintained Between the Two Communities in Northern Ireland', pp. 219–34 *Ethnic and Racial Studies* Vol. 9 No. 2.

Whyte, J. (1991) *Interpreting Northern Ireland*. London: Clarendon.

Wichert, S. (1991), *Northern Ireland Since 1945*. Harlow: Longman.

Wiener, R. (1980), *The Rape and Plunder of the Shankill.* Belfast: Farset.

Wilford, R. (1996), 'Representing Women' in Democratic Dialogue, Report No 4: *Power, Politics, Positionings.* Belfast.

Wilford, R. and Y. Galligan, (1999), 'Gender and Party Politics in Northern Ireland', pp. 169–84 in Y. Galligan, E. Ward and R. Wilford (eds) *Contesting Politics: Women in Ireland, North and South.* Oxford: Westview Press.

Wilson, T. (1989), *Ulster: Conflict and Consent.* London: Blackwell.

The Women of the Irish Republican Movement (WIRM), (1991), 'Fighting the Oppression of Women Must Go Together With the Republican Fight', pp. 133–70 in E. MacDonald (ed.) *Shoot the Women First.* London: Fourth Estate.

Wright, F. (1987), *Northern Ireland: A Comparative Analysis.* Dublin: Gill & Macmillan.

Ziff, T. (1991), 'Photographs at War', pp. 187–206 in B. Rolston (ed.) *The Media and Northern Ireland: Covering the Troubles.* London: Macmillan.

Index

Compiled by Judith Lavender